THE CHALLENGES OF MULTILATERALISM

The Challenges of Multilateralism

KATHRYN C. LAVELLE

Yale

UNIVERSITY PRESS

NEW HAVEN AND LONDON

Published with assistance from the Mary Cady Tew Memorial Fund.

Yale University Press books may be purchased in quantity for educational, business, or promotional use. For information, please e-mail sales.press@yale.edu (US office) or sales@yaleup.co.uk (UK office).

Set in Electra type by IDS Infotech Ltd., Chandigarh, India.
Printed in the United States of America.

Library of Congress Control Number: 2019945865
ISBN 978-0-300-23045-1 (paperbound : alk. paper)

A catalogue record for this book is available from the British Library.

This paper meets the requirements of ANSI/NISO Z39.48-1992 (Permanence of Paper).

10 9 8 7 6 5 4 3 2 1

To Jim

CONTENTS

CONTENTS

Multilateralism is a study of contrasts in motion. The term usually refers to states' efforts at coordinating relations according to a set of
commonly agreed on principles. Yet goals change, principles change, and
understandings about how to pursue goals according to different principles
evolve across time. In response, multilateral initiatives have brought about
striking, yet diverging, results. On the one hand, nationalist impulses have
always pulled states apart, and violent conflict remains a feature of the international landscape. Countries do not always honor their international
commitments, and the principles that underpin multilateral agreements
can appear hypocritical when they are contrasted with how countries actually behave. At its worst, multilateralism can offer a thin disguise for what
powerful states would have done anyway. On the other hand, the desire to
seek peace, reduce poverty, and promote the global health of people and
the planet pushes states to work together. Since the signing of the United
Nations Charter, the world community has not been eclipsed by the type
of system-wide war that threatened humanity twice in the three decades
preceding it. Notions of universal human rights have emerged. Trade has
flourished, and finance is free to pursue higher rates of return in competitive environments. Some diseases have been eradicated, others curtailed.
Understandings of common responsibilities for the global ecosystem have
become apparent. Thus, although multilateralism has plenty of defects and
limitations, it is the only solution for certain kinds of transnational problems.

In this book, the narrative thread that knits together the appearance and growth of multilateralism is the interplay among the societal changes associated with industrialization, capitalist production, globalization, and war in the nation-state system. As I see it, the challenges of multilateralism come from the dynamic progress associated with scientific discovery and the industrial production of goods and services. This advance alters politics within individual states, and among them, as it pushes forward across time, geographic space, and an expanding number of political concerns. The incredible part of the story is that despite catastrophic failures along the way, humanity keeps trying to construct new ways to cooperate and to include more groups into these attempts.

In the international organizations that facilitate multilateralism, decisions are made through voting and not from the conquest of war or bilateral diplomacy. The transformed decision making can undercut the range of choices individual democratic states can make by themselves. Nondemocratic states are members of many international organizations, introducing tension over who participates and what legitimacy they have to speak to certain ideals. International organizations are large bureaucracies, and like all bureaucracies, they can be seen as unresponsive to their environments, obsessed with their own rules, and self-defeating.[1] As political participation has grown at the local level, grassroots democratic initiatives both push multilateral processes to open up to citizen demands and pull at states to retreat from them. Given the competition and cooperation among public and private, national and international forces pushing and pulling in pursuit of goals that none can achieve alone, a history of the field at either the domestic or international level alone would offer an incomplete picture of what is going on.

In order to provide a foundation across several fields, I comingle a vision of politics at both levels rather than focusing exclusively on what international organizations do at the international level or reviewing theories of global governance offered in distinct social sciences. Although multilateralism should not be confused with formal international organization, most multilateral arrangements have formal treaties and international organizations attached to them, particularly those that appeared in the post–World

War II era.[2] This book thus focuses on the creation and evolution of the preeminent problem-solving international organizations in order to understand the contemporary governmental challenges they confront from both domestic and transnational constituencies. It also considers major, yet less formal arrangements that have operated alongside them and nongovernmental organizations that facilitate their work.

The book aims to instruct a wide audience. That group includes students majoring in a variety of disciplines, those pursuing an assortment of careers both inside and outside the academy, and anyone with an interest in the origins and political operations of multilateral international organizations, particularly as they operate in relation to each other. Contemporary trends in workforce participation point to a future where those engaged in international relations will do so on interdisciplinary teams of scientists, social scientists, politicians, legal experts, and other groups of professionals. Thus, the book speaks to students at either the upper-class undergraduate or interdisciplinary masters' level who anticipate their careers will involve working with multilateral arrangements across a diverse set of professions. The book's focus on the features of the governments of member states and politics within international organizations will therefore equip readers to situate their own interests within a web of interconnected institutions of global governance. This approach is not limited to security arrangements and not framed by the narrower theoretical debates of the discipline of political science. Therefore, it should help students with respective interests in global development, public health, the environment, trade, international finance, humanitarian law, and security studies as they grapple with the future of multilateralism.

The book is divided into ten chapters. The first three address the historical context for multilateralism before World War I, the interwar period, and after World War II by focusing on the postwar alliances that seek to maintain stability and dilute the nationalism that repeatedly pushed Europe into violent conflict. These chapters lay the foundation for understanding the politics of domestic support for multilateralism in advanced, industrial economies and then the postcolonial world. The next five chapters connect this narrative to the present multilateral order in each of eight issue areas that include global and regional security, trade, finance, the environment, global health, the European Union, and global justice. Chapter 9 questions the passing of the era of "big multilateralism" across issue areas. It considers challenges posed by regional initiatives and populist movements from below. The tenth chapter reviews the narrative theme built in the preceding chapters and considers the growing number of state and nonstate participants in multilateral processes over time. The analysis concludes with a look to the future of multilateralism, given changes in the interplay between industrialization and globalization in contemporary domestic and international politics.

The time frame for the book coincides with its central argument about industrialization and thus begins before the period of US leadership. Many of multilateralism's challenges have been present since the nineteenth century as industrialization has progressed within and across states. American ambivalence concerning international organizations was present before the United States became a world power. Groups within European countries have also questioned their worth and do so increasingly in the present era, particularly with respect to the European Union. Moreover, newer challenges spring from the democratic dilemmas within the international organizations themselves, which make them a target for many members, even when the states rendering criticism are not themselves democratic. Voting arrangements are not all "one member, one vote." Nor is population necessarily a factor. For example, weighted voting in the International Monetary Fund allocates 16.5 percent to the United States and 2.6 percent to India according to a complex formula agreed to at the end of World War II including a consideration for a state's GDP. Conversely, the United Nations General Assembly operates according to the egalitarian principle of sovereign equality, which results in its own asymmetries. The one vote of Andorra, with a population of approximately 80,000 people, is equal to the one vote of China, with a population of approximately 1.4 billion people. These arrangements strike many outside observers as inherently unfair and reinforce attacks on the institutions from a variety of sources. Finally, the growing participation of China in multilateral arrangements poses a new existential question about whether the liberal international order can be championed by a state that does not share the same domestic political values that previous champions have promoted.

The upshot is that multilateralism has reached an impasse. There has been no major multilateral trade agreement since the Uruguay Round concluded in 1994. The United Nations did not offer any radical policy initiatives in the wake of the 2008 financial crisis that began in US housing markets, or in response to the European sovereign debt crisis that followed in 2010. Moreover, long-standing international arrangements are in danger of unraveling, evidenced most dramatically by the 2016 United Kingdom vote to exit the European Union and the 2017 US decision to exit the Paris Climate Accord. Even informal arrangements experience tension, such as the 2018 Group of Seven meeting where the US president declined to sign the summit communiqué and later sent inflammatory messages via social media about American allies.

Therefore, the study of the history of multilateralism offers an expansive opening into the study of interstate relations and international organizations today. Peoples and states in each historical period have found their own unique resolutions to the dilemmas of democratic political challenges at home, where national politicians must respond to the need of their constituencies, and internationally, where states must find a basis of cooperation for problems that they cannot solve by themselves. No individual resolution of any given problem will last forever, and international organizations will continue to evolve in response to their environment. Understanding how politicians have moved beyond past predicaments serves to illuminate possible ways forward in the future.

AFL-CIO	American Federation of Labor and Congress of Industrialized Unions
BASIC	Brazil, South Africa, India, and China
BCBS	Basel Committee on Banking Supervision
BIS	Bank for International Settlements
CFCs	chlorofluorocarbons
CO_2	carbon dioxide
COMECON	Council of Mutual Economic Assistance
CP	contracting party
DALY	disability-adjusted life year
ECB	European Central Bank
ECOSOC	Economic and Social Council
ECSC	European Coal and Steel Community
EEC	European Economic Community
EMS	European Monetary System
EU	European Union
FSB	Financial Stability Board
FSF	Financial Stability Forum
G5	Group of Five
G7	Group of Seven
G8	Group of Eight
G10	Group of Ten

G20	Group of Twenty
G24	Group of Twenty-Four
G77	Group of Seventy-Seven
GATT	General Agreement on Tariffs and Trade
IBRD	International Bank for Reconstruction and Development
ICC	International Criminal Court
ICRC	International Committee of the Red Cross
ICTR	International Criminal Tribunal for Rwanda
ICTY	International Criminal Tribunal for the Former Yugoslavia
IDA	International Development Association
IFC	International Finance Corporation
ILO	International Labor Organization
IMF	International Monetary Fund
IO	international organization
IPCC	Intergovernmental Panel on Climate Change
ITO	International Trade Organization
NAFTA	North American Free Trade Agreement
NAM	Non-Aligned Movement
NATO	North Atlantic Treaty Organization
NGO	nongovernmental organization
NIEO	New International Economic Order
OECD	Organisation for Economic Co-operation and Development
OEEC	Organisation for European Economic Co-operation
SUNFED	Special United Nations Fund for Economic Development
UN	United Nations
UNCTAD	United Nations Conference on Trade and Development
UNDP	United Nations Development Programme
UNEP	United Nations Environment Programme
UNFCCC	United Nations Framework Convention on Climate Change
UNHCR	United Nations High Commissioner for Refugees
WHO	World Health Organization
WTO	World Trade Organization

THE CHALLENGES OF MULTILATERALISM

ONE

Early Movements toward Multilateralism

M ultilateralism arose at a time when the nation-state system in Europe confronted the simultaneous dilemmas of capitalist production and industrialization. In a capitalist system, factories are owned privately, investments are determined without government involvement, and market competition largely controls the price, production, and distribution of goods and services. The rise of new industrial economies in the nineteenth century freed millions from the daily tasks of survival and the limited prospects for social mobility of rural life. Along with capitalist industrialization, however, came dramatic social dislocation. Societies faced new challenges that governments could not solve on their own. As political systems grappled with these burgeoning issues, networks of individuals, international social movements, philanthropic associations, and international organizations among states sought to solve new problems connected to citizens' health, wealth, and security in light of the expansion of markets and trade.

Multilateralism has thus always comprised a range of governmental, quasi-governmental, and private, citizen-based activities. States act deliberately with others to realize objectives in particular issue areas according to common principles. These arrangements have defined and stabilized the international property rights of states, managed coordination problems among them, and helped to resolve the problems associated with collaboration.[1] Over time, codes of conduct became a defining characteristic of the concept; multilateralism thus became equated with more organized—or institutional—efforts at promoting particular causes or programs according to certain principles. Eventually states created even more formal universal international organizations (IOs), such as the League of Nations, with treaties, procedures, and physical headquarters.[2] Yet, as we will see in this chapter, the early movements toward multilateralism began with less formal efforts for states to act in concert with others. Although many such endeavors collapsed when World War II broke out, the advent of these transnational movements and organizations is important for their connection to social change, for the humanitarian vision of their founders, and because they set the course for contemporary efforts that transect official and private lines.

Nationalism and Industrialization in Europe

The Industrial Revolution was a transition from the hand production of goods to new manufacturing processes made possible by the invention of steam power and the development of factories. It began in Great Britain at the end of the 1700s and spread throughout Europe in waves during the nineteenth century. Rather than working on farms and crafting products one at a time or in small batches, people began to mass-produce goods with machines, work for wages, and buy food and other items with the money they earned. During these years, the advent of the steam engine and the use of machine tools displaced entire industries and pushed large numbers of people into the wage labor economy, resulting in entirely new ways of life for most who experienced it. The expansion of economic operations and extension of European colonial rule to distant territories overseas was an integral part of the process. Eventually, the mechanization of production generated great wealth and a higher quality of life for many through trade, employment, and scientific advance.

But the Industrial Revolution also fostered a nationalist connection between citizens and their governments, wherein many believed in their nation's cultural, economic, and military supremacy. Industrialization and nationalism thus converged in these years. Although earlier transnational governance arrangements had multilateral features, political scientist Craig Murphy argues that the end of the Napoleonic Wars and the Congress of

Vienna in 1815 can be taken as the starting point for multilateralism as we understand it today. When Napoleon was ultimately defeated at Waterloo, victors held the first of a series of multilateral conferences called to address European and interimperial conflicts. In the years that followed, public international unions began to appear, forming a nascent framework for the contemporary system of global governance through agencies established for both political and nonpolitical issues alike.[3]

Article 6 of the Second Treaty of Paris that emerged from the Congress of Vienna was a novelty in that it provided for periodic conferences of sovereigns or ministers to assure and facilitate the execution of the treaty and consolidate the relations among them for the good of the world. The implications of Article 6 were the ascendance of the Great Powers and the legal basis for "diplomacy by conference."[4] In what came later to be called the concert system, the major powers held ad hoc diplomatic conferences among themselves to regulate crises in Europe. During these same years, Prussia and Austria-Hungary repeatedly intervened in states' internal affairs to quell rising nationalism, radicalism, and liberalism, leading to disputes among the European powers. The concert system, therefore, was far from an unqualified success. Yet it remained the basis for international conduct throughout the nineteenth century.[5]

The concert system transformed European politics: it enabled multilateral treaty negotiations among key players, and it facilitated related meetings of representatives of ministries involved with almost any aspect of governance—transportation, communication, commerce, health, currency, and finance. Diplomats in this era were recruited mostly from a single, elite class of people and were often related to one another; they held a reasonably common sense of the limits of foreign policy, accepted mutual rules and restraints, and were loyal to something beyond the aims of their own state.[6] During these same years, even wider circles of private associations of transnationally oriented professionals and social activists also met to agree on voluntary international standards affecting every aspect of economic and social life in Europe and its empires. Eventually, many conferences established permanent administrations to carry out tasks assigned by the national representatives.[7] Thus, the early legislative and executive functions of modern IOs, as well as participation by nonstate actors, were forged as a combination of the building of economies, states, and transnational commerce.

States cooperated in three main issue areas during these years. The first was in business relations, seeking to facilitate trade and payment mechanisms among the industrial powers. The second addressed the rising health problems of populations moving to cities and conducting trade across longer distances. The third, and perhaps most extensive, area concerned how states conducted war. Although the period between the end of the Napoleonic Wars and World War I was relatively peaceful in European history, the initial Geneva and Hague Conventions were among the first formal statements concerning the treatment of individuals and use of weapons in the new body of secular international law.

Facilitating Trade and Commerce in the Industrial Revolution

Trade and commerce require money, or some store of value and unit of exchange that everyone agrees to use. Formal international cooperation among states was not always necessary in monetary relations, however, because for much of human history traders used coins minted from precious metal to make international payments. Thus, if residents in one country purchased more than they sold, they made up the difference with some form of precious metal, usually silver and gold. When trade expanded with industrialization, these early systems were not enough. Governments responded by raising and lowering the amount of gold or silver in the coins or their price at the mint. But problems with the connection between how many coins circulated and the prices of goods and services persisted. The discovery of gold in California in 1848 and Australia in 1851 increased the world's gold production by tenfold, leading to a fall in its price and further stress on the system. The difficulties of maintaining a metallic standard in the United States were particularly difficult in the 1800s, resulting in domestic political pressures to use only gold.[8] A gold standard developed among some states wherein the value of currency was defined in gold and that currency and gold were freely exchanged.

As economist Barry Eichengreen details, the Industrial Revolution propelled countries to adopt the gold standard because the one country already using it, Great Britain, was the world's leading economic power and main source of foreign finance in the late 1800s. When Germany, Europe's second leading industrial power, adopted the gold standard in 1871, the incentive of states to join was reinforced. Other early adopters (including Denmark, Holland, Norway, Sweden, and the Latin Monetary Union) were geographically close to Germany or major German trading partners.[9]

Therefore, although all national monetary systems were not alike at the turn of the twentieth century, an international system based on gold emerged, wherein national central banks cooperated to keep it going. These banks could pursue the policies they wanted to because they were mostly private institutions and were somewhat shielded from political interference. They operated by placing a priority on maintaining the ability to convert money in and out of gold and to defend their gold reserve.[10] Keeping prices stable was a lesser priority. At the time there was no clear theory of the relation between the policies of these banks, the broader economy, and the rate of unemployment. Moreover, when the central bank's policies resulted in unemployment, there was no real political mechanism for workers who suffered the most from its policies to respond, because most countries still limited the right to take part in elections to men who owned property.[11] The Bank of England stood at the center of the global system, and other banks cooperated to stabilize global credit. Such cooperation and coordination were less common outside the European core, such as in the United States and Latin America, where pressures to depreciate currency (or to change the exchange rate so that prices outside the country went up) were more profound.[12]

Other new issue areas in the Industrial Revolution were more practical than financial—such as delivering mail, operating telegraphs, and transporting goods across state lines—and called for more official, deliberate government action than that of central bankers who could cooperate privately. When national legislators confronted a new problem and developed legislation to address it, they needed to consult with those who understood the new ways of doing things. Thus, temporary experts would be needed to monitor both the problem and compliance with the new regulations. The new experts would often either turn toward new and better legislation or turn away from legislation and search for a new "science" or discipline to understand how the social evil could be eradicated.[13] These efforts extended beyond national borders. Therefore, the Industrial Revolution and bureaucracies of nation states grew alongside new fields of study and professions for individuals who could translate economic, social, and practical developments into areas of government action.

Murphy makes the case that the first agencies of international governance, the public international unions, were created at this time with members from several countries. They constructed ways of unifying transportation and communication across national boundaries in Western Europe so that their members could create larger markets. The new international governance agencies interpreted economic interests broadly, insofar as they supported higher wages for workers, peaceful settlement of international conflicts, and even some development assistance to poor nations.[14] More than thirty global IOs were founded between 1864 and World War I. Other regional agencies joined them, most of them in the Americas.[15]

The establishment of these agencies followed a familiar pattern: the problem emerged, early conferences were held, an international convention was eventually adopted, and then some type of more permanent secretariat was created. For example, the International Telegraph Union was born out of a conference held in Paris in 1865 when twenty delegates signed the first International Telegraph Convention. The convention is notable for setting common regulations, tariffs, and technology across Europe. A later conference established a permanent International Telegraph Union Bureau in Bern, Switzerland, so that members could exchange information.[16] Likewise, a series of bilateral treaties governed the exchange of mail during the seventeenth and eighteenth centuries. However, by the nineteenth century, the complexity of the bilateral agreements started to hold back rapid growth in trade and commerce. At the national level, countries created systems where postage on letters was prepaid and uniform, regardless of the distance between sender and recipient. After a few unsuccessful attempts at the international level, a conference held in Bern established the General Postal Union in 1874. So many members joined so quickly that it changed its name to the Universal Postal Union in 1878.[17]

Operating both within and across national governments, the elites who championed these efforts were part of a larger project of extending the powers of national government in the age of industrialization. In the scientific arena, worldwide needs converged on the necessity of a prime meridian for navigation purposes and to unify local times for railway timetables. Whereas some people had always needed to determine time accurately, most people before the Industrial Revolution did not need to. Their lives were governed by the movements of the sun, and they did not travel widely.[18] As the railways expanded, commerce needed to determine a common arrival and departure standard, known as railway time. As transportation grew, the need for standard longitudinal measurements came with it. These measurements had always been difficult to make at sea.[19] After a few efforts in this area did not result in standardization, the International Meridian Conference was held in Washington, DC, to determine a prime meridian for international use. In 1884, the conference selected the Greenwich meridian as the international standard for zero degrees longitude. Most European countries aligned their clocks with Greenwich in ten years. The Bureau International de l'Heure, or International Time Bureau, was established in Paris after World War I.

Preventing Disease in a Time of Migration

During the Industrial Revolution, many people moved from the countryside to towns and cities, and eventually to cities abroad.[20] They were now living closer together and in unsanitary conditions. The lack of urban infrastructure to provide clean water and sanitation, adequate housing, and basic health led to great epidemics, particularly of cholera, tuberculosis, and influenza, for much of the nineteenth century.[21] Quarantine began in the fourteenth century as a way to fight bubonic plague, and the use of quarantine expanded in the years before the Industrial Revolution to include other diseases, such as cholera. These efforts were popular but not effective.[22] Increased trade, while permitting people to access a greater variety of food, compounded the health effects of migration because those working along trade routes carried infectious diseases along with the goods traded. The consequences for all of these circumstances fell most heavily on disadvantaged individuals in towns and cities.

There thus emerged a new need to address disease both within and across borders. Yet the medical community could not agree either on the causes of disease or on the best way to prevent its spread. Eventually, governments called for coordination to address this public health issue and convened the first International Sanitary Conference in 1851. The twelve governments that met attempted to regulate the use of quarantine in a uniform manner and discussed the feasibility of establishing an international sanitary board for maritime activities. No one, however, ratified the convention, and thus, no one abided by the agreement.[23]

Theories about cholera's cause in the nineteenth century ranged from those emphasizing environmental conditions such as weather or climate to those stressing person-to-person communication and even to those based on supernatural suppositions about God's displeasure. When a scientific consensus on cholera's cause, spread, and treatment began to emerge, the seventh International Sanitary Conference, held in Venice in 1892, led to greater success than the first one, albeit limited. The convention ratified at the conference, and its later revisions, focused on efforts to protect states against the spread of infectious disease while minimizing interference with international trade and travel.[24] Later efforts led to the creation in Paris in 1907 of a permanent organization for maintaining and reporting epidemiological data and coordinating quarantine measures: the Office International d'Hygiène Publique, or International Office of Public Hygiene. An enlightened self-interest thus defined international health cooperation until the end of World War I. Powerful interests sought to safeguard and extend their political and economic reach through specific measures that protected trade and commerce.[25] For example, though peoples and governments feared cholera, they also did not want to impede trade and travel through the use of quarantine. The idea was to "protect" health, not to improve it.[26]

War and the Industrial Age

Just as industrialization triggered changes in the areas of trade, finance, and disease, so technological advances changed the nature of war. Yet the implications of these innovations were not as immediately apparent to the international community as those of other areas for much of the nineteenth century. The wars of previous centuries have been described as "hegemonic" insofar as they involved vast territories of the world and resulted in new international systems with new ideas and values that predominated. Yet Western Europe was relatively peaceful between 1815 and 1914. Conflicts such as the Crimean War, Franco-Prussian War, and Italian Wars of Independence arose but were of shorter duration and more confined in territory than the earlier catastrophic conflicts. The American Civil War, from 1861 to 1865, has had a lasting impact on US politics and society but was nonetheless just that—a civil war.

Much of this period of relative peace in Europe can be attributed to the diplomatic concert system formed among the coalition of powers established against Napoleon.[27] As with the central bank cooperation of the gold standard at the end of the century, cooperation of this type was possible among leaders because most workers lacked political rights. The diplomacy of the era was highly elitist in nature and took place among states with relatively equal military capabilities. Yet even though the formal system functioned for only a short time and had many flaws, it left behind intermediary bodies, values of acting in concert, and management of restraining alliances.[28]

In addition to the concert system of diplomacy, the relative lack of violent conflict among the major powers of Europe in the nineteenth century occurred because the production methods and scientific advances of the Industrial Revolution were not immediately translated into instruments of war. In most cases, mechanized production was used for *both* commercial and military uses and was not as advanced as it would become later in the century. For example, almost all explosives were used in both commercial and military settings, particularly black powder and dynamite. Gunpowder was used as early as the first half of the fifteenth century for blowing up the walls of fortifications and for land mines. Yet the development of the type of high explosives used in mining and engineering came after the American Civil War. These advances were not adopted for military purposes until later.[29] In another example, military versions of submersible ships had appeared before the Civil War and were deployed as offensive weapons during the American hostilities. Yet the Confederacy could not produce as many as needed before the end of the war, and the Union had nearly won the war by the time viable submarines were ready for action.[30] Therefore, they did not play a decisive role.

Politically, capitalist arms firms such as Krupp in Germany, Schneider-Creusot in France, Škoda in Austria-Hungary, and both Armstrong Whitworth and Vickers in England have been accused of provoking countries toward war to gain defense contracts; however, James Joll points to a more complex reality in the totality of their international business efforts. For example, Škoda had a lucrative arms business but also exported lock gates to the Suez Canal and power turbines to Niagara Falls. Hence, these firms' contracts in various countries would be affected by any outbreak of war, giving them a strong incentive to avoid conflict. Joll concludes that the governments needed arms firms more than the arms firms needed governments.[31]

Technological advances and industrial production affected the nature of war in ways other than the ability of countries to make more weapons; yet similarly, these influences were not immediately apparent. Photography, for example, was in its incipient stage in the mid-nineteenth century. War photography was born in the 1850s during the Crimean War when photographers documented logistics; these pictures, however, lacked the drama of later photographic expression.[32] The single bloodiest day of conflict in US history, the Battle of Antietam, fought on September 17, 1862, is notable because it was the first time that photographs forced Americans to confront the carnage of war. The work of photographer Mathew Brady played a major role in this transformation when he exhibited the pictures his assistant, Alexander Gardner, made after the battle. In 1863, Oliver Wendell Holmes wrote in the *Atlantic Monthly* that the sight of the pictures was a sharp commentary on civilization. The public reaction was as if the photographer had brought the bodies into people's dooryards.[33] People saw the reality of war in an entirely new way. Yet because the Civil War was an internecine conflict, the photographs galvanized a national, and not international, consciousness.

Efforts to Advance International Humanitarian Law and Universal Moral Codes

Although the wars of the late nineteenth century were not hegemonic, industrialization forced a major reappraisal of the human condition on all social levels. Efforts at international cooperation proceeded through governments, individuals, and public and private philanthropic organizations. Among the wars that took place in nineteenth-century Europe and the United States, the Italian Wars of Independence, Crimean War, and American Civil War prompted a combination of efforts among individuals and governments that resulted in the first manifestations of a body of international humanitarian law and new transnational advocacy networks that would offer opportunities for individuals to work to advance universal moral codes around the world. The process of mechanization and the creation of a working class transformed individuals' consciousness about themselves and their place in the international order in even more profound ways. Athletic competition that crossed races and socioeconomic classes would promote nationalism that was not bigoted. The sum of these efforts and developments forged the greatest humanitarian movement of the century.[34] Yet as we will see, the success and degree of controversy attached to these efforts varied considerably.

The formation of the Red Cross and signing of the first Geneva Convention for the "Amelioration of the Condition of the Wounded in Armies in the Field" are arguably among the first manifestations of international humanitarian law. Both grew out of the experiences of Swiss businessman Henry Dunant following the Battle of Solferino, which was fought as part of the wider war for unification of the Italian peninsula in the nineteenth century. On June 24, 1859, the alliance of France and Sardinia under Napoleon III met the Austrian army at the small village of Solferino in northern Italy. Fighting continued for fifteen hours until the Austrians retreated, leaving more than forty thousand killed or injured. The small medical service attached to the French and Sardinian forces was unable to cope. Many combatants died from simple wounds owing to a lack of knowledge or available care. Surrounding villages were overwhelmed with the walking wounded, with the largest number going to nearby Castiglione delle Stiviere. Dunant, who happened to be passing through on business, was appalled by what he saw. In his native Switzerland, he had been involved with charitable organizations, and now he worked with local women to help the wounded, bringing in supplies to wash dressings, food, water, and clean clothes.

Three years later, Dunant published A Memory of Solferino, relating what he had seen.[35] The narrative hammered home his desire to form volunteer relief societies to care for those wounded in war. These societies would be inactive in peacetime but ready for the possibility of war.[36] National committees would bring aid and relief on the battlefield and care for the wounded in hospitals afterward.[37] A *Memory of Solferino* specifically called for neutral protection to be guaranteed through an international agreement among governments and demonstrated by some type of identifying armband or symbol.[38]

Dunant's vision was not to abolish war but to take a practical step toward international cooperation with respect to its conduct.[39] Copies of the book were sent to important people in Geneva and throughout Europe, including royalty and ministers. Many welcomed Dunant's ideas. Advances in technology and the increasing use of firearms meant that warfare caused injuries never before seen. A body of trained volunteers would be a valuable asset to any military establishment. Within months of the publication of *A Memory of Solferino*, a temporary committee formed among five men in Geneva to begin organizing relief societies. In 1863—nine months after the publication of Dunant's book—an organizing conference was held in Geneva for the Red Cross.

In 1864, the Swiss government called for another conference to include the governments of all European countries, as well as the United States, Brazil, and Mexico. Although not all those invited attended, sixteen countries sent a total of twenty-six delegates. The conference drafted a treaty, the Geneva Convention, that, when ratified and agreed to by governments, bound them to give humane treatment to the sick and wounded in war regardless of their nationality and to protect those who cared for them. National relief societies would be recognized by the new International Committee of the Red Cross (ICRC). To be recognized, a society had to fulfill two specific requirements: it had to be recognized by its own national government as a relief society according to the Geneva Convention, and the national government must itself be a state party to the convention. The conference also proposed a standard emblem for the new ICRC in the form of a red cross on a white background. The first national relief societies were soon founded. In 1906, additional treaties expanded the terms of the convention.

The United States was embroiled in the Civil War during 1864 and sent no representatives to the conference that established the Geneva Convention.

In 1870, the Franco-Prussian War mobilized the newly founded ICRC, and American humanitarian Clara Barton, who had worked with soldiers on Civil War battlefields, interrupted a trip in Europe to join the volunteers in tending to the wounded. On her return to the United States, Barton worked to secure ratification of the 1864 Geneva Convention and founded the American Red Cross. Her efforts were rewarded in 1882, when the United States ratified the treaty. In its first decade, however, the fledgling American organization worked mostly on disaster relief.[40]

Although some believed that the ICRC could contribute to abolishing war through the development of international law, the ICRC's approach sought more to adjust to war-prone states than to try to change them. For some, the work of the national societies was seen as part of the war effort. During World War I, the ICRC attempted to stop reprisals against prisoners of war, but after that war, it adjusted its mission to address illness and misfortune more generally. Confrontation with belligerents might endanger the lives or operations of humanitarians. These early efforts thus sought to avoid judgment and political struggles. Many other organizations have followed in this tradition of attempting to provide humanitarian assistance without discrimination among those in need.[41]

In 1898, Czar Nicholas II of Russia called for another peace conference in The Hague that would add to the new body of international law. The aim of this conference was to discuss peace and disarmament; the treaties and negotiations that resulted from this and a later meeting are among the first written statements of the laws of war and war crimes. To do their work, participants drew on other statements and codes such as those prepared by Francis Lieber during the American Civil War—the *Instructions for the Government of Armies of the United States in the Field* (1863), known as the Lieber Code.[42] The First Hague Conference ended in 1899 with the adoption of a Convention on the Pacific Settlement of International Disputes, which provided for the creation of permanent machinery for tribunals to be set up, known as the Permanent Court of Arbitration. A permanent bureau at The Hague served as a court registrar or secretariat and laid down rules. In 1907, the Second Hague Conference revised the convention and improved the rules. If states were parties to the 1899 and

1907 conventions, they were obliged neither to submit their disputes to arbitration nor to follow the rules of procedure laid down.[43] Nonetheless, the 1899 and 1907 Hague Conventions are significant developments insofar as they sought to place boundaries around conduct in war by addressing the peaceful settlement of international disputes, arms limitation, and the laws of war that the larger scale of production and transport of armaments made possible.[44]

Therefore, the origins of the Red Cross, Geneva Conventions, and Hague Conventions are inextricably linked both to one another and to the relatively limited wars that raged at the time of their creation: the Italian Wars of Independence (1859, 1866), the Crimean War (1853–56), and the American Civil War (1861–65). In short, the Geneva Convention came to embody the principles that wounded and sick soldiers, their personnel, and their establishments are immune from capture and destruction; that all combatants are to be treated impartially; that civilians providing aid to the wounded are to be protected; and that the symbol of the Red Cross serves as a symbol identifying persons and equipment covered by the agreement. The Hague Conventions addressed weaponry and created a procedural means for allowing all participants, irrespective of size, economic power, or military might, to negotiate. This was a major step toward broadening international diplomacy beyond Europe and toward the community of states.[45] Later international humanitarian law negotiated in the twentieth century made advances toward the peaceful settlement of disputes, arms limitation, and the laws of war.[46]

In the area of sport, activists challenged notions of race and social class with international competition. Although he was not the only person to have the idea to revive the ancient games, Pierre de Coubertin proposed the idea of restoring the Olympic games in 1892. A French aristocrat, Coubertin became an advocate of participatory and spectator sports after he toured North America for the French government in 1889 to report on the organization of US and Canadian schools and universities.[47] Sports that cut across class lines were rare in Europe, and Coubertin was impressed with their mass popularity in North America. During the same year, he attended the opening of the Paris Exposition, the world's fair held on the hundred-year anniversary of the storming of the Bastille. The ceremony stirred in Coubertin a sense of how new symbols and rituals could excite a sense of history.[48]

When Coubertin proposed reviving the games, he hoped that the games would encourage political education by cultivating a nonchauvinistic nationalism. He saw sporting encounters as the free trade of the future, and athletes as "ambassadors of peace."[49] Nonetheless, Coubertin was reluctant to speak too openly of these goals to avoid asking too much of athletes or frightening pacifists. Not all of his contemporaries shared his views on the potential of the Olympic Games to unite the world's nations. Rather, authors such as Charles Maurras argued that the encounter with cultural differences encouraged by the games would divide human groups from each other.[50] In later years, Coubertin witnessed chauvinistic, nationalist displays among athletes that challenged his thinking. Eventually, some athletes came to demonstrate the problems of patriotism and nationalism as much as how to resolve them, thus exposing one of the fundamental problems of the Olympics—that they both unite humanity and divide it.[51]

Two years after Coubertin's proposal, leaders voted to create an international committee for the Olympic Games, an international, nongovernmental, nonprofit organization. The first modern games were held in Athens in 1896. Theodore Roosevelt was an early supporter and honorary president of the 1904 games in Saint Louis.[52] Originally based in Paris, the administrative headquarters of the International Olympic Committee have been based in Lausanne, Switzerland, since April 10, 1915. The contradictions inherent in athletes demonstrating both nationalism and the transnational Olympic spirit persist to this day.

The process of mechanization and the creation of a working class thus transformed individuals' consciousness about themselves and their place in the international order beyond treaties and nascent international law. Although scholars debate whether a true global civil society began to form in the nineteenth century, Margaret Keck and Kathryn Sikkink argue that the conduct of international relations changed during this time. A transnational civil society began to emerge, albeit fragmented, that struggled over which citizens and groups would be considered legitimate.[53] These movements challenged notions about races and social classes in areas as diverse as slavery, women's suffrage, foot binding, and female circumcision.

Given the diversity of issues confronted, the persistence of controversy attached to them is not surprising. Where some observers interpret the links among activists from different nationalities and cultures as people engaging in moral campaigns, others see the same people trying to impose their will on others through various forms of cultural imperialism. That is, were these activists promoting universal moral standards, or were they forcing their way of life on others? Others ask if the early campaigns even produced any substantive change. Regardless, the new technologies and institutions made it possible to alter the moral universe in which people act by changing how the individual thinks about responsibility and guilt. Most of the activists and missionaries who led the antislavery, foot binding, and female circumcision campaigns justified their actions on religious beliefs. Although those beliefs had a humanitarian side, they could also be intolerant.[54]

The Interwar Period and Universal Solutions
to National Problems

Despite the humanitarian initiatives of the nineteenth century, hegemonic war returned to Europe early in the twentieth century with the outbreak of World War I, a conflict sparked by the assassination of the heir to the throne of the Austro-Hungarian Empire that turned into one for control of the entire world order. The productive and scientific advances of the Industrial Revolution were now translated into instruments of violent conflict, and technology changed the nature of war. The scale of the carnage was unexpected and unprecedented. In the aftermath, world leaders attempted to forge stronger international institutions to end war and promote a sense of international community through transportation, communication, education, and health. During the 1920s, liberal fundamentalists surmised that the greatest resistance to plans for peace would come, not from the periphery of the world's industrial economies, but from the appeal of Bolshevism to the working class. International organizations could be used to assuage the masses in a different way.[55] The interwar period was thus shaped not

Fig. 1.1. Scene on the Somme front, October 1916. British Photographs of World War I. Courtesy of the National Archives and Records Administration (16579101).

only by the Treaty of Versailles with its Covenant for a League of Nations but by the introduction of additional committees, commissions, and IOs—many of them associated with the League—that would address the conditions of the working class, as well as by the active participation of transnational philanthropies engaged in humanitarian endeavors that would advance the ideals of peace and wellness through a variety of mechanisms.

The Treaty of Versailles and the League of Nations

Proposals for an organization to end war appeared before World War I even began. The industrialist and philanthropist Andrew Carnegie used the words "League of Peace" in speaking to the students of Saint Andrew's University as early as 1905. At the Second Hague Conference, José Batlle y Ordóñez, the former president of Uruguay, introduced a proposition for a federation of nations. President Theodore Roosevelt proposed a league of peace, maintained by force if necessary, in his Nobel Prize address in 1910.[56]

Those seeking a formal league of peace envisioned it proceeding in four stages. The first had been accomplished by The Hague movement in creating a machinery. Next, states would need to agree to use this machinery. The third step would place a sanction behind the tribunals established, and the fourth would put a sanction behind the decisions of the courts and councils. The league would compel nations to submit their quarrels to the organization before fighting.[57] Formed in 1915 at a conference held at Independence Hall in Philadelphia, the League to Enforce Peace elected Republican William Howard Taft as its first president. Republican senator Henry Cabot Lodge addressed the league's first national assembly in positive terms. When the United States entered World War I in April 1917, the organization adopted a "win the war" program.[58] Pacifists did not support the program, believing that peace could not come from coercion. Many Republicans, including Lodge, who had initially supported it, did not ultimately support the next movement, President Woodrow Wilson's proposed League of Nations.

Wilson incorporated the idea of an international organization as a mechanism for organizing the peace into his broader crusade for the law of nations over the tyranny of war.[59] He outlined his principles for peace in a speech before Congress in 1918 as Fourteen Points. As World War I drew to a close, Wilson's Fourteen Points formed the basis for the armistice. Wilson knew that some in the Senate would oppose the League of Nations. When the opposition came, he appealed directly to the American people. He ruined his health in the process and stubbornly refused to compromise with Congress. Although the treaty achieved a majority of votes in the Senate on two attempts, it failed to receive the two-thirds necessary for ratification. The fundamental hurdle for ratification was not necessarily opposition to multilateralism in all its forms; rather, those in the Senate who opposed either the Treaty of Versailles or the League could not separate the two.[60] The United States eventually concluded a separate treaty with Germany, and it had an ambivalent relationship with the League of Nations throughout its existence.[61]

Despite the failure of American ratification, the League of Nations embodied the principles of joint action by member states against an aggressor, arbitration of international disputes, reduction of armaments, and open diplomacy. Headquartered in Geneva, the new organization had an assembly of representatives of all members (roughly corresponding to a parliament), a council of permanent representatives of the leading Allied powers and additional rotating members (roughly corresponding to a cabinet), and an executive agency presided over by a secretary-general. It also provided for a Permanent Court of International Justice and a system of mandates to address issues in colonial Asia and Africa.

The League's organs and operating procedures systematized the earlier methods of peaceful cooperation that had emerged in the nineteenth century, including the Hague Conferences, Permanent Court of Arbitration, and public international unions. The League assembly and council also followed in the tradition of the Concert of Europe, with four innovations: a compromise between larger and smaller governments, clearly defined procedures, regular meetings, and links to other parts of the system of international organization touching all aspects of international life. Whereas governments working through the Concert of Europe might attend a meeting during a crisis, the members of the League pledged to attend the assembly or council and recognize the right of those bodies to address disputes, impose delays, call for sanctions against an aggressor, and discharge other functions.[62]

As stipulated in the Covenant of the League of Nations, the council was to formulate plans for establishing a Permanent Court of International Justice. The court would hear and determine any international dispute the parties submitted and give advisory opinions on any dispute the council referred to it. In 1921, the Permanent Court of International Justice was established with its permanent seat in the Peace Palace in The Hague, which it shares with the Permanent Court of Arbitration. Although the League of Nations brought the Permanent Court of International Justice into being and was closely associated with it, it was not a part of the League.[63]

The Treaty of Versailles also created an International Labour Organization (ILO) in 1919 as part of the belief that universal and lasting peace can only be based in social justice. The Peace Conference set up a labor commission, which Samuel Gompers, head of the American Federation of Labor, chaired. The constitution provided for a tripartite organization, or one that brings together representatives of governments, employers, and workers in its executive bodies. The early ILO adopted International Labour Conventions dealing with hours of work in industry, unemployment, maternity protection, night work for women, and minimum age and night work for children. In 1920, the ILO was located in Geneva. As further evidence of the American ambivalence toward IOs in the interwar period, the United States became a member of the ILO in 1934 but continued to refrain from formal membership in the League of Nations.[64]

Other international efforts grew out of the Covenant of the League of Nations, a document that implied that such entities would eventually be established to address questions of a technical nature in subsequent years. These included a Health Organization, Mandates Commission, an Economic and Financial Organization, and Communications and Transit Organization, alongside a host of other bureaus and committees, such as the Permanent Central Opium Board, Advisory Committee on the Traffic in Women and Children, Slavery Commission, Refugees Commission, Disarmament Commission, and Committee for the Study of the Legal Status of Women. These efforts, as well as the public and private participation in them, are significant in their own right, but they are also significant because they formed a bridge between the nineteenth-century social movements, the League, and the later institutions of the United Nations when World War II concluded.

As mentioned above, the International Office of Public Hygiene, which collected and distributed information from health departments around the world, had been established in Paris before the war. In accordance with Article 23, the League of Nations established a Health Committee and Health Section. Because of disagreements between the United States and some member states, the Paris office and League committee were not associated with each other. Nonetheless, after existing as a provisional committee, the League of Nations Health Organization was fully established in 1924. Headed by Polish bacteriologist Ludwik Rajchman, the organization attracted reformers who took an international perspective on public health.[65]

Another initiative sought to address the economic and financial conditions of European countries. The League of Nations' economic work is often overlooked because the covenant says little about it and the work mandate of the section was narrow. It is significant, however, in foreshadowing many

Fig. 1.2. League of Nations building under construction, undated, photo by Alfred Pasche. Woodrow Wilson Presidential Library Photo Collection, Woodrow Wilson Presidential Library & Museum, Staunton, Virginia.

operations of the International Monetary Fund (IMF) and World Bank following World War II and in shaping a nascent core of support for them.[66] In 1920, the Council of the League called for a financial conference to be held that year in Brussels, and the First Assembly at Geneva created an economic and financial advisory committee to provide the requisite information to the Brussels conference. Although League members resisted the creation of permanent committees, the Economic and Financial Organization came into being in 1923 and soon grew into a considerable operation.[67] By 1938, the organization had a staff of sixty-five in Geneva. By way of comparison, the Health Organization, Organization for Communication and Transit, and drug control and social questions organizations had a *combined* staff of sixty.[68]

The Rockefeller Foundation and the League of Nations

The connection between the League of Nations and the Rockefeller Foundation speaks to the early and continual nature of public and private associations in the growth of multilateralism, even when the country where the private association is located is not a formal member. This connection did not come about accidentally. The League had prominent supporters within the Wilson administration who felt that the new organization could resolve the inadequacies of the Treaty of Versailles. One supporter was Raymond Fosdick, who had served as a civilian aide to General John Pershing and then worked as the US representative with Eric Drummond of Great Britain and Jean Monnet of France to construct the League.[69] When it was clear that the United States would not join, Fosdick returned to the United States, where he worked on behalf of the organization in a private capacity. He continued to visit Drummond in Geneva to keep current on League affairs and advise him about US sentiment.[70] One of Fosdick's first legal clients was John D. Rockefeller, a Republican who initially had not been a wholehearted supporter of the League.[71] Fosdick eventually became president of the Rockefeller Foundation, and its subsequent collaboration with the League on health issues was a natural fit, despite Rockefeller's mixed feelings about the young IO overall.

The Rockefeller Foundation formed an International Health Division because it saw a need for cross-border cooperation to address health challenges and because it felt that promoting public health internationally would lead to greater political and economic stability. John D. Rockefeller had earlier founded the Rockefeller International Health Board in 1913. The board's work centered on the eradication of hookworm, first in the American South and later in countries dominated by US commercial interests such as Panama, Costa Rica, Colombia, and Nicaragua.[72] Rockefeller trustees likewise connected increased support for health programs with weakening support for radical labor and socialist movements. If capitalist, democratic governments responded to citizens' health needs, the populace would be less likely to revolt.[73] Not surprisingly, the Rockefeller Foundation became a major supporter of the League of Nations Health Organization in its efforts to internationalize public health. Representatives from American universities served on its committees. During the 1930s, the Rockefeller Foundation funded approximately 25 percent of the budget for the League's international health work.[74]

Rockefeller Foundation assistance was also significant in other areas of the League's work. In 1927, when the League was developing plans for headquarters buildings in Geneva, Fosdick thought of Rockefeller's interest in funding libraries. He worked through the State Department and the League membership to ensure that neither entity would object to a private donation. Eventually, Rockefeller endowed a library in the new headquarters that would come to be considered the finest collection of works on international affairs in Europe. When a villa became available for purchase near the headquarters location, Rockefeller bought it to serve as a tennis club that would improve the lives of diplomats in Geneva and would prevent speculative building in the area.[75] The League's economic section and the Rockefeller Foundation deepened their association through the existing relationships among individuals at the foundation, the League, and a variety of research institutions. The foundation considered the research work of the economic section to be quite good, and its inquiries into economic stabilization at the start of the Great Depression aligned with those of the foundation. At its peak, the foundation provided up to one third of the section's budget for additional work on economic depressions.[76]

Reparations and the Treaty of Versailles

The Treaty of Versailles that ended World War I called for Germany to pay reparations, or compensation, to the victors for war costs, although it did not specify the total sum of reparations expected or how the funds were to be distributed among the victors. Initially, these questions were left for a reparations committee that was to be formed shortly thereafter but that the United States did not join.[77] Later in the 1920s, the US government agreed to cooperate with European governments in trying to create conditions for peace and economic growth in Europe. As with other areas, however, this cooperation was ambiguous. The issue of German reparations thus forged even more public and private associations in early international organizations.

The reparations issue was inseparable from that of central bank cooperation. As with other forms of international cooperation, central bank cooperation increased after World War I, particularly between 1922 and 1930, when exchange rates among different countries' currencies needed to be stabilized. Central banks provided special stabilization credits, some in connection with the reconstruction work of the Financial Committee of the League of Nations, some outside of it. Eventually, monetary and political authorities sought a more permanent system of cooperation, particularly with respect to the problem of German reparations, which festered throughout the decade.[78] Because the United States did not ratify the Treaty of Versailles, questions of Allied war debts and reparations had to be considered separately, wherein the United States maintained an interest in one but not the other. When relevant committees formed, the US government could not appoint members; American citizens could, and did, serve in their private capacities, however. First Charles Dawes and later Owen D. Young chaired reparations committees to create the Dawes Plan and Young Plan.[79]

The idea for a Bank for International Settlements (BIS) came from Young's committee. To be founded by the principal central banks of the countries involved, it was to be an international bank that would promote cooperation among them and facilitate international financial settlements. The proposed bank could execute the Young Plan as those governments' agent. However, the administration of President Herbert Hoover opposed the formation of such a bank if it were to include questions of reparations alongside war debt. Hoover also opposed the participation of the Federal Reserve.[80] As the negotiations progressed, other members of the US delegation to the negotiations in Paris convinced the administration to allow some participation from the Federal Reserve. Nonetheless, the American obstinacy on the question of reparations made it difficult to find an institutional solution to the repayment of Germany's debt.

The Young Plan was accepted at a conference held at The Hague in January 1930. The BIS began operations May 17, 1930. American ambivalence over participation persisted. Unlike other countries, whose central banks joined the BIS, a banking group formed by three American banks—J. P. Morgan and Company, the First National Bank of New York, and the First National Bank of Chicago—guaranteed the original US subscription to the BIS.[81] Among the bank's original tasks was the receipt and distribution of reparation payments provided for in the Hague Agreements and the Young Plan. Although the BIS performed these functions at first, the Young Plan came to a standstill when the financial crisis associated with the Great Depression broke out.[82] From 1931 onward, the BIS attempted to counteract the effects of the financial crisis.

The Great Depression and the Collapse of Prewar International Efforts

The Great Depression posed an existential threat to the nascent system of international organizations. Industrialization played a significant role in their foundations, purposes, and values. And so, when industrial production crashed, the associated economic fallout threatened the politics of their members as well as the nascent international governance system that had formed to mitigate the worst excesses of war and market forces. Of course, there had been ebbs and flows in the business cycle before the Depression, yet the problems associated with the 1930s stand out for their severity, duration, political effects, and international nature. By the end of the interwar era, the center of gravity in the international system had shifted toward the United States, although not yet in a way that fostered a harmonious environment because of the ambivalent US relationship to multilateral efforts during the 1920s and 1930s. World War II pushed any efforts at cooperation to their limits, forcing some to collapse altogether.

The Great Depression of the 1930s

Between 1929 and 1932, American industrial production fell by 48 percent. German production fell by 39 percent. Unemployment peaked at 25 and 44 percent in the United States and Germany, respectively.[83] In 1930, the United States imposed the Smoot-Hawley Tariff, the highest in the nation's history. Other countries retaliated with their own tariffs, igniting a destructive trade war among industrial economies. Although the gold standard had been reestablished in the interwar period, the strain of the economic collapse limited the range of policy solutions possible for central banks of the day. The mechanisms that had been used to manage prewar crises were not available to them when the entire system was under duress. The BIS held negotiations for coordinating assistance to Austria in 1931; however, the relationship between the BIS and the transfer of German reparations made its deliberations appear political.[84] The crisis spread to Hungary and Germany. Eventually, the gold standard collapsed.

The League of Nations secretariat grappled with the appropriate mechanisms through which to institutionalize political and economic coordination for much of its history. The Great Depression only made these considerations more complicated. In response, the League tried to find a more permanent solution on its technical side. These efforts resonated with the United States, which had always been more comfortable with the League's technical work than with its collective security apparatus. As part of this overall project, the League technical organizations would collect data on national efforts to improve nutrition; in turn, a committee of agricultural, economic, and health experts would report findings on the agricultural and economic effects of improved nutrition. Subsequent reports on the problem of nutrition in 1936 and 1937 linked the problems of poverty, poor eating habits, bad health, and early death. Similar work was done on the protection and welfare of children and on rural hygiene.

Toward the late 1930s, a set of proposals for reorienting the work mandate of the League of Nations called for a distinct reorganization of the machinery of its economic and social work. Known colloquially as the Bruce Committee Report, the Report of the Special Committee for the Development of International Cooperation in Economic and Social Affairs sought the active participation of nonmember states such as the United States in these affairs and embodied the notion that international economic policies should be directed toward improving the well-being of the masses. While the Bruce Committee appeared to deemphasize the League's political work, it acknowledged that political issues dwell in a variety of social and economic problems.[85]

Despite its efforts to prevent war, reduce poverty, expand demand for industrial goods, and end the global depression, the League of Nations faced great political pressure. When Adolf Hitler took power in 1933, he withdrew Germany from membership. Italian dictator Benito Mussolini invaded Abyssinia (modern-day Ethiopia) in 1935. Emperor Haile Selassie asked the League for help, and it voted to impose sanctions on Italy, but Britain and France refused to embargo oil shipments. The League thus failed a critical test to organize its collective security mechanism. In 1936, Germany occupied the Rhineland in direct violation of the Versailles Treaty. By then the League was not taken seriously as a factor for peace and stability.[86]

International Organizations in World War II

Members entered and exited the League of Nations throughout its existence. Afghanistan, Ecuador, and the Union of Soviet Socialist Republics (USSR) were the last three members to join in September 1934. Before that time, Costa Rica and Brazil had given notice of withdrawal (effective after two years) in 1925 and 1926, respectively, over regional disputes and Brazil's failure to gain a permanent seat on the council. Withdrawals escalated in the 1930s, beginning with Germany and Japan in 1933. Paraguay followed with a notice in 1935; Guatemala, Honduras, and Nicaragua offered notice in 1936. Italy and Salvador followed in 1937, Chile and Venezuela in 1938. During 1938, Germany annexed Austria, and in 1939, Italy annexed Albania. Hungary, Peru, and Spain offered notice of withdrawal in 1939. During that year, the council declared that the Union of Soviet Socialist Republics would no longer be a League member. Romania offered notice of withdrawal in 1940, and Haiti in 1942.[87] The work of the Permanent Court of International Justice had diminished in the years before the war. Its last public sitting was on December 4, 1939, after which time it did not deal with any judicial business and no further elections of judges were held. The court moved to Geneva in 1940, with a sole judge and some registry officials remaining at The Hague.[88]

Once the war was under way, the League's finances were seriously strained, and the lives of many working in Geneva were jeopardized because Switzerland was surrounded by German troops. Acting Secretary-General Sean Lester and others sought to continue its work outside the country. The twentieth session of the assembly prolonged the terms of office of members until further notice. From December 1939, when the assembly adjourned, until April 1946, when a new (and final) session was called, a skeleton secretariat functioned in Geneva headed by Lester. The Treasury and High Commission for Refugees operated from London.

Two of the sections that conducted technical work of the League operated in Canada and the United States. The International Labour Organization's director, John Winant, did not want his organization to become an instrument of the totalitarian states. In August 1939, the Canadian government allowed the temporary transfer of ILO staff to Montreal. Forty staff members from eighteen countries left for McGill University, and the rest returned to their own countries as national correspondents or went to branch offices.[89] American supporters of the League thought that a transfer to the territorial United States would encourage American membership in any multilateral organization that might emerge when the war ended. Working with the Rockefeller Foundation, Princeton University, and the Institute for Advanced Study, they negotiated the move of the Economic Section to Princeton, New Jersey. Since the move was unofficial, Congress was not involved. The Rockefeller Foundation continued to fund approximately one third of the section's activities and to supplement expenses that the Institute for Advanced Study incurred as hosts.[90]

World War II effectively ended the existing arrangements in the area of health governance. The International Office of Public Hygiene in Paris could not carry out its mission, and it was nearly impossible to operate during the war. Delegates could not travel, so the office stopped holding meetings after 1939. The Health Unit of the League of Nations was similarly curtailed by the war. Many of the staff left for their home countries.[91]

Arguably the most controversial international organization during the war was the Bank for International Settlements. As war approached, the relatively new bank found itself in an unprecedented position. Its managers were committed to its survival, which meant that it must maintain neutrality while the bank's board members were at war with each other. In reality, however, survival also would depend on the BIS's usefulness to each side. Gianni Toniolo points to the difficulty in reconciling these postures.[92] When regular board meetings ceased, members had to be informed about management decisions by mail. Many were in countries whose central banks were under Axis control. Yet the BIS had to preserve the special privileges it was granted by The Hague agreement under which it was established. Even in wartime, its assets and deposits were exempt from confiscation, expropriation, or other restriction.[93]

Although the BIS managers kept the organization alive, the bank's wartime conduct has been criticized for its dealings with Nazi Germany. First of all, historians question whether the BIS received gold looted from countries conquered by Germany, private citizens, or concentration camps. On that account, there is proof that the BIS received looted Belgian and Dutch gold from the Reichsbank. Second, historians ask about bank neutrality—that is, did BIS services help Germany's war effort? Here, too, there is suspicious activity on the part of the bank. The most serious allegation against the BIS, however, concerns the transfer of Czechoslovak gold and German interest payments that occurred before the war.[94] These activities jeopardized the BIS in the negotiations immediately after the war for a new set of organizations that would manage the global economy.

Conclusion

The dynamic elements of nineteenth-century Europe—the Industrial Revolution, nation-state building, and transnational movements among private groups and early philanthropies—interacted in complex ways to forge early forms of multilateralism. Individuals and governments began to try to resolve the new problems that came along with these processes. Early international organizations grew out of diplomatic conferences convened to address new intergovernmental and social problems that accompanied the movement of peoples, expansion of trade, and technological progress of the age. Just as national bureaucracies developed at this time, so did international ones, staffed by experts in the new issue areas. Controversies accompanied these efforts, however. The diplomatic and philanthropic efforts were elitist in nature. The entire endeavor was pulled apart by the catastrophe of World War I. Although the international organizations of the interwar League of Nations era may have sought universal membership, states reserved individual prerogatives. The movement toward multilateralism was decimated again by World War II and the devastation of the nuclear age. Nonetheless, in the aftermath of the war, states and peoples tried again.

TWO

The Embryonic Plan for
Postwar Multilateralism

The spirit that would embody postwar international organizations emerged with the formation of an alliance among the United States, Great Britain, and the Union of Soviet Socialist Republics to fight World War II.[1] Even before the Americans formally joined the war effort, President Franklin D. Roosevelt set an ideological and moral course for the future by closing his 1941 State of the Union message with a declaration of hope for a world founded on four essential human freedoms: freedom of speech and expression, freedom of religion, freedom from want, and freedom from fear. Tensions related to these essential freedoms existed among the three major Allies from the outset and persisted throughout the war. Chief questions among them concerned the fate of Poland, Germany, and smaller states. Chief debates persisted over democracy versus totalitarianism and capitalism versus communism in the postwar world. Yet despite their differences, the Allies succeeded in advancing nascent plans for a framework of formal international organizations that would preserve connections among them. When the Soviet and Chinese ambassadors met with Franklin Roosevelt and Prime Minister Winston Churchill in January 1942, they signed the "Declaration by United Nations." Twenty-two other nations at war with the Axis powers added their signatures, creating an alliance of states that pledged to wage war with all their combined resources. That is, they would not sign separate peace agreements.[2] These documents laid the groundwork

for the modern United Nations, which includes economic, social, and security organizations.

When Franklin Roosevelt ran as the Democratic vice-presidential nominee earlier in his life, he made more than eight hundred speeches supporting the League of Nations. He argued that it was a practical necessity.[3] After
the war, planners constructed a blueprint for a new international order that
advanced elements of the philosophy, substance, and form of Franklin Roosevelt's New Deal regulatory state. The new multilateralism addressed the
political challenges of industrialization at the domestic level as before, yet
transformed their solutions through existing conceptions of cooperation at
the international level. That is, many of the same policy makers from the
New Deal advanced the same solutions for the world's problems as they had
in domestic American politics, specialized administrative organizations, at
the international level. The most comprehensive designs were drawn up in
Washington.[4] Once the geopolitical rivalry of the Cold War was apparent,
later pillars of the Western alliance, NATO (the North Atlantic Treaty Organization) and the European Community, were born. Each in its own way
ensured the ongoing engagement of the United States in world affairs and
prevented a retreat into American isolationism.

The postwar plans for formal organizations were neither entirely new nor
exclusively American, but they did constitute an innovative pattern of multilateral diplomacy. Scholars at the time, such as David Mitrany, argued for
a functional approach to cooperation that would bind authority to a specific
activity and thus break the link between authority and a definite territory.[5]
The formal organizations that were created took on issues where a consensus on norms and principles did not yet exist. They could place issues on the
global agenda and convene states with conference diplomacy. Finally, despite opposition from states and nonstate groups, the formal organizations
could confer their own distinctive legitimacy in certain circumstances.[6] Although the Cold War challenged the Allies' vision of a universal international organization that would preserve the connections among them, it did
not completely undermine attempts at coordinating relations among like-
minded democratic and capitalist states.

Negotiating Multilateral Organizations among Uneasy Allies and Asymmetrical Economies

As we saw in chapter 1, few examples of multilateralism became formal organizations before the League of Nations. The Concert of Europe had been a series of great power consultations. Free trade and the gold standard functioned through ad hoc bilateral and unilateral means. The League was the first multipurpose, universal membership organization, but it failed in its most fundamental security objective: to prevent another cataclysmic conflict through collective security.[7] For Mark Mazower, the League of Nations began a history of world organization, and the United Nations introduced a new chapter. The UN was linked to the League by questions of empire and the visions of global order in the final decades of the British Empire. The United States played a role in setting up the organization, but what emerged was not as much what Roosevelt thought of as "Four Policemen," or world government, or an alliance of democracies. It was an organization that kept the wartime alliance of the Big Three (the United States, United Kingdom, and Soviet Union) together.[8]

The formal institutions that comprise the UN system created immediately following War II thus resulted from negotiations among states with very definite interests at a particular moment in time. Initially, the men who designed the organizations were actively engaged in the final campaigns of the war. They sought to build a better world with a clear-eyed sense of how horrific events can turn. As the war wound down, the leaders of the Big Three, Roosevelt, Churchill, and Soviet premier Joseph Stalin, continued to meet. In addition, diplomatic conferences were held among officials from all of the Allied countries. In economic affairs, the Allies' delegates met at Bretton Woods, New Hampshire, at the United Nations Monetary and Financial Conference to reconstruct an international trade and financial system. The plans sketched at Bretton Woods eventually became the International Monetary Fund, World Bank Group, and General Agreement on Tariffs and Trade (GATT). With respect to security, the Allies held talks at Dumbarton Oaks in Washington, DC, to flesh out the details of what became the six organs of the United Nations.

Two cross-cutting divisions affected the negotiations at Bretton Woods and Dumbarton Oaks: the persistent difference of economic ideologies among wartime allies on communism, imperialism, and capitalism, and the regional strains among the United States and Latin American countries, where levels of industrialization varied dramatically and all states had not engaged in the allied war effort against Germany as enthusiastically. Compromises cut across these divisions led to the advancement of developmental activities within the new International Bank for Reconstruction and Development (now part of the World Bank Group). The ongoing mix of public and private sector organizations' interests in world organizations also continued through this period.

Franklin Roosevelt entered his presidency predisposed toward multilateralism. As assistant secretary of the navy in the Wilson administration, he had supported US membership in the League. Members of his administration had communicated regularly with those individuals in the US private sector who had supported its technical activities when the Bruce Committee reforms on the technical work of the League of Nations were suggested at the end of the 1930s. Nonetheless, Roosevelt downplayed open discussions of his post–World War II plans, multilateral or otherwise, even after the United States entered the war. Tensions among the Allies were rooted both in the Bolshevik Revolution and the nature of British imperialism. The New York Council on Foreign Relations, a private organization of business leaders, government officials, and academics, offered to study postwar issues, including multilateralism, in secret and report on its findings to the State Department. Secretary of State Cordell Hull accepted the council's offer, and the council created four committees in the area of postwar armaments, economic relations, colonial territories, and cross-border aggression. The Rockefeller Foundation provided financial support for the project, and diplomat Norman Davis was responsible for coordinating the studies and presenting them to the State Department. The private nature of the council facilitated these arrangements and allowed them to remain secret.[9]

As many historians have documented, the United States held a more integrated view of the postwar world than the British and Soviets did. The latter two viewed the world in terms of "spheres of influence," with the British placing priority on the Commonwealth, that is, the territories of its former empire, and the Soviets on Eastern Europe. As the war progressed and the Allies embarked on more substantive plans for the future, the Big Three met in Tehran, Iran, in 1943 and commenced substantive discussions of a postwar organization. Although the Allies accepted the principle that the postwar organization would include nonmilitary issues such as public health and food relief, differences among them, as well as within the Roosevelt administration, persisted. Hull envisioned a more democratic world organization, and Stalin and Roosevelt envisioned one with special rights for the great powers.

The Soviet Union's history with international organizations was much less clear in the early 1940s. Although the Soviets were initially hostile to the League of Nations, in the five years from 1934 to 1939 the Soviet government became a major proponent due to the threat of German and Japanese attacks. Moreover, the Soviet Union also cooperated with many of the organizations and conferences of the League on health, sanitation, and communications. Although the USSR did not cooperate with the Permanent Court for International Justice, it considered itself to be in a transitional period in 1942 with respect to the court. It recognized and practiced many accepted principles of international law at the time. It appeared that as Soviet ideology shifted from world revolution to building communism in the USSR alone, the country had better relations with some of its former adversaries.[10]

The task of individuals planning the United Nations was challenged from the start, therefore, by the fundamental incompatibility of economic systems in the United States, United Kingdom, and USSR, but not necessarily their orientations toward all efforts at legal formulations that would coordinate relations for one or more needs. Although the countries were allies, the planners were essentially charged with the task of designing an organization that would be strong enough to stop conflicts quickly yet flexible enough to allow American policy to operate freely.[11] At the State Department, planners used the experiences of the League in their preparations for a multilateral organization. These men judged that the League's problem was not its design but the actions of its member states.[12] They thus took several key organizational features from the League, shifted responsibility from the assembly to the executive body, and increased the League's emphasis on peacekeeping.

Economic Development and Planning for a United Nations

Differing levels of economic development among allied states, specifically those in Latin America, challenged the planning for the United Nations in a different way. The Spanish colonial empire in North and South America had disintegrated in the nineteenth century, leaving a group of states that were sovereign yet subject to European and American financial and military influence through investment patterns and the Monroe Doctrine. The United States had begun to alter its policy toward Latin America in the late 1920s when President-Elect Herbert Hoover began to talk of the United States acting as a "good neighbor." At the time, Hoover was referring to the deployment of US armed forces there, but the term expanded when Hoover specifically repudiated intervention to protect US investors in Mexico.[13] As secretary of commerce and later as president, Hoover redirected US policy away from the military focus of the Theodore Roosevelt–William Howard Taft era and toward a broader business orientation that emphasized foreign trade and investment.[14] Yet American attitudes toward Latin America changed considerably during the Great Depression, when hearings were held on the activities of New York financiers vis-à-vis Latin America in the 1920s. The more sympathetic attitudes helped to forge political support for some kind of "New Deal" across the region.[15]

As had been the case with League supporters, many prominent Americans saw business and security interests in the Latin American region as a unified whole. Among these, John D. Rockefeller Jr.'s son, Nelson Rockefeller, had visited Mexico in 1933. He developed a much more serious interest in inter-American relations when he later was appointed to the board of Creole Petroleum. He took a three-month tour of seven countries in the region in 1937 and was briefed along the way by experts from Chase Bank and the Standard Oil Company. During this trip, he was impressed by the strong anti-American sentiment he encountered. He returned to the United States convinced that the behavior of US firms in South America would ultimately endanger their assets and that the private enterprise system itself would be challenged if the humanitarian needs of the poor were not met.[16] In 1938, he urged Roosevelt to respond to German business activities in the region with an American propaganda counteroffensive.[17]

Therefore, in the 1930s, the Good Neighbor policy began to take on elements of an economic development program to combat radical left- and right-wing economic ideologies. Public financial assistance to these governments would secure alliances and promote political and economic stability in a region that was an important source of raw materials and a profitable investment location for American businesses.[18] In 1939, American officials pushed for the creation of a permanent Inter-American Financial and Economic Advisory Committee, which would include financial experts from each country. Talks also began on an Inter-American Bank that would facilitate lending under better conditions than had existed in the 1920s and that would facilitate the "development" goals of national governments.[19] Finally, the Committee created an Inter-American Development Commission to promote enterprises to promote Latin American mineral, agricultural, and industrial production for hemispheric markets.

In mid-1940, Roosevelt created the Office for the Coordination of Commercial and Cultural Relations between the American Republics and appointed Nelson Rockefeller its director.[20] While viewed by some as a propaganda mechanism that operated outside normal diplomatic channels, the office also served an important role as the initial US economic aid program in the region. Rockefeller proposed that development assistance was necessary for US national security shortly after the attack on Pearl Harbor. He argued that to defend the hemisphere, the United States needed an effective communications apparatus. Thus, those Americans engaged in this effort would need to maintain their health in parts of the world where tropical diseases were endemic. The United States would have to help pay for the eradication of these diseases because Latin American governments simply did not possess the resources to do so themselves. Although many of the early disease, sanitation, water, and other public works programs were criticized within the United States, they established an important tradition for the next fifty years.[21]

The attack on Pearl Harbor on December 7, 1941, brought the United States formally into World War II, and the question of Latin American defense became more pronounced. At the 1942 Rio de Janeiro meeting of Latin American ministers of foreign affairs, Roosevelt sought a unanimous resolution that the Latin American states would break diplomatic relations with the Axis powers. Argentina and Chile did not do so. Argentina had profited from remaining neutral during World War I, and a significant number of first-generation Italian and Germans lived there. Moreover, the country was geographically removed from the conflict and received propaganda from both sides. While they received reports of Nazi atrocities, they also received reports of US internment camps. Thus, they refused to endorse a US resolution simply because the United States had been attacked by Japan in the middle of the Pacific.[22]

This brief review of US–Latin American relations in the early twentieth century shows that when formal negotiations for multilateral organizations commenced toward the conclusion of the war, significant strains existed among the Big Three allies, as well as among the Big Three and Latin American states. Regional security issues were strained by lingering colonial relationships, as well as by asymmetries in levels of economic development that created numerous cross-cutting cleavages.

Diplomacy at Bretton Woods

Regional strains were played out initially in the negotiations for the Bretton Woods institutions that would shape the new international economic order and later in the Dumbarton Oaks talks that would shape the UN organizations. Nonetheless, domestic politics in the United States also shaped the early contours of the postwar multilateral system. Discussions for the Bretton Woods financial institutions commenced with the circulation of various memorandums by American Treasury official Harry Dexter White and British economist and Bank of England official John Maynard Keynes as early as 1941.[23] Eventually held in July 1944 at the Mount Washington Hotel in Bretton Woods, the United Nations Monetary and Financial Conference sought to fix currency rates to facilitate an expansion in international trade following the war along the lines of Keynes's and White's plans. The final act of the conference laid the groundwork for what would have had three pillars, if each had been created as planned.

The first pillar was a stabilization fund—which became the International Monetary Fund—that would restore a market for the foreign exchange of currencies pegged to a gold standard, yet would be adjustable if a state needed to correct a fundamental disequilibrium. At the Bretton Woods conference, the decision to use a state's quota, or what it contributed, to determine its voting power was a compromise between two approaches: one that related to members' contributions and the other that related to the legal principle of the sovereign equality of states. Politically, the wartime allies wanted to achieve a ranking they had agreed upon. In early formulations, the United States was to have the largest quota, Great Britain and its colonies about half the US quota, the Soviet Union below that of the United Kingdom, and China somewhat less again.[24] Yet basic votes were also considered to be necessary for the regulatory functions of the IMF. At the time, basic votes gave smaller countries a degree of influence because they constituted 11.3 percent of the total. Planners combined the two approaches in giving each member country one vote for every one hundred thousand dollars of quota, plus 250 basic votes. Since then, as membership in the IMF has quadrupled and quotas have increased, the share of basic votes in the total has declined to approximately 2.1 percent of the total, rendering the participation of small states negligible in the governance structure.[25]

The second pillar of the Bretton Woods system was an international bank—which became the World Bank—to finance the reconstruction efforts of war-torn European nations. Nineteen of the forty-four states invited to the conference were from Latin America. Constituting the largest regional bloc, they sought to address the role of economic development in the bank's charter by encouraging equal weight for development assistance to be given to areas both affected and not affected by the war.[26] Specifically, Mexico sought to have the term "development" included in the initial title of the World Bank: the International Bank for Reconstruction and Development (IBRD).[27] Despite additional differences over relative quota positions, the role of silver, and commodity price stabilization, the Latin American states became strong supporters of the Bretton Woods negotiations.[28]

The final pillar of the Bretton Woods system would have been for the governments to reach an agreement to restore free trade. Ultimately, an

International Trade Organization (ITO) would have complemented the IMF and World Bank by addressing the totality of issues surrounding trade, not limited to but including labor rights and anticompetitive business practices. In March 1948, a planned charter for the ITO was completed and set out the basic parameters for trade and other international economic concerns. It faced stiff opposition in the US Congress. By December 1950, President Truman announced he would no longer pursue approval of the charter. The planned organization never came into existence, and countries relied on an interim agreement with periodic negotiations for new trade treaties, the General Agreement on Tariffs and Trade, until the end of the twentieth century.

Smoothing the Differences among Allies in the United Nations

The Dumbarton Oaks talks, held from August to October 1944, were the first step in constructing an international organization to succeed the League of Nations. Although many of the same cross-cutting political cleavages existed at both Bretton Woods and Dumbarton Oaks, there were several key differences.[29] An obvious one was the physical location of the meetings: Washington, DC, versus New Hampshire. Roosevelt could follow, and intervene in, the Dumbarton Oaks talks more readily, whereas he had much less interest in the progress at Bretton Woods. In addition, the planners at Bretton Woods had commenced their talks with a more substantive agenda, derived from the Keynes and White discussions. The negotiators at Dumbarton Oaks lacked the same initial unified vision. Last, the planners faced different sets of political opponents. At Dumbarton Oaks, the Soviets sought to design a peace and security organization that would ensure postwar cooperation among the Allies. The Soviets did not pose a challenge to the design of the IMF because they did not join the organization.

Initial differences at Dumbarton Oaks among the Big Three were immediately apparent in each of the major security and membership concerns they sought to address. First of all, the United States wanted a broad scope for the new organization, including an Economic and Social Council (ECOSOC) to promote the best use of the world's economic resources. The Soviets called for a UN more focused on security affairs. Second, the Soviets proposed an international air force to continue the wartime alliance. Third, the negotiators differed over the founding members of the new organization. The United States wanted to include pro-Allied nations who had not signed the declaration, whereas the Soviets explored the possibility of including all sixteen Soviet republics among the initial members so that the USSR would not feel a sense of isolation in the General Assembly. Finally, the negotiators considered the issue of voting procedures in the Security Council. The issue arose as to how the voting would be handled when a permanent member was directly involved.[30]

When concluded, the Dumbarton Oaks agreements contained something for each of the Big Three. For Roosevelt, they contained an institutional framework for US cooperation with foreign states after World War II ended, meaning that states would have certain roles, expectations, and limits on their behavior. For the US Senate, they provided for a collective security arrangement that would allow US troops to return home when hostilities ceased. For Churchill, the United Nations would be weak enough not to interfere with the Commonwealth, and for Stalin, the same organization would ensure the state's superpower status.[31]

The final details of the organization were worked out at the conference of the Big Three at Yalta, on the Crimean Peninsula, and then later at the first meeting of the nascent United Nations organization in San Francisco. Roosevelt died on April 12, 1945, between the meetings. President Harry Truman asked Eleanor Roosevelt to join the American delegation headed by Secretary of State James Byrnes and former secretary of state Edward Stettinius. She was assigned to the Committee on Humanitarian, Social and Cultural Concerns, which became significant due to the refugee and repatriation issues it handled. When the delegates met in April in San Francisco, relations among the Big Three were tense, and many small nations were opposed to concentrating power in the permanent members of the Security Council.

The issue of communism also intruded on the conference. Latin American states sought to establish a regional security system to deal with communist threats from inside and outside the hemisphere. They wanted this system to be independent of the UN and to be put in place quickly.[32] The Latin American states had not been invited to the Dumbarton Oaks talks

Fig. 2.1. Winston Churchill, Franklin D. Roosevelt, and Joseph Stalin at Yalta, February 9, 1945. Courtesy of the Franklin D. Roosevelt Presidential Library and Museum, Hyde Park, New York.

and, contrary to the Good Neighbor policy, were not consulted by the United States. At the Inter-American Conference on Problems of War and Peace, held in Mexico City in early 1945, the United States wanted delegates to endorse the Dumbarton Oaks proposals. Slighted by the fact that they had not been consulted earlier, the Latin American states sought to issue remarks critical of Dumbarton Oaks. In general, the Latins worried about Soviet clout in the new organization.[33] They sought an inter-American peace system and saw no need for the UN to play a role in hemispheric disputes. The resolution of differences among allies would have a profound impact on the future of the organization. The involvement of Nelson Rockefeller, acting in a quasi-official capacity, would play a significant role in organizing the first bloc of developing states and creating a consciousness among them of their own ability to use their voting power to their advantage.

His family's wealth would also play a role in securing a permanent home for the UN Secretariat in New York.

Tensions between the Latin American delegation and the Soviets surfaced in the months before the San Francisco conference. Stalin had gained acceptance for the seating of delegates from Ukraine and White Russia (Belarus) at Yalta in exchange for the seating of some British Commonwealth states. Argentine admission also posed a problem: the Latin American countries favored it, but the Russians opposed it. President Juan Perón had sided with the Axis powers during the war, and Roosevelt had reassured Stalin that Argentina would not attend the conference. In the intervening months, however, Roosevelt's health deteriorated. Before his death, he initialed a memo allowing Argentina to sign the UN declaration.

Nelson Rockefeller had encouraged Roosevelt to sign the memo as a part of his greater zeal for a "unity of the Americas" concept. Having moved in and out of the New Deal administration, by late 1943 Rockefeller was concerned that the State Department had deemphasized Latin America in favor of Europe in its postwar planning. He advocated a "special status and emphasis" for inter-American affairs, through the appointment of one person to take responsibility for the combined economic and political affairs of Latin America.[34] For nine months starting in 1944, he became assistant secretary of state and head of the State Department's division of Latin American affairs. When the United Nations Conference was held in San Francisco, Rockefeller was not selected to act as an official delegate. He arrived at the conference in a private capacity and chose to stay in the same hotel as the Latin American delegation. While there, he entertained delegates in his hotel and otherwise antagonized Cordell Hull's successor at the State Department, Edward Stettinius.[35] The Latin American states posed a delicate problem for the American diplomats because they were nineteen of the forty-six states attending the conference. Hence, the United States needed them to vote as a bloc to outvote the Soviet states. As the conference progressed, Rockefeller was so successful in unifying the Latin votes that he was referred to as their "ringmaster."[36] It is debatable whether they would have organized themselves in this fashion had Rockefeller not played this role.

In general, development issues did not dominate the San Francisco conference because there was no self-aware group of so-called developing countries. Although it was widely known that economic disparities existed, economic strategy proposed the same solution for all countries seeking to improve their fortunes.[37] In organizing as a regional bloc, however, the Latin American states demonstrated that their voting power was disproportionate to their political power, which would have long-term consequences for the promotion of development in the organization that followed. The organization also exacerbated the Cold War insofar as the Soviets realized that they would have to hold firm on other issues when facing this formidable voting bloc.[38]

Having always supported the technical work of the League, the United States envisioned an ECOSOC that would act on information provided by neutral research of the Department of Economic Affairs. Others shared the American view. Individuals from the League's economic section felt that the League's technical work had been its most successful yet underappreciated work. A representative of the Canadian government, Louis Rasminsky, was assigned to the San Francisco committee considering the purpose and structure of the ECOSOC. Although Rasminsky did not seek to design the type of international organization that the UN would become, he was convinced of the connection between economic distress and war. He thus sought to encourage the importance of the UN's technical capabilities. Problems arose when countries wished to distort statistics for political purposes. Therefore, although the United States had endorsed the creation of ECOSOC, small states upgraded its status to a principal organ of the UN at the San Francisco meeting.[39]

The work of the new United Nations was at last under way, with six main organs: the General Assembly, Security Council, ECOSOC, Trusteeship Council, International Court of Justice, and Secretariat. The General Assembly serves as the main deliberative organ of all member states, each having one vote. The Security Council would maintain international peace and security; thus, it could be convened at any time. Of the fifteen members, five are permanent (China, France, USSR [now Russia], the United Kingdom, and the United States). ECOSOC would coordinate the economic and social work of the UN. The Trusteeship Council would supervise the administration of the Trust Territories. The International Court of Justice would be the main judicial organ, located in The Hague. Last, the Secretariat would be where an international staff worked at UN headquarters to carry out the day-to-day work of the organization.

The role of the Rockefeller family in the formation of the UN persisted well after Nelson left the Roosevelt administration. When the UN was temporarily headquartered on Long Island, New York, and considering competing bids from Philadelphia and San Francisco to make its permanent home in those cities, Mayor William O'Dwyer asked him to join a committee of New York civic leaders who were encouraging the UN to stay in the area. As the negotiations heated up and it appeared that the organization might move, Rockefeller scrambled to offer a parcel of land on the family estate at Pocantico Hills. Upon hearing that the UN would not likely accept this offer, Nelson raised the possibility of purchasing a tract of land on the East River that had been purchased by a developer. Although the property had some disadvantages, his father, John D. Rockefeller Jr., offered to buy it for $8.5 million and donate it to the United Nations. Recalling an earlier gift of the library to the League of Nations, for which he had been responsible for a considerable Swiss tax liability, he stipulated that the transfer would have to be free of any gift tax. The offer was accepted.[40] Nelson would continue to play a role in Latin American affairs, as well as in the formation of an International Finance Corporation (IFC) as part of the young World Bank Group.

The principle of NGO (nongovernmental organization) representation had been introduced at the San Francisco conference, and provisions were made for consultative arrangements to the ECOSOC. These provisions were controversial from the start in terms of both the criteria that would define NGO eligibility and the status NGOs would be accorded. In the early years of the ECOSOC, a further difficulty arose with respect to national organizations. The International Chamber of Commerce from the League era was granted Category A consultative status with the ECOSOC in 1947. It still holds this position, although the Cold War caused relations to deteriorate in the interim. The International Chamber of Commerce was the only NGO that could address plenary sessions and meetings at the United

Nations Conference on Trade and Employment, held in Havana from November 1947 to February 1948. Later, when the ITO charter failed, the International Chamber of Commerce concentrated on building the GATT into a permanent organization.[41] By 1967, of approximately 378 NGOs with consultative status, only about a dozen could have been considered national, yet most of the 12 were American, including the US Chamber of Commerce and the National Association of Manufacturers.[42]

Ensuring American Participation in the New International Organizations

Inis Claude argues that the nature of both the League of Nations and the United Nations was set by the prevailing understanding of the wars that prompted their creation. With the UN, the sense was that the dictators who started the war would not have done so if the great powers of the day had been aligned in determined opposition to any breach of the peace.[43] Given the American ambivalence toward multilateral arrangements and failure to join the League of Nations, the system needed to secure US membership and a domestic base of support in American politics. Efforts were under way from the start. With approval from the White House, the State Department initiated a public relations blitz for the United Nations. In the late summer of 1943, the Postwar Advisory Council of the Republican Party adopted a resolution favoring responsible participation by the United States in a postwar cooperative organization among sovereign nations. Senator Arthur Vandenberg (R-Michigan) desired a middle ground between isolation and international organization. He went on to become a major figure in creating the UN.[44] Leaders from the foreign policy establishment invited fifty organizations to meet in New York to discuss a pro-UN strategy in September 1944. Forty groups assembled and agreed to back a common campaign for it.[45]

Similar efforts were under way to secure passage of the Bretton Woods Agreement. When Keynes's and White's early proposals for international financial institutions had begun to circulate, the chief opponents had been in the US Senate and the American banking community. Among these opponents, the American Bankers Association supported the formation of the IBRD but not the IMF. The association challenged the IMF on the grounds that the way the new organization would govern exchange rates effectively made the dollar the only viable world currency. The United States would thus be obliged to provide dollars for any country that asked.[46] The New York banking community opposed the creation of a public fund by its very nature as a public entity and because the proposals contained the possibility of mandatory controls on the movement of capital. Although the bankers could not prevent the IMF from forming, they were able to tone down proposals for obligatory cooperative controls. In the final agreement, the US government would not be required to introduce capital controls.[47] New Deal industrialists were much more supportive of the Bretton Woods plan, and this division between bankers and industrialists was repeated in other industrialized countries.[48]

At the inaugural meeting of the IBRD and the IMF in Savannah, Georgia, in March 1946, what participants termed a "bad spirit" developed between the US delegation and practically all of the other delegations.[49] The Europeans and Canadians were particularly disturbed that the IMF headquarters would be located in Washington, DC. To these delegations, the Americans appeared to consider every technical question with reference to US politics; the fund thus had to be located in Washington near the Federal Reserve Board and the Treasury.[50] In a separate debate, the United Kingdom sought an IMF that would preserve sovereignty in financial affairs, and the United States sought one that would be more interventionist.[51] Nonetheless, in the years following the war, the United States held nearly all of the global financial resources. There were no drawings from the IMF in 1950 at all. Eventually, the members accommodated the United States.[52]

The Cold War and the Western Alliance

The initial outline of a system of international organizations was drawn when the allies were still fighting World War II. The planners therefore created IOs that were a mix of cooperative efforts with a heavy dose of the reality of the atrocities of war and the spoils of victory. Once the hostilities ceased, however, the rapid deterioration of relations between two of the Big Three powers shaped the operation of many of the newly formed organizations and compelled governments on each side to participate in new ones. These initiatives progressed in parallel, and there was little overlapping administrative purview. Funding for the different organizations also came from diverse processes and sources.

After the Cold War tensions were out in the open, additional pillars of the postwar settlement became a necessity to cement the Western alliance. NATO and the predecessor to the European Union have origins in this need. Both of these arrangements were influenced by a desire to keep the United States involved and engaged in European security against the perceived Soviet threat. But the latter also allowed European states to compete with the United States. Despite the focus on resisting a communist threat in Europe throughout much of the American planning, the first armed confrontation that would test the new system occurred in Asia with the outbreak of the Korean conflict.

The Cold War

After Germany invaded the USSR in June 1941, the United States, Soviet Union, and Great Britain identified Nazi Germany as a threat to their joint survival, and the Allies' military alliance was a necessary arrangement. There had been bitter opposition among the three before the war, particularly between Winston Churchill and the Communist regime. Disputes continued throughout the war. Thus, it is not surprising that once Germany was defeated, the alliance fractured. The main divisions were over Poland and the states in regions liberated by the Allies. The USSR wanted to prevent another Western European invasion through Central and Eastern Europe. For Stalin, therefore, security came from Soviet control over all the states the Red Army occupied at the end of hostilities. Such control would prevent Germany from posing a future threat.[53]

Relations continued to deteriorate in 1946 and 1947. In March 1946, Harry Truman saw a turning point in American foreign policy with the Greek civil war. Fearing a communist victory, Truman addressed a joint session of Congress to present his case that the war there was not just between Greeks but one of outside aggression. Truman argued that the United States has a duty to support free peoples who are resisting attempted subjugation by armed minorities or outside pressures. Although it was not clear that Stalin masterminded the Greek revolution, for Truman and the US public, revolutions in the name of Karl Marx were connected to Moscow. A bipartisan, anticommunist consensus was formed that remained until the 1960s.[54] Churchill likewise argued that an "Iron Curtain" had descended across Europe.[55]

Three months after Truman's speech, the United States sought further to protect its interests in Europe. In April 1948, the United States launched an initiative to aid Western Europe, the European Recovery Program, or Marshall Plan. Its goals were to rebuild the regions that had been devastated by war, remove trade barriers among them, and make Europe prosperous again to prevent the spread of communism. In addition, a prosperous Europe would be able to purchase American goods. Stalin was suspicious of US-British ties that would result in a US-dominated Western Bloc, as well as the American establishment of overseas military bases that enabled the United States to control the Atlantic and Pacific Oceans, particularly in Japan.[56] The United States offered Marshall Plan assistance to the Soviet Union and Eastern countries, but the USSR refused it and prevented East Germany, Poland, and others from accepting: acceptance would have come with preconditions, including demands on Soviet behavior, that were unacceptable.[57] Despite substantive limits on Soviet power, one effect of the Marshall Plan was to halt any advance of Communist parties in Western Europe, from which Stalin gained his influence. The next year, tensions mounted with Stalin's creation of the Cominform, or Communist Information System, to coordinate the activities of Communist parties that the Soviets directed.

The first test of the American willingness to mobilize against communism occurred outside the expressed US defense perimeter in South Korea when North Korea invaded on June 25, 1950. The Truman administration acted as if it were a "surprise attack" and concluded that the invasion represented another case of Soviet aggression. Although the evidence for these claims has been argued since that time, Truman reacted by ordering naval and air support from Japan to bolster the retreating South Korean army. He took the issue to an emergency session of the UN Security Council, which passed a resolution condemning the invasion and calling for a withdrawal of

North Korean forces from South Korea. On June 27, the Security Council passed another resolution for UN members to contribute forces for a "police action" to repel the invaders. The resolutions were facilitated because the Soviet delegation was boycotting the Security Council in protest of its refusal to seat the People's Republic of China on the world body. With the second resolution, the UN authorized military involvement in Korea.[58]

The North Atlantic Treaty Organization

When the Nazis invaded Poland in September 1939, the concept of collective security as defined by the League of Nations was definitively discredited. As wartime collaboration between the United States, Great Britain, and the USSR collapsed, the UN Security Council embodied a modified type of collective security with the concept of a "veto" by the five permanent members. The veto ensures that the Security Council will never declare one of those five to be an aggressor, since they can simply vote against the resolution. As the Cold War escalated, a series of events led to the construction of the North Atlantic Treaty Organization. The new organization entailed collective security arrangements unlike the League of Nations or United Nations because it rejected the notion of universal membership and the goal of preventing all wars from the outset. Rather, the concept of collective defense in NATO aimed to create a spirit of solidarity and cohesion among its members as an alliance against common enemies.

The reality for the West was that the USSR appeared to present a first-order threat, particularly as tensions heightened with the Greek civil war and Korean conflict in 1949 and 1950. Therefore, the outlines of the new international organizations shifted from the vision of the Allies fighting the common enemy of Nazi Germany to one of the new alignments and divisions among them. Each camp set about creating its own institutions and unity within it. In March 1948, the governments of Belgium, Great Britain, France, the Netherlands, and Luxembourg signed the Treaty of Brussels, establishing a collective defense alliance among them. They hoped to signal to the Americans that they were willing to stand against the Soviet Union and persuade the United States to agree to a direct commitment in this regard.[59]

Although the United States still contained isolationist political elements, both Democrats and Republicans were predisposed toward establishing a formal alliance with Europe because those involved with the postwar occupation came to share the belief that the USSR constituted a growing threat to the vital interests of both the United States and Western Europe.[60] Exemplifying this American ambivalence, the Senate's leading Republican on national security issues, Arthur Vandenberg, had doubts about unfettered support for Europe but nonetheless saw the Soviets as a threat. In a one-page document, the Vandenberg Resolution declared the Senate's intent to pursue collective defense arrangements. Some elements of the foreign policy establishment, such as diplomat George Kennan and Senator Robert Taft (R-OH) opposed a formal alliance and preferred a unilateral declaration.[61]

Much of the debate centered around the treaty's Article 5 wherein an attack on one state would be considered an attack on all.[62] Despite these challenges, the Washington Treaty, or North Atlantic Treaty, was signed in Washington on April 4, 1949, by twelve founding members. It derives its authority from Article 51 of the United Nations Charter, which affirms the right of states to individual or collective defense.[63] Article 5's reference to the UN Charter is ambiguous. Regardless, NATO was established because the states concluded that the Soviet Union threatened their existence. Lord Hastings Ismay, NATO's first secretary-general, joked that the organization's purpose was "to keep the Americans in, the Russians out, and the Germans down."[64]

Germany had been an issue from the start. The postwar country had been divided into four occupation zones, yet the Soviet zone was closed off from the three others. The creation of a West German state became a high priority for the US government as the first line of defense against Soviet expansion. The United States created a parliamentary government there in 1949. Soon thereafter, the United States integrated the new state into the international trading system, supplied it with Marshall Plan aid, and introduced a new currency. Its new chancellor, Konrad Adenauer, attempted to integrate the Federal Republic of Germany into the Western European community.[65]

Although West German territory was covered by the initial NATO security guarantee, the new state was not a treaty member. It remained under Allied

Fig. 2.2. Official flag of the Allied Atlantic Command, North Atlantic Treaty Organization, April 7, 1952. United States Navy. Harry S. Truman Library & Museum, Accession Number 96-752.

military occupation until 1952 and had no armed forces of its own. The French and other Europeans were reluctant to allow Germany to rearm. The Soviet Union also opposed the rearmament of Western Germany. Nonetheless, the fear of German militarism was met with the fear of potential Soviet aggression. German troops were needed to reinforce NATO ground forces. Eventually, NATO members agreed on West Germany's entry by the end of 1954, with the condition that it supply twelve divisions of ground forces and that it be prohibited from developing nuclear, bacteriological, or chemical weapons, warships, and long-range missiles and bombers.[66]

Within the NATO alliance, fissures existed among members. Most notable was tension created through the assertive French nationalism of Charles de Gaulle. De Gaulle argued that the Americans, along with their ally Great Britain, were too dominant in NATO. He questioned the American commitment to defend Europe. He rejected a US offer to put nuclear weapons in France and created his own nuclear arsenal, the *force de frappe*, or strike force. In so doing, de Gaulle made France a nuclear power. Yet in the 1960s, he would not join other countries' nuclear arms control agreements. In 1966, he withdrew all French troops from NATO, although he did not withdraw from the alliance.[67]

As the West deepened its integration, the USSR developed its own program of economic and political integration in Eastern Europe. The Soviets had developed the Council of Mutual Economic Aid, or COMECON, to integrate Poland, Hungary, Romania, Czechoslovakia, and Bulgaria (and later Albania). The economies emphasized war industries, and not consumer goods. The estates of nobles and churches were confiscated. Political changes accompanied the economic ones. Opposition parties were declared illegal. In the early years of the COMECON, intellectual property rights were also weakened in such a way that each country's technological advances were made available to others for a small charge. This principle of intellectual exchange benefitted the less industrialized, less technologically advanced countries such as the Soviet Union to the detriment of the more advanced countries in the Soviet Bloc such as East Germany and Czechoslovakia. In 1955, the Soviet Union created the Warsaw Treaty Organization, or Warsaw Pact, in response to the German inclusion in NATO. Its members could not withdraw. The Soviet army underpinned these arrangements.[68] The Soviets therefore also attempted to coordinate relations, but in a more coercive manner than the institutions that developed in the West.

The European Economic Community

The other element that cemented the Western alliance was the unification of Western Europe in pursuit of economic, political, and social relations. The earliest efforts to unify Europe could be attributed to the emperor Charlemagne (742–814) or to military efforts at conquest, such as Napoleon or Hitler. However, the devastation caused by World War II convinced many that a new type of political arrangement was needed to prevent further ruinous conflict among these states. As with NATO, American involvement shaped the outcome, both in a positive sense—in promoting integration—

and negative sense—in serving as an entity against which Europe was integrated.[69] The United States saw integration was a way of promoting prosperity,
strengthening Western Europe's resistance to communism, and reconciling
old enemies.

At first, the United States used the Marshall Plan as an instrument to encourage the European recipients to coordinate plans for using the aid.[70] After the Soviet Union declined to participate, the sixteen countries that did
join convened a Conference on European Economic Cooperation in Paris.
The conference established a committee and a variety of technical groups to
sketch the recovery program presented to the US government in September
1947. An Organisation for European Economic Co-operation (OEEC) was
established in order to administer the aid.[71] Allocating aid proved to be such
a difficult task for the OEEC that it ceded this responsibility to a US government agency three years later. Nonetheless, in the early years of the organization, intra-OEEC trade rose by 272 percent and propelled the European
recovery. The problems it encountered forced it to experiment with working
routines that remain a part of its successor organization's surveillance practices.[72] Officials learned the habit of cooperating with one another and taking the interests of others into consideration when they returned to make
policy in their own states. Finally, the early OEEC expressed a community
sense of capitalism and democracy.[73] Therefore, although the OEEC's legacy is debatable, it remains a fixture on the landscape of international organizations through its successor organization, the OECD.

In 1949, states established the Council of Europe (an organization separate from what became the European Economic Community and its body
of ministers, the European Council of the European Union) as a consultative body; nonetheless, it was the first post-1945 European political organization. The Council of Europe's notable achievement was the signing in
November 1950 of the European Convention on Human Rights, which
some authors regard as the true start of a modern human rights movement.[74]
The convention was a sophisticated treaty for its time because it provided
for a commission, which determines the admissibility of petitions, and a
Court of Human Rights. The court sits at Strasbourg, France, to provide rulings on the cases presented. While the European Court has been criticized

for its relative lack of enforcement mechanism, it is nonetheless significant because it can be seen as a role model for future world bodies under the United Nations.[75]

In May 1950, it was apparent that a union with a stronger political objective would not be acceptable to all European states. Nonetheless, the effort took on new energy when French foreign minister Robert Schuman proposed combining coal and steel resources in the Schuman Plan, which became the blueprint for the European Coal and Steel Community (ECSC). Drafted by Jean Monnet, who had worked in national economic planning in postwar France, it embodied the view that economic prosperity and development could be best achieved at the European, rather than national, level. Writing at a time when most French people distrusted Germany, Monnet had also argued that peace and stability in Europe could be achieved only through a joint venture of France and Germany. It would reconcile Franco-German interests by pooling coal and steel resources under one high authority.

West German chancellor Konrad Adenauer accepted the plan and thus helped to form the precursor to the European Community: the ECSC was established in April 1951. Although the ECSC was limited, it provided a psychological space for some in Europe to move forward.[76] Moreover, it was Western Europe's first organization that redistributed a degree of state sovereignty to a supranational authority. Although all Western European states were invited to join, only Belgium, Italy, Luxembourg, and the Netherlands accepted the supranational principle of the ECSC.[77] Other communities were proposed, including a European Defense Community and a European Political Community, but were rejected by the French parliament.

France and Germany thus played key roles in forming the European Community, although ideology was not a major motive at first. In the mid-1950s, the effort at integrating European defense fell short, but intra-European trade rose, due to the successes of the OEEC and the GATT. In response, negotiations began to establish a European Economic Community (EEC). To gain domestic support for the more comprehensive integration, those involved insisted on a special regime for agriculture in the common market, assistance for French overseas territories, and the establishment of a European nuclear power body. Great Britain did not participate. Hence, the Treaty of Rome, signed in March 1957 and establishing the EEC, was a typical political compromise.[78] The same day, the same countries signed the treaty establishing the European Atomic Energy Community for the purpose of developing peaceful applications of atomic energy. Together, the two treaties are sometimes called the Treaties of Rome.

The institutional structure of the EEC followed the lines of the ECSC. A supranational European commission was intended to be the driving force of integration, counterbalanced by a council of ministers representing the member states. An assembly and the European Court of Justice were added, and they asserted themselves within the arrangements to enlarge their own authority. The European Court ruled that EEC law took precedence over national law and thus became a major bonding force.[79]

From the start, the new project faced issues of democratic legitimacy of the kind that would later be addressed with direct elections to provide accountability to the institutions of unification. The European Parliament was originally the Common Assembly of the earlier ECSC. Yet a legislative body was not central to the founders' plans. The assembly had very limited and specific powers and mostly could only give opinions on laws. It was not elected by voters but was drawn from the member states' national parliaments. When the Treaty of Rome was signed, governments were cautious about stronger European-level institutions; officials felt that an elected parliament might use this democratic legitimacy to argue for other prerogatives. Thus, there were no provisions for direct elections in the early European Community.[80]

In 1958, when the EEC was established, the collapse of the French Fourth Republic and return of General Charles de Gaulle in France was bigger news. De Gaulle wanted to see a common agricultural policy in the EEC.[81] However, he had fought the ECSC and European defense efforts. He favored European integration in order to contain Germany and counter American power, but only so far as it served French interests. De Gaulle twice rebuffed the United Kingdom's attempt to join. In 1965, he boycotted the work of the organization, creating a crisis in its early history. When he resigned from office in 1969, the EEC was economically strong but politically weak. For much of the 1970s, the EEC appeared to be stagnant.[82]

Once established, the EEC's institutions began to consolidate. The integration of Europe followed no master plan but occurred in response to domestic and international pressures, as well as competing visions of the future. Yet in these early years, the EEC confronted issues that have remained central to the unification of Europe ever since. On one hand, deepening the community would allow for more intensive integration; on the other, broadening it would cover a wider territory. However, issues connected to the rate of integration and how integration relates to enlargement are highly contentious.[83]

Conclusion

The landscape of international organizations changed significantly after World War II, initially due to the relations among the Allies as the war progressed, and later due to the division of the world into the two Cold War blocs that hindered the operations of some international organizations and called for the creation of other entirely new ones. However, once established, the successes of the IOs initiated the creation of others along the same lines. Hence, the ideological underpinnings of the IOs were subject to constant change and ranged from the broad idealism of Roosevelt's four freedoms to the more practical necessity of the early ECSC on the part of Germany and France. The consequence is that the domestic bases of political support for this budding system of IOs likewise continually shifted.

The process of forming an embryonic framework of IOs was thus far from preordained. Development did not move toward a predetermined goal. When the Allies' wartime alliance broke apart in the Cold War, most of these IOs failed to embody the vision of their founders. But other attempts to coordinate relations among groups of states according to shared principles grew alongside them, or in their place. For example, the proposed collective security apparatus of the United Nations — the Security Council — was eventually accompanied by the collective defense treaties of NATO and the Warsaw Pact. The International Bank for Reconstruction and Development was subsumed by the Marshall Plan and morphed into a World Bank Group of institutions. Some other questions of German reconstruction were taken up by the ECSC, which became the European Economic Community, where the rate of progress has not been consistent. Every advance has had a powerful countervailing force pulling in the opposite direction.[84] Some organizations became cornerstones of the postwar order, while others have receded or never developed as envisioned. All remain subject to recurring modification.

THREE

Decolonization and Development

At the time the postwar planners constructed a framework for formal international organizations, most of the people living in Africa and Asia were governed by some kind of colonial arrangement where ultimate political decisions were made overseas. The origins of these arrangements were economic and commenced with the earliest activities of European joint-stock companies that traded around the globe and consolidated political control to protect their business operations.[1] As Europe industrialized, imperial powers expanded their control over the governments and economies of their overseas territories. Colonial markets grew. Yet the industrialization that occurred later was different because it occurred in a world economy where some parts of the world had already done so. Thus, the later industrializers had relationships (colonial and otherwise) with the industrial economies that now existed. Since one side now had more advanced technology and organization, it could preempt the opportunities of the other. Albert O. Hirschman and other political economists have described these as "structural," "dependent," or "late" development patterns where the context of the world economy and political associations influenced who became entrepreneurs and what types of products they produced.[2]

Once the formal colonial arrangements began to unravel after the two world wars, they quickly fell apart. At the domestic level, people fought for their liberation. At the international level, the military defeat of fascism and discovery of human rights abuses in Nazi Germany discredited the laws and

policies of racial discrimination in the Western societies that exercised colonial rule.[3] The United Nations Charter institutionalized the notion of self-
determination in a growing body of international law. The UN General
Assembly incorporated various declarations and resolutions that acquired
moral and legal force. Once the process of decolonization was under way,
the new states called for more of it in the new international forums. In 1960,
the process was inevitable; by 1980, it was essentially complete.[4] And IOs
had helped to make it happen in the political sphere.

The economic strings were much more difficult to disentangle, however,
and the role of IOs in the economic sphere has been much less tidy. The
entry of so many new and diverse states into the multilateral political system
nonetheless transformed it internally and externally. The rapidly expanding
number of state members of IOs were less culturally and ethnically homogenous than they had been at the end of the war. Some were wealthier and
others poorer. The new numbers changed the balance among voting majorities, which brought a whole new set of issues to the fore—chief among
them the need for technical assistance from the West and the advancement
of economic development in terms of money and strategies to promote industrialization. Therefore, as imperial operations wound down, IOs took on
many colonial tasks, with the exception that they did not directly administer
territory.[5] The new states worked in a coalition on some issues, but this coalition broke down on others. The new settings gave former colonies voting
advantages where they frequently did not have corresponding power or economic capacity. In response, developed states changed their strategies, insofar as they sought to bring their own issues to IOs where they retained a
voting advantage. The upshot is that by the 1970s, the Bretton Woods institutions that had struggled earlier in their existence became more significant
players than the United Nations system. The UN organs became fragmented and were underfunded, particularly in the field of economic development.

This chapter explores how multilateralism accommodated and facilitated the expansion of the state system with the end of colonialism. It considers how the concept of development that accompanied these changes
was shaped by the American response to Cold War competition as it both

heated up and then cooled off. In some respects, the UN's most successful project has been to usher in the major transition to sovereign statehood that has rendered one of its six organs—the Trusteeship Council—obsolete. Yet in another sense, efforts to reduce global inequality have revealed the depth of some of the associated problems that plague the world community to this day. While some would argue that multilateralism birthed many developing states, others would claim that as development became a part of the multilateral project, the predicament of less developed states grew worse.

Decolonization, Development, and the International Framework

The sovereign representation of peoples in the developing world is a relatively recent historical phenomenon. Before the formal independence of India in 1947, much of the world's population in developing countries was represented in international organizations through some colonial vehicle. Although Latin American states participated directly in the League of Nations because they were formally independent from European rule a century earlier, any notion of development in Latin America came along with the New Deal and Good Neighbor policies of the US government in the 1930s that sought to counter the Nazi economic and military influence in the region.[6] As we saw in chapter 2, the initial state advocates for development within the UN were the Latin American states working as a voting bloc at the San Francisco conference. The United States took their concerns seriously at the time in order to counter the Soviet strength. In the African and Asian context, development evolved along with decolonization and was propelled as more new states entered IOs.

The introduction of so many new states into the working of IOs, together with the new numbers, revolutionized the multilateral system. First of all, the new states meant that UN representatives were no longer as racially homogenous. Second, their membership meant a shift in programmatic focus to development at the international level. Third, entirely new IOs were created. With new organizations and overlapping areas of expertise and action, states became strategic about where they raised their concerns and sought remedies.

Colonial Territories in International Organizations

In the interwar period, the League of Nations covenant set an international precedent for some form of eventual participation of subject peoples in their own government. A European government acting as a "mandatory power" would "tutor" them for an indeterminate period of time before that participation would become a reality. The first League assembly created a Permanent Mandates Commission to review reports that were required annually. Although the United States did not participate in the Mandates Commission and the colonies of the Allies were not included in its oversight, many features of the League of Nations Mandates Commission carried over into the United Nations.[7]

Chapter XI (on Non-Self-Governing Territories) of the UN Charter established the Trusteeship Council according to the explicit principle that the interests of inhabitants of nonsovereign territories would take precedence in matters pertaining to governance. Administering authorities agreed to "accept a direct responsibility to the UN for administering the trustee territories, in accordance with the principles in the UN Charter." As a part of these responsibilities, the authorities would promote the well-being of inhabitants by ensuring their advancement, just treatment, and protection against abuses. Authorities would develop self-government as well as economic development. Along the lines of the League, the authorities would submit information concerning the economic, social, and educational conditions and would conduct research accordingly. Finally, the authorities would encourage respect for human rights. Nonetheless, the Charter was primarily concerned with the powers to be exercised by the administering authorities and not the rights of the people in the trust territories.

When the San Francisco conference establishing the UN was held, representatives from China, India, Syria, Poland, and Byelorussia raised the issue of the participation of indigenous inhabitants of colonies. In particular, the representative of China advocated for representation of the people of trust territories in meetings of the Trusteeship Council when matters affecting a particular territory were being considered. The Chinese proposal, however, was neither discussed nor considered. It did not appear in the drafts examined by the committee that formed the contents of Chapter XIII (on the Trusteeship Council) of the Charter.[8]

Thus, in the years immediately preceding independence, the UN found itself in a paradoxical situation with respect to colonialism. In its trusteeship responsibilities, it was engaged with, and responsible for, individuals living there; yet, the organization continued to show deference to the colonial authorities. Its structure blocked any comprehensive change because the different UN organs responsible—the Trusteeship Council, Security Council, and General Assembly—did not always agree among themselves on the best manner to handle a given situation. There was a particular degree of conflict between the Trusteeship Council and the Fourth Committee of the General Assembly, the Special Political and Decolonization Committee.

Limited as it was in the UN, participation by indigenous peoples was even more restricted in the early IMF and World Bank. The early IMF sought to foster stable exchange rates, and most colonies' currency was managed through a currency board or other regional arrangement. Their status in the IMF therefore derived from the colonial power's acceptance of the IMF Articles of Agreement. The World Bank could, and did, make loans to colonies. However, metropolitan governments (or those in the parent country) controlled the entry of external capital, "to protect the native inhabitants from exploitation and sometimes in the interest of their own investors or enterprises."[9] Foreign enterprises therefore had to negotiate with the metropolitan country before they could embark on any new venture. This posed a considerable obstacle if each side had to negotiate from scratch.

Postcolonial Territories in International Organizations

The UN Charter declares that all people have the right to national self-determination. However, what constitutes a "people" or a "national self"? Benyamin Neuberger makes the point that the British who opposed Irish independence saw only one "national self," whereas the Irish saw themselves as distinct.[10] Moreover, internal and external self-determination are not easily separated, nor is political self-determination easily separated from economic.[11] Self-determination in the UN came to be identified with a very specific type: the liberation of nonwhite peoples from European rule.[12]

The connection between decolonization and multilateralism gave rise to arguments for a new understanding of sovereignty after decolonization, wherein changing assumptions and beliefs about the right to sovereignty became embodied in institutions, laws, treaties, and conferences. Robert H. Jackson argues that what were then referred to as third world states (according to their status in terms of wealth and class) were more appropriately termed "quasi-states," meaning that they were not self-standing structures with domestic foundations but territorial jurisdictions supported from above by international law and material aid. In that sense, they were more juridical entities than empirical ones.[13]

Once the post–World War II decolonization movement was under way, it gained momentum from the existence of representatives of new states who spoke out against colonialism in IOs. Among these, India (along with other semiautonomous dominion territories in the British Empire— Canada, South Africa, New Zealand, and Australia) had been a founding member of the UN. Formally independent after Britain's passage of the Indian Independence Act of 1947, India played a major role in the struggle against colonialism and apartheid in the UN. Notably, an Indian representative served as the first chair of the Decolonization Committee.[14]

Although the new states were all former colonies, the similarities ended there. Their colonial experiences varied dramatically in terms of duration, what stage of economic development the rest of the world experienced at the time, and how the colonial power in question had administered the territory when it had political control. In addition, these states possessed little real knowledge of one another. Many had few or no democratic features in their domestic governments. Gross asymmetries of levels of technological capacity and wealth now existed, as well as more authoritarian governments in these states that prevented a genuine civil society from emerging. Independent organizations such as church groups, clubs, community organizations, and professional organizations that could have provided services or participated in NGO forums like those in the industrial state members of the 1940s simply did not exist in many of the newly admitted states.

At the same time that decolonization was gaining steam, development became a key component of US foreign policy. Harry Truman's "Four

Point" inaugural speech on January 20, 1949, marked the turning point. In it, Truman advocated sharing scientific advances and industrial progress to advance the growth of underdeveloped areas as part of a larger effort seeking peace and freedom. Foreign aid thus accompanied the US strategy for world economic recovery alongside the Marshall Plan and NATO.[15] Within the UN, Truman's speech marked a change of course, and the specialized agencies received a new impetus when the ECOSOC created the Expanded Programme of Technical Assistance for Economic Development with larger appropriations.[16]

The so-called free technical assistance was not without controversy. Stephen Browne argues that this assistance made recipients believe that they could not have managed without it and then became ingrained as a "natural" basis for development cooperation. In many cases, technical assistance of this type actually reflects what donors are best able to provide, and not necessarily what a developing country needs. Over time, recipients look to foreign solutions rather than developing their own capacities according to their own objectives.[17]

Despite the controversies connected to the concept of development, the involvement of the UN provided an outlet for economists from the developing world to continue to generate new thinking on the position of these states in the structure of the global economy. The Prebisch-Singer thesis was one such idea, formulated by Argentinian economist Raul Prebisch and British development theorist Hans Singer, who were then working at the United Nations—Prebisch at the Economic Commission for Latin America in Chile and Singer in New York.[18] According to the thesis, the net barter terms of trade (or the ratio between the price of a country's export and import goods) trends downward for developing countries that export primary commodities and import manufactured goods. Thus, developing countries exporting primary products will find themselves at a structural disadvantage to manufactured goods no matter how many primary commodities they export. Publications started to distinguish groups of countries between "center" and "periphery" wherein the core, or center, held certain structural advantages and the periphery disadvantages. Some form of intervention would be needed to rectify this situation.

SUNFED, IDA, and IFC

The combination of new states in the UN, new thinking about self-determination and development, and the American shift in support for development as a component of its broader policy agenda eventually resulted in more substantive UN policy initiatives, notably attempts to gain access to development funding on easy terms within the UN.[19] The results of these and other efforts put the UN and the World Bank on a path in financing development that eventually encompassed a wide-ranging landscape of agencies, banks, and funding agencies, each serving the differing interests of donors and recipients.

One of the earliest initiatives was a 1949 proposal for creating an international agency within the UN to provide and coordinate technical assistance to developing countries, assist them in obtaining requisite materials for economic development, finance national development projects, and direct and finance regional development projects. Variations on this proposal dominated economic discussions in the UN in the 1950s, notably the Special United Nations Fund for Economic Development (SUNFED). Led by China, India, and Yugoslavia, developing countries argued that SUNFED should be available to all countries, and not serve as a means of foreign economic and political interference in their internal affairs.[20] The United States was finally convinced to create a low-interest, long-term lending facility. However, when it did, it did so under the auspices of the World Bank Group, in the form of the International Development Association (IDA) and not the UN.[21]

Other debates about the institutional environment for development took place during these years. As with the creation of IDA, the United States continued to prefer to create new institutions under the umbrella of the World Bank Group, where it held several advantages, such as the preferential voting allocation for wealthier states and the participation of Americans in bank leadership. Once development moved onto the US foreign policy agenda, the Truman administration's International Development Advisory Board, headed by Nelson Rockefeller, sought to increase the flow of private investment from the United States and Europe to Latin America, Asia, and Africa.[22] An International Finance Corporation was part of this proposal. Others in the administration opposed it, however, because it would have allowed for the IFC to buy stock in a corporation—and in effect own a private business, which ran counter to American ideas about free enterprise. After a delay of several years and the rise of rival development assistance by the USSR and its satellites in the form of long-term exchange contracts for their products, pressures again grew for some type of facility.[23] The United States eventually gave in and offered support for an IFC. Nonetheless, for the first five years of operation (1956–61), the new IO approved few loans.[24]

The debate over the establishment of SUNFED likewise taught developing countries several significant lessons in the conduct of multilateral diplomacy and the advantage of their growing voting strength in some forums. Not until the 1960s, however, would the influx of large numbers of new states allow them to use the one-state-one-vote feature of the General Assembly to their advantage.[25]

Formal Proposals for Action from Developing Countries

Once the number of newly independent states reached a critical mass, they organized in groups and sought forums in which they could press for their interests more effectively. The form of organization varied according to the IO in question. A coalition that comprised regional blocs, known as the Group of Seventy-Seven (G77), operated in the United Nations, and the Group of Twenty-Four (G24) pressed for developing country interests in the Bretton Woods organizations. The coalitions sought distributive justice not for *peoples* but for *states* connected through their status as former colonial subjects, regardless of whether some indigenous subjects had accrued wealth in the colonial regime. Tension among and within blocs ran high on some issues; therefore, proposals were extremely vague so all could agree, as opposed to addressing the substantive needs of the coalition. The culmination of organized diplomatic efforts by the third world to press for these claims was the New International Economic Order (NIEO), a policy program that contained many of the internal contradictions of the G77 coalition.

Working in a Coalition: The Group of Seventy-Seven

Early efforts at organization in IOs sought to strike a middle ground in the Cold War between East and West. The African-Asian Bandung Conference in 1955 was notable for seeking to further the progress of decolonization and foster goals of economic development. Later efforts in this regard came to fruition in the Non-Aligned Movement, which sought mutual peace and security throughout the Cold War. Yet the most inclusive and organized coalition of developing countries to operate in IOs is the G77 coalition, which emerged from the regional consultations and general preparatory consultations held before the first meeting of the United Nations Conference on Trade and Development (UNCTAD). The G77 combination of regional groups was a significant innovation because it was the first time that all developing countries, aside from their regimes and alliances, acted in concert; earlier initiatives such as the Bandung Conference had been confined to the African and Asian regions.

When all five regional groups convened at the general preparatory committee meeting for the first UNCTAD conference, in May–June 1963, the three developing regions considered their economic problems to diverge from those of developed countries. At the closing session of this general committee, the representatives of the developing countries summarized their views, needs, and aspirations with regard to the upcoming UNCTAD conference. Later they submitted this document (which came to be regarded as the Geneva Declaration and prelude to the establishment of the G77) to the UN General Assembly as a joint declaration on behalf of the seventy-five developing-country member states of the UN.[26]

Regional representative systems had been used in the General Assembly and International Labour Organization to ensure equitable geographic representation: Group A represented Eastern Europe excluding Yugoslavia; Group B represented Western Europe, the United States, and Commonwealth countries not included in Groups C or D; Group C represented African and Asian countries and Yugoslavia; and Group D represented Latin American countries. The UNCTAD preparatory committee meetings were different, though, because these groups were based less on geographical representation than on the varying political and economic systems and different stages of economic development of the states themselves. Thus, they had a political character as well as a geographic one.[27] "A" represented industrialized communist states, "B" represented industrialized market economies, and "C" and "D" represented developing countries.

When the regional group representation system used for the UNCTAD preparatory committee meetings later became enshrined in UNCTAD workings as the "group system," the groups did retain a certain degree of their administrative origins. That is, for election purposes and for the definition of their own regional interests, the regional groups always acted separately; for intergroup negotiation purposes, they acted in unison. While Group C represented African countries, Asian countries, and Yugoslavia, it never met as such; rather the African Group and Asian Group met separately, and the Group C delineation was used solely for election to offices within the organization. Therefore, the groups either operated as three "political parties" (East, West, and South) or five (East, West, Latin America, Africa, and Asia).

Institutionalizing the Coalition in UNCTAD

The United Nations called for the first UN Conference on Trade and Development to address issues of trade and development in an integrated manner. As we saw in chapter 2, an organization for this purpose did not exist because the United States had not ratified the Havana Charter signed in 1948 after the UN Conference on Trade and Employment, and the planned International Trade Organization had never materialized with the other Bretton Woods international financial institutions. The USSR, with Eastern Bloc support, had been an early advocate for holding a UN Conference on Trade and Development to form an entirely new and independent institution. The Soviets claimed that the GATT, as it had evolved from the aborted ITO, lacked membership universality. Privately the Soviets had hoped that a new organization would promote an increase in East-West trade, increase the legitimacy of the Soviet state in the system of international trade, and afford them oversight of the multilateral organizations attached to that system.[28] Given Cold War considerations, the United States did not favor creating a new institution as the Soviets did, but preferred to expand the capacities of the GATT, IMF, and World Bank.[29]

Although developing countries failed to set up UNCTAD as an independent institution and in a sense "replace" the GATT, the first conference was successful in instituting UNCTAD as an organ of the UN General Assembly with a trade mandate that encompassed development. Founding

Fig. 3.1. Raul Prebisch, secretary-general of the UNCTAD conference in Geneva, reads his opening statement, March 24, 1964. United Nations Photo #368107.

Secretary-General Raul Prebisch sought to create a body that would advocate for the entire developing world. Thus, in practice, a new organization was created, albeit one whose mission was subject to interpretation. Interpretation meant that while UNCTAD's stated mandate was to promote trade, the West interpreted "promotion" in terms of discussion and not negotiation.

The G77's public display of unity at the first conference meant that the seventy-seven countries did not just act as an unofficial group bound together by common interests but they openly set up a conference within a conference.[30] A pattern developed: a few months before the ministerial meeting of the G77 in preparation for an UNCTAD conference, the regional groups would meet, thus involving a wide array of UN agencies. The

Economic Commission for Africa and Organization for African Unity led the African Group. The Latin American Group had the best institutional support for UNCTAD conferences in the Economic Commission for Latin America. The Asian Group was the weakest in this respect since there was no singular regional organization to provide group unity, with some questioning whether Asia actually constitutes a region. Moreover, the Asians were fragmented into subregional groups wherein the Association of South East Asian Nations and the League of Arab States (which included part of the African region, too) were the most prominent. Japan met with the Asian Group and developed country groups for various purposes in different forums. While individual Asian countries carried weight, and the Economic and Social Commission for Asia and the Pacific attempted to play a coordinating role, intragroup problems meant that a substantial part of the coordinating work of the Asian Group took place either during meetings of the G77 itself or in negotiations with Group B, Group D, and China.[31]

Nonetheless, the key feature of the ideology among the G77, which cemented a strikingly heterogeneous institutional alliance, was not a point of theory upon which all *agreed* but rather one upon which all agreed *not* to agree. Developing countries refused to accept a universal model of development. Third world governments argued that a country's economic system should reflect its cultural history. The only valid interpretation of a country's culture, according to this view, was a government's own.[32] Thus the operative principle was to maintain the world's cultural diversity as a value fostered by the global economic system. Economic principles such as free markets promoting economic efficiency were not themselves universal values to be fostered. In fostering *diversity*, the alliance had a built-in, prior moral justification for the inevitable disagreements that the members of the broad alliance would have. Rather than resolving differences, the preservation of cultural diversity provided a cooperative way to accept those differences.[33]

Although a unified model of economic development did not appear during UNCTAD's first two decades, a unified development ideology did emerge among developing states. The ideology was based on notions of the exploitation of poorer countries by wealthier ones and the unequal exchange between rich and poor in the face of market forces. The secretariat espoused strategies to restructure the entire trading system for the betterment of the G77. The upshot of this development ideology and UNCTAD's one-nation, one-vote system was a politicization of economic relations between North and South in the organization despite deep division within the G77 on both material *and* normative issues throughout its existence in UNCTAD and other international organizations.[34]

Nonetheless, cross-cutting cleavages divided the coalition within UNCTAD's committee work and conference preparation. Overall, India, Pakistan, and the Latin American countries were considered to be "moderates" despite their inflammatory rhetoric. They were essentially countries that had been independent longer, were contracting parties to the GATT, and possessed a relatively higher level of economic development relative to other developing countries. Similarly grouped, the "African 18" were those mostly francophone African countries associated with the European Economic Community whose interests diverged from African Commonwealth countries. In addition, the "extremists" were newly independent countries with a lower level of economic development such as Ghana, Burma, and Indonesia.[35]

UNCTAD and the GATT

The GATT system established at Bretton Woods struggled with the lingering perception through the 1970s and into the 1980s that it was a part of the system created by the victors of World War II that promoted their needs, whereas UNCTAD was a part of the United Nations that resonated with developing countries' concerns. The issues with developing countries were perpetrated by the functioning of the GATT system. Developing countries had been excluded from the earliest GATT negotiations because most were colonies when they were held. Of the twenty-three original GATT signatories, eleven were less developed contracting parties. Two (Lebanon and Syria) dropped out and a third, China (Taiwan) withdrew in 1951.

At decolonization, the new countries all joined the UN and most joined the IMF/IBRD, but few joined the GATT. It was possible to sidestep formal GATT membership because if the General Agreement had been applied in a colonial territory, the postindependence state could continue to apply the GATT treaty on a de facto basis and postpone formalizing its status.[36] Even if a newly independent country wished to participate, its opportunities were limited. Participation in the GATT negotiations were generally at the ambassadorial level. Countries lacking the resources to field ambassadors were often represented by junior officials. These junior officials often were expected only to take notes and were discouraged from more active participation in the decision-making process. Called "green room" consultations, these negotiations were named after the wallpaper in the GATT director-general's conference room in Geneva where they took place. Understandings reached there were presented formally to others, often only with very short notice.[37] One observer described the presence of any developing countries in the GATT in this way: "For the most part they (negotiators from the South) are like extras on the GATT stage: the show can't go on without them, but nobody is remotely interested in what they have to say."[38] Although each contracting party (CP) was technically entitled to one vote under Article 25 of the General Agreement, the CPs rarely voted, except on amendments to the agreement, accession of new members, and waivers.

Despite the thinly veiled rivalry between the GATT and UNCTAD during the 1970s, the GATT was a fundamentally different institution from both UNCTAD and other international financial organizations due to its nature as a binding treaty. The GATT also differed from UNCTAD in that it never recognized a regional group system as UNCTAD did. However, it did recognize a "least developed country" classification.[39] Incorporating these countries more formally into the GATT system would not become a priority for another ten to twenty years, when debt would put serious strains on the G77 coalition, and the GATT would not be able to move forward without the developing world.

The New International Economic Order

Following a directive in the Charter of Algiers in 1967, informal coordinating groups of the Group of Seventy-Seven were established in all headquarters of various UN specialized agencies. By the beginning of the 1970s, the G77 had broadened its scope of activity, and thus its influence, but had decreased the importance of UNCTAD as a group forum since UNCTAD was no longer the only place the coalition operated.[40] As chapters of the G77 fanned out into other IOs and cities, developing countries established the G24 in 1971 to coordinate the positions of developing countries on monetary and finance development issues in the IMF and World Bank. The G24 is a smaller and more specialized body than the G77 and comprises finance ministries and central banks.[41]

During these years, the G77 issued three documents in the UN General Assembly that articulated concrete proposals for the NIEO across IOs: the Declaration on the Establishment of a New International Economic Order, the Programme of Action on the Establishment of a New International Economic Order, and the Charter of the Economic Rights and Duties of States.[42] They advanced five main objectives: to raise the price and volume of developing country exports; change the role of foreign capital through limits in the scope of multinational corporation operations and increased access to capital markets for development finance; increase the flow of public resources to developing countries from developed countries; change the international monetary system; and change the decision-making structure of international economic institutions by revising vote allocation in the IMF, IBRD, and GATT.

The World Bank, Wall Street, the UN, and Development Finance in the 1970s

Although the expansion of G77 activity to include all areas of the UN and other IOs marked a change from its previous exclusive identification with UNCTAD, the ideas contained in the NIEO were not new. However, the old ideas received new *attention* in the West during the 1970s, when the prices of many of the primary commodities that developing countries exported shot up and created vulnerabilities in the developed countries that imported them. During these years, therefore, the growth in what the World Bank did, and what position it held among IOs, shifted because its leadership responded to the new circumstances and the ongoing policy preferences of the US government. The United States had always preferred to promote its development efforts through the bank. By the end of the 1970s, the World Bank would be an important institutional location for development lending and thinking. The UN would likewise take on different roles in response to American actions and its own internal initiatives.

The World Bank and Development Finance

The World Bank's president has always been an American by gentleman's agreement. Nonetheless, the Truman administration had trouble finding an American to serve as the first president of the new organization. Secretary of State James Byrnes offered it to a former Wall Street executive and publisher, Eugene Meyer, most likely because Meyer had organized a high-level famine emergency committee with Truman's sanction.[43] One of the most immediate problems Meyer confronted was in working out the internal governance arrangements in the new institution, chiefly the balance between the president and the board. Under the system of weighted votes established by the World Bank's articles of agreement, the board member with the greatest percentage of votes would also be an American. If the board controlled the organization, the US executive director would have greater influence over its lending policies than the World Bank president would, whereas if the board deferred to the president, the president would have greater influence. Meyer clashed with the first American executive director, Emilio Collado, and resigned, suddenly, in December 1946. At the time, his departure was considered to be a setback from which the young World Bank could never recover.[44] John J. McCloy took the position next but insisted on executive authority, thus settling the question of whether it would rest with the president or the executive directors sent by member states. Eugene Black became the American executive director, and Robert Garner was appointed vice president at the same time.

With the new management arrangements in place, the next step in expanding the reach of the institution would be to borrow money and then lend it out.[45] To expand available capital, McCloy, Garner, and Black decided to issues securities in April 1947. Next, the men moved beyond selling loans from the World Bank's portfolio to underwriting a public bond sale, further expanding the bank's activities.[46] Yet a requirement that governments issue guarantees and other political issues complicated early bank policies. Private enterprise would not seek bank financing for fear that the government guarantee required by the bank would subject them to closer government scrutiny and interference. Governments were likewise skeptical because giving a guarantee also gave the appearance that they were playing favorites. They also wanted to be free to submit their own proposals because government-owned facilities would enhance their own prestige. Some of these hurdles contributed to proposals for an IFC. However, currency was also a problem in that the borrower had to pay in the same currency borrowed. The Latins worried from the start that the bank would be more for reconstruction (of countries recovering from the war) and less for development (of countries needing to catch up in terms of industrialization).[47]

The early and ongoing connections between the IBRD and Wall Street affected the types of loans that were made. In the early years, a sound loan meant that the project would produce earnings that would contribute to repayment. The early lending in developing countries was thus overwhelmingly directed toward such capital infrastructure as railways, communication facilities, power plants, and port facilities. A deeper examination of development needs might have produced a wider range of lending, such as education and urban development; however, some bank officials felt that to lend in the social field would hurt the bank's position in the financial community.[48]

When the first UNCTAD conference met in Geneva, the North-South struggle had virtually replaced the East-West Cold War conflict in economic forums. World Bank president George Woods attempted to strike a cooperative attitude on relations with other international agencies by declaring to the group that the bank would participate actively and affirmatively in UNCTAD deliberations. Furthermore, the bank would move beyond financing infrastructure and would increase its assistance to agricultural and industrial production. Program loans would finance programs to import individual pieces of equipment, components, and spare parts in cases where existing industrial capacity lacked foreign exchange with which to buy equipment. Lending for educational purposes would likewise be expanded.[49] In so doing, Woods worked to make the bank much more of a development institution.[50]

The bank's next president, Robert McNamara, continued in this direction and transformed the organization during his thirteen years at the helm.

Once in office, McNamara sought to develop an intellectual underpinning or foundation for what the World Bank would do under his leadership. His thinking was influenced by Barbara Ward, whom he had first heard speak to Kennedy cabinet members at Robert and Ethel Kennedy's home. A British journalist who had covered the Marshall Plan for Europe, Ward was an admirer of the United States and someone who believed in the potential of foreign aid. As a result of his forays into the topic, McNamara transformed the World Bank into a major center of thinking about development. He also placed an early emphasis on population planning.[51]

For McNamara, the World Bank should seek to address certain objectives in terms of social and economic advance in the developing countries. Achieving those objectives required not only action by the developing countries and their leaders but also external assistance.[52] The effect was that the bank moved beyond infrastructure projects and into a variety of other areas that sought poverty alleviation, investments in human capital, and policy reforms from the top. In addition, McNamara was willing to attach conditions to the organization's work.[53]

The United Nations and Development Finance

During the years that the World Bank grew in prominence in development circles, the United Nations agencies outside of UNCTAD lacked a clear direction. Among them, the United Nations Development Programme (UNDP) had been formed out of the original UN technical assistance programs. Yet UNDP was plagued from the start by the voluntary nature of its funding contribution system. It was always more of a fund than a program, and it lacked a development specialist at its helm.[54] Its top administrators were sympathetic to the NIEO debates, but UNDP largely stayed out of the arena, other than to provide technical assistance to UN bodies such as UNCTAD.[55]

By 1987, at the seventh UNCTAD conference, meetings were held in informal committees. This change opened up the rigid bloc system whereby consensus had been reached within regional groups and could not be altered once the group meeting ended.[56] Yet despite an outward acceptance of the ideas associated with the resolution of their common concerns, states and peoples remained genuinely divided over the merits of the specific policies that the IMF and World Bank were advocating, then known as the Washington Consensus. For example, bringing government spending in line meant cuts in health and education budgets. Economists argued that the Washington Consensus would promote economic growth, but other development experts questioned what social cost countries would have to pay for growth.

In response to this question, the concept of development came to encompass two different yet overlapping aspects: economic and social. As we will see in future chapters, in the 1980s the world experienced a debt crisis, and countries increasingly turned to the IMF and World Bank for assistance. It appeared that the Bretton Woods institutions focused far more on the economic side of the equation. UNDP and other UN agencies based in the field came to represent the social side. UNDP had carried on its work in providing technical assistance during the NIEO years as the World Bank rose in prominence. Whereas the bank became a development agency, UNDP was still not considered to be one. The Reagan administration nominated William H. Draper III to head UNDP. As a Reagan nominee, he came with a conservative perspective on economics, free markets, and the private sector. Draper withdrew support from UNDP for the technical agencies of the UN and made it a more independent institution. At the same time, he tried to build expertise within the institution, putting it in competition with the World Bank. He initiated a program of cost sharing in an attempt to ensure that technical assistance would satisfy the real needs of the country and that UNDP would prove to be a competitive supplier of such services.[57]

Notably, Draper introduced the concept of human development to UNDP through the Human Development Reports. According to this thinking, people are not means to development ends but are themselves the ends. The Human Development Index would provide a measure of human capabilities in terms of longevity, knowledge, and decent living standards.[58] With its move toward human development, UNDP became more of an advocacy institution than it had been in the past. This move would open the door to including additional concepts, such as protection of the environment and the battle against AIDS, into a broader conception of development.

Therefore, the disparate economic problems developing countries confronted eventually reshaped understandings of development and how its economic and social components were promoted through different institutions in the multilateral system. The G77 coalition and notions of common interests in the global South persist to the present day but are generally segmented by region or other interests once an actual proposal is made. There are no longer calls from a universal coalition of developing countries to turn the United Nations into a development fund or agency. We will see that further changes in the global economy cemented the new arrangements.

Conclusion

Participation in international organizations changed dramatically with the decolonization movement after World War II, since the movement itself was fostered within them. As new states joined the United Nations, International Monetary Fund, and World Bank, they organized their interests together with a unified development ideology and a systematic plan of action to attain them. Nonetheless, the bloc system of participation contained the seeds of its own disintegration. It was successful because it was comprehensive, yet its comprehensive nature meant that its proposals were the least common denominator among them. Hence, the NIEO program appealed to everyone, and to no one. As the G77 appeared in more IOs, it could advance a program of action in all of them, but developed countries could devote resources to the IOs where they held the greatest advantage, thus undercutting institutions such as UNCTAD. As such, UNCTAD faded as the intellectual source for G77 ideology and the locus for negotiations.

The historic record shows that the G77 coalition was deeply divided on both material *and* normative issues throughout its existence in UNCTAD and other international organizations. The commonly held meanings within the coalition were the products of the more advanced industrial economies like Brazil and India, and they advanced the interests of elites within those societies. The G77 was forced to minimize differences on issues like restitution for colonialism because the colonial period had ended at such different times and in different ways for the African, Asian, and Latin

American regions. The benefits of the NIEO, such as the Integrated Pro-gramme for Commodities, as well as the Common Fund, would have ac-crued disproportionately to Latin American states. Africans and Latin Americans thus divided over these plans. Different colonial languages fur-ther divided the African Group internally.[59]

As we will see in the next chapter, the recovery of the world trading sys-tem reinforced these movements in multilateral institutions. Trade negotia-tions are even more specific than development policies; thus, they create entirely new allies out of states. The IOs that had been seen as instruments of liberation came to be seen as instruments of postcolonial oppression in some quarters, particularly as the GATT system began to play a more cen-tral role in the multilateral system alongside the IMF and World Bank.[60]

FOUR

Restoring Free Trade in the World Economy

Nationalism and industrialization shaped the initial emergence of multilateral forms of international cooperation in the nineteenth century as well as the range of issues they tried to address. Politics and economics likewise influenced the contours of multilateralism in the way the world economy recovered from the ravages of the two hegemonic wars of the twentieth century. Deepening trade relations, together with the rise of American multinational corporations, prompted the need for new types of international agreements and mechanisms to handle disputes. This postwar movement was driven by transnational insurance, transport, and financial corporations. National chambers of commerce and cooperative government officials engaged in competitive deregulation to create a permissive and voluntary regulatory network.[1]

As we saw in chapter 2, the initial GATT system was based on the principles of multilateralism, reciprocity, and nondiscrimination. These principles meant that trade rules were to be extended without bias to all members. Unilateralism, bilateralism, and trading blocs were prohibited except in unusual cases. Reciprocity would ensure that rules would be determined by mutually balanced concessions.[2] The initial treaty was successful in helping to establish rules to reduce trade conflict. Successive rounds of trade negotiations resulted in agreements based on compromise and not unilateral actions by the strong. Thus, the GATT system sought an open form of multilateralism, one that provided for the extension of negotiated trade rules for all members, although candidates did have to meet certain criteria and agree to obey its rules.[3]

Smaller trading arrangements among countries in a region were important steps along the way to larger ones with more members that covered more goods and services. The initial move toward economic regionalism occurred with the 1957 Treaty of Rome, which created the European Economic Community. The EEC's intent was to build a more integrated Europe, primarily through a common external tariff and common agriculture policy. Yet in order for the GATT system to expand to provide the new rules and decision-making procedures in the new environment, it was necessary to forge political coalitions in advanced industrial democracies to support the expansion of trade. Multinational corporations were an integral part of this process in both domestic and international politics, as was the eventual embrace of less developed countries in the free trade system. By the early 1970s, international production by American multinational corporations surpassed trade as the main component of the country's international economic exchange.[4] Eventually, the activities of multinationals provoked criticism that they contributed to the deindustrialization of the US economy.[5]

Thus, the politics that shape contemporary dynamics have roots in the changing domestic politics of wealthy states, the politics among IOs, and the demands of the changing world economy with new business forms and lowered costs of communication and transportation. Regional trading blocs have been important steps along the way, both for the benefits they provide to their own members and for the pressure they put on the GATT system to respond. When the GATT system became institutionalized in the World Trade Organization (WTO), these same dynamics eventually undercut the premise of the original GATT framework that members should apply the same tariff to imports from all WTO members. We will see that a global trade system managed exclusively within this framework became unrealistic, and preferential trade areas and regional trade agreements must be considered in contemporary economic relations.

Trade, Domestic European and American Politics, and Multinational Corporations in the 1960s and 1970s

The United States and its allies promoted free trade as a cornerstone of the postwar economic order and grounded the free trade regime in more than one international organization. As mentioned in chapter 2, the GATT system originated following the failure of attempts to establish an International Trade Organization as a third pillar of the Bretton Woods system. It operated as a treaty, growing more expansive in successive rounds of negotiations that lowered tariffs and addressed additional barriers to trade as they arose. Conversely, in chapter 3 we saw how UNCTAD was an initiative of developing countries established by the UN General Assembly to address economic issues related to trade and development in a comprehensive manner. It is part of the UN Secretariat, reporting to the General Assembly and the ECOSOC with its own membership, leadership, and budget. In their early years, the two appealed to different sets of states—the GATT perceived as the rich man's club, and UNCTAD perceived as the poor man's club.

The initial intent of the 1947 GATT was simply to show how far the consensus on international trade policies could go. It did not provide for a permanent IO, and the lack of a treaty establishing the GATT as one meant that it technically never had "members." It had "contracting parties" to the treaty.[6] When the United States announced in 1950 that it would not continue to seek congressional approval of the ITO, the GATT was forced to fill the void. Thus, it grew to *resemble* an international organization, yet it retained key differences. For example, there was no provision in the General Agreement for a secretariat. After the Havana conference, an interim commission had been created to prepare for the work of the ITO. Performing secretariat services for the GATT, this commission became the de facto GATT secretariat under an arrangement that technically existed until the Marrakesh Accords were signed in 1994. Likewise, the position of director-general within the GATT was one of conciliator and not one of compulsory legal power. He or she could hold consultations and information negotiations with CPs to reach a consensus yet had to rely on the power of persuasion to achieve results.[7]

Despite these limitations, the GATT was successful at liberalizing trade. Initially, its members addressed tariffs, which had been raised during the Great Depression and World War II. Over the years, the number of CPs expanded, as well as the issues they were willing to take on.[8] However, the legal status of the GATT was not the only impediment to the free trade regime in the postwar years. Strong nationalist sentiments remained.

Nonetheless, we have seen that interest in European unity was also renewed after World War II. Although European states were initially concerned with rebuilding their own national economies, the rising hostilities between the United States and Soviet Union helped Western Europe to define itself as an entity with common interests vis-à-vis the United States as well as the USSR. As the states recovered, the belief spread that further recovery would require assistance from the United States and collaboration across Western European states.

The governments in exile of Belgium, the Netherlands, and Luxembourg took an early step at collaboration by forming a customs union—that is, by allowing free trade among themselves.[9] The European Recovery Program, or Marshall Plan, contributed to ideas for a federal Europe since the American offer of aid was contingent on the administration of a common relief program among participating countries to maximize its benefits. The United States also insisted that the European participants decide among themselves how to distribute aid across the countries, tasks assigned to the Organisation for European Economic Co-operation, established in April 1948.[10]

Promoting Free Trade in US Politics

Economists generally agree on the merits of free trade in theory, yet politicians find it extremely difficult to work out in practice, because its beneficiaries are not well organized but its opponents are. That is, citizens who benefit from lower prices may not be aware that their ability to purchase what they do comes from trade, and those hurt by it are aware that trade is the reason, particularly when jobs are at stake. Over time, the United States overcame the internal political barriers to free trade by reshaping the balance among domestic political institutions that make trade policy in the Congress and executive branches.

This process was gradual. After the passage of the Reciprocal Trade Agreements Act in 1934, Congress authorized the president to negotiate and implement agreements internationally in which each affected country would cut its tariffs. In 1945, the reciprocal negotiating authority was updated to allow further reductions of up to 50 percent from that year's rates. The efforts grew less effective by the 1950s. Congress responded by authorizing negotiators to cut tariffs across the board. During those years, Congress also saw a need for a focal point for trade policy management within the executive branch—a role played by Secretary of State Cordell Hull until 1944—that could balance foreign and domestic concerns. House Ways and Means chairman Wilbur D. Mills (D-AR) proposed that the president designate a special representative for trade negotiations. Although the office of special trade representative was not closely connected to the president, the individual holding the office would work with legislators along and across party lines. With its position between the executive and legislative branches, the office could tilt trade policy in the liberal, market-expanding direction.[11]

Both the legislative and executive branches, moreover, encouraged trade. Congressional efforts in the immediate postwar era benefitted from the lack of partisanship in American trade policy-making. Elites agreed on the need to open markets and expand trade. With the general public relatively uninterested in the issue, neither political party used trade as an issue against the other.[12] "Protectionist" groups were on the defensive, and only a limited number of groups sought protection for themselves. During the 1960s, President John F. Kennedy's administration pursued free trade as a foreign policy issue. He understood the costs of free trade to textile producers and other industries that competed with imports in his home state of Massachusetts. When the six-nation EEC was unified on the borders of Communist Eastern Europe, he argued that free trade would benefit poorer countries and unify the West in the fight against communism. Rather than working on an item-by-item basis, Kennedy sought permission to reduce tariffs across the board. And he sought authority to negotiate for five years without congressional interference.[13] Kennedy named Christian Herter as the White House special trade representative with a staff to assist him. The office later became permanent and expanded to eliminate other barriers to trade. Over time, the power of the office grew.[14]

The United States thus participated in a series of successive multilateral trade negotiations in the GATT system in response to the global environment yet supported by a tacit alliance between domestic business and labor. The changing relations among the branches of government in the office of the special trade representative facilitated the alliance. In 1967, negotiators completed what was named the Kennedy Round of multilateral trade negotiations and cut duties on average of 35 percent.[15] The Kennedy Round marked the high point of tariff negotiations in the GATT, with cuts on specific items and manufacturers of approximately 33 percent as well as a number of additional reforms. For example, the round included rules on dumping—that is, the practice of pricing exports below their price in the home market or below the cost of production in order to gain market share. It also attempted to address some of the issues of less developed countries by giving their exports preferential treatment.[16] Later GATT rounds continued the process of freeing trade (table 4.1).

The Rise of Multinational Corporations and Changing Balance of Trade in the Global Economy

The workings of the global economy changed significantly after World War II with the rise of the multinational corporation as a business form. This change has had important implications for international trade. A multinational corporation, also known as a multinational company, multinational enterprise, or transnational corporation, is one that owns and controls production facilities in more than one country. Such firms usually require foreign direct investment, meaning that they *control* the businesses in the other country and do not just purchase their securities (such as stocks and bonds).[17] Although businesses of this type have existed since the start of the capitalist era, these early companies were mostly involved in agricultural products and extractive industries in specific regions of the world.[18] The Dutch East India Company and Massachusetts Bay Company, for example, each had its own foreign policies and controlled territories overseas. Contemporary multinational systems of supply, production, marketing,

Table 4.1 Rounds of multilateral trade negotiations in GATT/WTO

Years	Place or name	Countries	Chief subjects
1947	Geneva	23	Tariffs
1949	Annecy	13	Tariffs
1951	Torquay	38	Tariffs
1956	Geneva	26	Tariffs
1960–61	Dillon Round	26	Tariffs
1964–67	Kennedy Round	62	Tariffs and antidumping measures
1973–79	Tokyo Round	102	Tariffs, nontariff measures, "framework" agreements
1986–94	Uruguay Round	123	Tariffs, nontariff measures, rules, services, intellectual property, dispute settlement, textiles, agriculture, creation of WTO, etc.
2001–	Doha Round	157	Agriculture, nonagricultural market access, trade facilitation, rules, the environment, multilateral register for wines and spirits, other intellectual property issues, dispute settlement

Source: World Trade Organization

investment, information transfer, and management construct the paths along which the world's transnational activities flow and transform trade within them.[19]

After World War II, multinationals became the major institutional form of transnational practices. The acceleration of foreign direct investment was pivotal after the war; promotion of this form of business organization became part of US foreign policy during the Cold War, reflecting American interests.[20] Most multinationals were initially American, although in the 1960s, European and Japanese enterprises joined the trend. At the end of the 1970s, newly industrializing countries such as Brazil, India, and South Korea became home countries (those with the business's headquarters and central management) to multinationals.[21] Advances in technology escalated the growth of foreign direct investment as it spread across the globe. Time and space became compressed as transportation and communications networks grew. Government policies grew friendlier to serving as host countries (countries that received foreign direct investment), and American corporations wanted to establish operations overseas to maintain access to closed yet growing markets, the European Common Market in particular.[22]

Regardless of the country that exports foreign direct investment (or home country), multinationals invest in another country because the firm perceives that there are advantages in doing business there. These might be natural resources, cheap labor, geographical location, skill levels, political and financial stability, or the regulatory environment. Many host countries, therefore, may be other industrialized countries. In more recent years, developing countries have seen an increase in manufacturing operations. Multinationals may also be more likely to invest in and produce goods in states that restrict imports, thereby avoiding import restrictions.[23] Multinational companies can be organized horizontally, where plants around the world make the same or similar goods everywhere. Or they can be vertically integrated, where the outputs of some plants become the inputs for other plants in the same firm. Many multinationals are integrated along both lines.[24]

As the multinational form of business organization spread and the world economy continued its recovery from the devastation of the war, the balance of trade shifted between the United States and other countries, in turn changing domestic American political alignments. As we saw, the major US labor and business associations held free trade positions in the 1960s, with the exception of textile unions. Big business and labor were thus allied in support of free trade. Urban Democrats who opposed liberalized trade did so quietly, with the exception of Indiana senator Vance Hartke. By the end of the 1960s, however, the AFL-CIO and a number of major industrial unions became concerned with US trade policy. They no longer saw free trade as an unconditional good for their members. This domestic political shift in the United States had worldwide ramifications, particularly with respect to American support and participation in multilateral institutions promoting free trade.

The global story was shaped by the recovery of Japan after World War II. Japanese per capita income grew rapidly after the war, to the point where the country's economy was comparable to those of advanced industrial Western European nations. Japan achieved this growth through massive increases in national production and trade. The rapid growth rate led Japan to be perceived as a special trade problem for many reasons. Among them were the problems associated with absorbing Japan into the world system. As a non-Western island nation, Japanese culture had been more closed and close-knit throughout its expansion. In the 1960s, it still maintained a high degree of barriers to entry. The country came to be regarded as a free rider on the system, exploiting market opportunities abroad while making only minor changes at home. Japanese businesses also appeared to benefit from some form of government-business cooperation. As other countries, such as the Republic of Korea, Taiwan, Singapore, Brazil, and Mexico followed the Japanese example, American firms faced a different global playing field in the 1970s than they did in the 1960s when the Kennedy Round was negotiated and signed.[25] The GATT had difficulty responding to these pressures because the lead trading countries were less homogeneous than they had been when the original agreements were reached.

The growing imbalance between American imports and exports put additional pressure on the system in the 1970s. For only the second time in the century, the United States ran a deficit. Trade policy became much more overtly partisan. The AFL-CIO supported trade restrictions more openly, and more industries sought trade action.[26] Moreover, the political shift followed a deeper change in the geographic bases of support for the two major American political parties. The Nixon-Kennedy election began to reverse the pattern where the Republican base was strongest in the industrial Northeast and Midwest. Democrats gained ground where organized labor was strongest, and these changes began to influence the party's policies on trade, making it more protectionist in response to the industrial workers who now saw free trade as a threat to their jobs. As the Republican Party gained strength in the South and West, it associated itself with free trade policies.

A signpost for the changing times was the 1971 Foreign Trade and Investment Act, otherwise known as the Burke-Hartke Bill after its lead sponsors, Senators James Burke (D-MA) and Vance Hartke (D-IN). Supported by the AFL-CIO, the bill sought a sharp change in the direction of US trade policy.

It would have imposed comprehensive import quotas on goods that competed with American-made products. Thus, ball bearings would have been subject to a quota, whereas bananas would not. It would also have slowed the mobility of capital and technology. The president would have the authority to stop any overseas transfer of capital or technology that could cause a net reduction in US employment. It would have also changed the way overseas income was taxed, making overseas investments less attractive. Nearly every US-based multinational corporation considered it punitive.[27]

Burke-Hartke could be described as the highwater mark of post–World War II protectionism in the United States. Although the bill did not become law, it changed the way the trade policy debate operated in the Washington establishment. Multinational corporations increased their lobbying presence. Many private groups sponsored studies in think tanks on what multinationals did for the US economy. The debate over the bill stimulated academic work on trade that brought together ideas about multinationals, intrafirm trade, economies of scale, and other factors. Eventually, a new field of strategic trade theory emerged that influenced the American debate over competitiveness in the 1980s and incorporated technology policy.[28]

After Richard Nixon was reelected president in 1972, his administration moved to pass a bill that would allow US participation in the next GATT round. In so doing, the administration could augment the existing export expansion program. Cabinet officials in the Commerce and Labor Departments supported provisions that would slow the rate of imports, although others in the administration did not want to compromise.[29]

The Tokyo Round of Multilateral Trade Negotiations

The next major GATT set of negotiations was the Tokyo Round from 1973 to 1979. It was more comprehensive than earlier efforts. The Tokyo Round negotiators used an across-the-board approach to tariff reductions and combined it with a broader agenda of nontariff issues and preferences for developing countries. It achieved tariff reductions on most industrial products and liberalized agricultural trade.

However, tariff reduction can be a victim of its own success. Even when tariffs are lowered to zero, barriers to trade still exist. During the 1970s, many unfair trade practices grew and became larger obstacles to trade than tariffs. For example, export subsidies (where the government provides financial incentives to companies so that they can export goods), government procurement limits, and safety standards can be imposed to discourage importing certain goods. The Tokyo Round successfully introduced codes of conduct to address the issue of nontariff barriers. In this regard, it was more comprehensive than earlier efforts. However, all GATT members did not accept the obligations of these new codes, and enforcement of them was laborious. The GATT system of the 1970s was also undercut with respect to nondiscrimination, or the idea that each national government would treat the products of all others the same within the GATT system. The advance of the European Community, in particular, eroded the GATT system because European members gave one another more favorable market access and tariff preferences to less developed countries.[30]

The results of the Tokyo Round were mixed at best. There seemed to be a lack of commitment from all members to implementing the agreements. And even if they were committed, implementation was confounded by the myriad dispute settlement mechanisms associated with each of the Tokyo Round codes of conduct. There was particular dissatisfaction with the round on the part of developing countries, which felt that their aspirations had not been addressed. Significantly, developing countries sought a more expanded agricultural policy in the GATT, one area the agreement had traditionally avoided. Textiles and bilateral quantitative restrictions on imports imposed outside GATT rules meant that the dispute settlement mechanism hadn't kept pace with the realities of the international trading environment.[31] The results of the negotiations thus revealed that the limits of the GATT framework were being reached.[32]

Within the American political system, calls for protectionist measures grew louder in Congress, and the trade policy-making system grew more dependent on the executive branch officials. They participated in the legislative process by arguing with, resisting, and bargaining with those who sought protection for a specific industry. In 1979, Congress compelled the Jimmy Carter administration to reorganize the office of the special trade representative in terms of size and power, including a new name: the Office of the United

States Trade Representative.[33] Nonetheless, the office remains awkwardly situated between the two branches of the federal government. Given that the office is independent from the day-to-day activities of the chief of staff in the White House and must also take direction from Congress, any individual holding the post confronts a fundamental dilemma between the two.[34]

In the 1980s, the trade situation had grown so dire that Americans were spending more than three dollars on foreign goods for every two dollars foreigners spent on theirs. Demands grew for Congress to change the state of affairs. The executive branch increased ad hoc restrictions on behalf of automobiles and steel and tightened enforcement of textile agreements.[35] By 1982, partisan differences grew more open. The economy was suffering from a recession, and the industrial Midwest was hit particularly hard. The dollar was strong. In the 1984 presidential election, the Democratic nominee, Walter Mondale, began to argue that the United States had played by international trade rules even as other countries—such as Japan—took advantage of them. Although Mondale lost the election, growing numbers of Americans began to see a direct connection between imports and the loss of jobs.[36]

Launching the Uruguay Round in Developed and Developing Countries

After Ronald Reagan won reelection against Walter Mondale in 1984, his administration argued that the US trade deficit could be resolved by expanding opportunities where the United States could be internationally competitive but was restricted by domestic regulations and trade barriers imposed elsewhere.[37] As with the American economy, the situation of developing countries had changed from its heyday in the 1970s. One key driver of change was a series of debt and liquidity crises that began with the Mexican debt crisis of 1982 and continued through the 1990s. The debt crisis was a seminal event: it could have resulted in a collapse of the commercial banking system in developing and developed countries alike. Solutions for all parties concerned would be found by expanding opportunities for trade and investment among them.

Therefore, developed and developing countries alike were pushed to find new solutions to the old problem of how to achieve free trade in the

face of protectionist interests. Shifting alliances in international organizations made the negotiations possible. The initial Mexican default was a pivotal event for developing countries in IOs because it reconfigured the way
the G77 coalition operates in IOs to the present day. Although the G77 did
not disband, states within each region responded to the debt crisis by coping
in a manner that would resolve the type of sovereign debt they had taken on.
And within regions, IOs and private banks worked on a country-by-country
basis to resolve their individual debt exposure. The result was the ascendance of the Bretton Woods institutions in the development field and the rel-
egation of UN agencies to supporting roles. These changes had important
implications for the unfolding Uruguay Round negotiations during the
same years.

Changes in the World Economy and the GATT System

Arthur Dunkel took over the directorship of the GATT secretariat from Ol-
ivier Long in 1980. Despite Dunkel's energetic leadership style, by 1983, the
GATT's provisions had been enlarged and reinterpreted so extensively that
even international law experts could not to agree on what contractual obligations the treaty imposed. Moreover, the structure of the international
economy changed in many ways during the mid- to late 1980s, over and
above the changes that accompanied the debt crisis in developing countries. These wider changes called for modifications in the agenda of the
GATT negotiations and required that developing countries play a greater
role in the GATT for the system to survive.

These independent economic developments' interaction magnified their
separate impacts. First of all, a deeper and broader integration of the world
economy occurred with the changes in the organization of business operations in multinational corporations. The spread of this form of business operation across the globe made it easier to transfer the skills, knowledge,
management, and research necessary to build and run a manufacturing operation. Advances in computer technology and telecommunications meant
that a firm could trade skills internationally without physically relocating
key employees. Second, differing demographic trends between the advanced, industrial countries and the rest of the world made the developing

Fig. 4.1. Arthur Dunkel (center), GATT director-general, 1980–93. Courtesy of the World Trade Organization.

world more important to GATT negotiations. The GATT secretariat perceived that low growth rates in wealthy countries would have serious implications for national pension schemes. As for developing countries, of the nearly two billion people who would be added to the world's population from 1995 to 2015, ninety-five out of one hundred were predicted to be born outside the membership of the Organisation for Economic Co-operation and Development (OECD, successor to the OEEC) area as it then existed. Thus, the GATT secretariat perceived a need to create jobs in the developing world and to make those countries that had high population growth more competitive in labor-intensive activities.[38]

When the new round of negotiations, the Uruguay Round, commenced in 1986, it was different for developing countries than previous rounds for a variety of reasons. First, agriculture and textiles were included, which provided an incentive for participation. In the area of tropical products and natural resource–based products, negotiators aimed at the fullest possible liberalization.[39] The textiles and clothing negotiations aimed at formulating modalities that would permit the eventual integration of this sector into the

GATT on the basis of strengthened GATT rules and disciplines. Similarly, the agricultural negotiations aimed at liberalization by improving market access, disciplining the use of all direct and indirect subsidies, and minimizing the adverse effects that sanitary and phytosanitary regulations (those related to pests and pathogens in agricultural goods) and barriers can have on trade in agriculture. In addition, international financial institutions were pressuring developing countries to expand their exports to repay their external debt. They had the example of the successful export-led growth strategy of the Asian countries that encouraged participation. Finally, developing countries received technical assistance from UNDP through UNCTAD in the Uruguay Round that helped them to identify their interests and strengthen their position.[40]

Unlike the previous Tokyo Round in the 1970s, the UNCTAD secretariat supported the Uruguay Round negotiations at their inception in 1986. A variety of causes, both internal and external, contributed to the changed relationship between the two institutions. Members of the secretariat noted that attendance at regular UNCTAD meetings had dropped and that the diplomatic rank of those who did attend had fallen significantly, indicating national leaders no longer saw those meetings as a top priority. The implied threats to the organization accompanied the open and undignified debate about the past performance on both the political and management levels.[41] Staff warned that in order to survive, the secretariat needed to become an authentic development think tank.[42] As early as 1985, concerned parties suggested that UNCTAD begin to search for "complementarity" with other institutions—such as in keeping the performance of other multilateral institutions under constant and honest scrutiny, and in paying particular attention to the impact of any new measures on developing countries.[43]

Therefore, when the Uruguay Round commenced, UNCTAD filled a role in providing technical assistance that the GATT could not. An important distinction existed between the two organizations' technical cooperation activities. The GATT made no evaluation of the outcome of the negotiations, nor did it attempt to. The GATT secretariat, as custodian of a contractual arrangement, was forced to maintain a maximum level of impartiality in this process—that is, to act as a referee. An institution cannot be *both* a coach and a referee. In extending technical expertise, UNCTAD could act as a coach for developing countries. However, the G77 coalition never functioned in the Uruguay Round. Broad and fluid alliances spanning the global North-South divide emerged, such as the fourteen agricultural exporters that formed the Cairns Group (Argentina, Australia, Brazil, Canada, Chile, Colombia, Fiji, Hungary, Indonesia, Malaysia, New Zealand, the Philippines, Thailand, and Uruguay) of "fair traders." The Cairns Group provided powerful backing for the US demands on agricultural liberalization. Conversely, South Korea supported the EEC's position. Likewise, sub-Saharan African countries sought to maintain their preferences in Europe against encroachments from Latin America and Asia.[44] So while the G77 supported technical assistance initiatives in UNCTAD, the UNCTAD programs that resulted aggregated the needs of a region, or a state, and not the needs of the G77 as a whole.

Multinational Corporations and Services in the Uruguay Round

One of the greatest obstacles to the proposed round was the liberalization of trade in services. The capacity to trade in services has been inextricably linked to information and communications technology. The first category of services trade consisted of transport services, including shipping and civil aviation. The second category comprised tourism services, and the third category covered producer services, including those used by companies in the production of final goods like telecommunications, financial services like banking and insurance, and other consultancy services like architecture and accountancy. The United States proposed to liberalize service restrictions because it was one of the most dynamic sectors of the American economy. Although the share by volume of services in the US economy had grown only from 50.4 percent to 54.6 percent from 1953 to 1983, the service industries in 1983 absorbed 66.75 percent of all workers, as opposed to 49.5 percent in 1953. Multinationals were the most successful in synthesizing three categories of services into the production process.[45]

To support its initiatives in bringing services onto the GATT agenda, the United States attempted to develop an international consensus for negotiations on services, among others, by supporting academic research and high-level seminars and through a work program initiated in the OECD. These various activities shared a common characteristic: service issues were invariably presented in the context of trade, using terminology and concepts borrowed from the GATT and other trade agreements.[46] Although the United States was the primary motivator for talks on trade in services, Europe and Japan supported the American initiative.

Developing countries objected to the US action because they feared that their domestic service industries would be frozen at the level of inequality that existed before the round. Furthermore, they did not want to have to justify domestic policies concerning services they had already established. For their part, they had introduced services into UNCTAD from its first conference, and UNCTAD had maintained its long-standing expertise in this area.

The negotiators eventually reached a compromise at Punta del Este, Uruguay. France agreed to allow agricultural products on the negotiating agenda. While the group of developing countries led by Brazil and India had resisted the US moves on services negotiations, they were able to exploit US-EEC differences on other issues to form a tactical alliance with the EEC.[47] The resulting compromise was that negotiations would follow a positive list or bottom-up approach wherein countries would agree to areas where they were willing to liberalize. This compromise represented a significant departure from the way GATT negotiations had usually been conducted, wherein negotiations followed a negative list or top-down approach and all sectors and subsectors of services would have to be included in the schedule of commitments with the possibility of reserving some modes of delivery. Furthermore, market access and national treatment are fundamental obligations in the GATT paradigm, with exceptions for departure in certain circumstances. In services obligations, these two areas are bilaterally negotiated and included in the schedule of commitments. Therefore, unlike traditional obligations, a CP can commit to market access on services with limits and conditions on national treatment and can allay concerns about particular service sectors with suitable conditions. Separate talks on services would commence at the same time as talks on trade in goods, although the two might be merged at some future date. Thus, India and Brazil could say that they had kept the service issue apart from traditional negotiations while satisfying the demand by the United States, European Economic Community, and Japan for GATT-linked talks on services.

The CPs thus agreed to launch a new round of multilateral negotiations in September 1986 with the ministerial declaration agreed to in Punta del Este. The Uruguayan resort had been chosen for the GATT meeting in a deliberate political gesture toward the developing world. The confident handling by some delegates suggests that the move may indeed have helped to alleviate third world mistrust of the GATT and preference for the more cumbersome UNCTAD. Overall, developing countries could point to some success in influencing how the negotiations were conducted. The compromise on the inclusion of foreign investment was that negotiations were conducted on two tracks, so that services could not affect exports of manufactured goods. The Uruguay Round of multilateral trade negotiations thus began with the goal of introducing new issues under the umbrella of the GATT, which would address the needs of developed and developing countries alike. These issues included trade in services, foreign investment, and intellectual property rights.

The Evolution of the GATT System in the Uruguay Round

The Uruguay Round did not progress smoothly. As with each of the previous GATT rounds, the initial agreement on what would be covered took more time to conclude. And each round took more time to negotiate than planned once it began. Yet the Uruguay Round was particularly difficult. The preliminary negotiations to launch the Uruguay Round took four years, and the round itself stretched from 1986 to 1994. During these years, the talks broke down over the issue of agriculture and, later, over services, market access, antidumping, and a proposal for a new IO to resolve the GATT's institutional inadequacies. Many deadlines passed before a final agreement was reached. Although tariffs had been lowered after World War II, commentators began to speak of a "new protectionism," wherein an array of nontariff barriers such as domestic content legislation and governmental attempts to expand exports and support specific sectors became a major obstacle to world trade.[48] In addition, a "new regionalism" emerged in response to the slow-moving Uruguay Round negotiations. Participants grew apprehensive that any agreement would be reached.[49]

The result was a variety of forms of regional integration, driven by different causes, and the perception that the world was moving toward regional economic blocs. Different institutions emerged to create new entities, contributing to a growing number of places where economic issues of concern are addressed. Along the way, the Cold War ended and an entirely new group of states began to join the liberal trading order. Thus, when the Uruguay Round came into effect, it operated in a different global political economy than that which existed when it began.

The Growth of Regional Trading Blocs: The EEC and NAFTA

The original goal of the leaders who established the GATT regime in 1947 was to eliminate regional trading blocs. However, Article 24 of the General Agreement allowed for the creation of customs unions and free trade areas with proper notification to the GATT. An early effort at economic regionalism had been the European Economic Community, intending to integrate the European market among the six countries that signed the Treaty of Rome in 1957, establishing a customs union and external tariff. The EEC's intent was to build a more integrated Europe, primarily through the common external tariff and common agriculture policy. Although some GATT CPs argued that it conflicted with GATT principles, the United States tolerated discrimination against its exports in exchange for other aspects of its foreign policy. The Americans sought to increase European sales by proposing further rounds of multilateral talks, which became the Dillon Round and then the Kennedy Round. In 1986, the Single European Act in Europe posed a new kind of threat to the United States, insofar as it could create a united, and possibly closed, West European market. In response, the United States began to deepen its own regional ties.

In October 1987, the United States and Canada signed a bilateral free trade agreement. It was the first of its kind in that it was economically significant for both countries. It contained many groundbreaking provisions, including those that banned the imposition of performance requirements (such as local content, import substitution, or local sourcing requirements), provided national treatment for covered services providers, and liberalized the financial services trade. Controversy surrounding the agreement in Canada led to the so-called free trade election in 1988 in which Progressive Conservative prime minister Brian Mulroney defeated Liberal Party leader John Turner. Turner had vowed to reject the agreement if he were elected. The Free Trade Agreement passed the Canadian parliament in December 1988.[50]

When the Uruguay Round negotiations faltered, the United States sought to proceed with trade liberalization in the form of continental free trade. The North American Free Trade Agreement (NAFTA) would group the United States with Canada and Mexico. American political interests were immediately skeptical that the United States could mesh with such a different economy, and Mexican interests were wary of US power. However, a new Mexican president, Carlos Salinas de Gortari, was elected in 1988 and sought to open Mexico's economy and privatize state-run enterprises after the debt crisis of that period. The George H. W. Bush administration was interested in the concept as a way to stabilize the United States' neighbor to the south. When the 1990 ministerial meeting did not complete the Uruguay Round negotiations, work on NAFTA moved to the forefront.[51]

Domestic political opposition in the United States emerged before the Bush administration had even received the negotiating authority for the talks. Labor and environmental groups did not want the agreement to move further jobs out of the United States and contribute to the environmental degradation that they argued Mexico would allow. President Bush assured the groups that the government would create a fund for American worker assistance and retraining, as well as work with Mexico on environmental issues.[52] However, because Mexican tariffs were much higher than those of the United States at the time, observers expected that the agreement would cause US exports to grow at a faster rate than imports from Mexico would grow.[53]

The NAFTA text was approved in August 1992. The most significant changes were negotiated in the textiles, apparel, automotive, and agricultural industries. To generate domestic support for the agreement, the Bush administration created several special deals so that Mexico would not become an export platform for non–North American firms. The pact appeared to be a regional trading bloc like the EEC, albeit less comprehensive. It thus began to appear as if antagonistic trading blocs would emerge around the world. Proponents of NAFTA argued that the level of global trade was high enough that everyone could be satisfied. Most likely, NAFTA was merely accelerating trends that were already in place, since the United States had already invested considerable sums in the Mexican economy, and tariffs were already low.[54] After a substantive national debate, NAFTA was approved in November 1993 under a new presidential administration, that of Democrat Bill Clinton. Free trade thus advanced in the United States with an outward display of bipartisan support.

One of the important legacies of NAFTA is that it served as a template for other multilateral trade negotiations as part of the Uruguay Round. It also helped American manufacturing industries, especially the auto industry, become more competitive globally through the development of integrated supply chains in a North American region. Specialization has taken place as manufacturing and assembly plants have reoriented to take advantage of economies of scale. Work is performed where it is most efficient.[55] The Mexican economy has also realized benefits, but they have not been evenly distributed within the country or between the country and its northern neighbors. The most persistent questions have arisen over the agricultural sector in Mexico.[56] Moreover, the NAFTA legacies fostered political divisions in the United States and elsewhere that would be exacerbated in the twenty-first century.

The Role of Transnational Corporations in the Uruguay Round

The new areas of the Uruguay Round negotiations (trade-related intellectual property measures, trade-related investment measures, and services) had proven to be of continuing importance to developing countries, but they were more important for transnational corporations. During the Uruguay Round, American transnational corporations became increasingly involved in the *process* of the negotiations. The linkages among firms engaged in international production allowed for a diverse set of special interests favorable to the negotiations to become more active as they took place.[57] During the same years that business coalitions chose to focus on developing a broadly shared position and participate in the negotiations, product-specific interests in the United States (both pro and con) held back and preferred to participate after the final deal was proposed.[58]

On the intellectual property issue, which was one of the highest-priority items to the US business community, the American business coalition defined its objectives and strategies clearly. Toward this end, the members agreed that they sought a code of minimum standards for copyrights, trademarks, patents, and appellation of origin issues. They also desired an enforcement mechanism and a dispute settlement mechanism. Next, they sought to forge a consensus with the business communities of Japan and Europe, which were initially reluctant to include intellectual property under the auspices of GATT but shared an interest in influencing the actions of the developing world, where the theft of intellectual property was rampant.[59] Therefore, Congress remained susceptible to protectionist sentiment. But the American business advisory system was designed to work on behalf of the whole against individual protectionist sentiments. This system could be considered either a device for coopting the business community or exactly the opposite. In either case, the system enhanced the understanding by the private sector of the constraints on the negotiators and created a degree of personal identification with its success.[60]

The Final Agreement Is Reached

The Uruguay Round was concluded in Marrakesh, Morocco, in June 1994. The final phase had been a bitter confrontation between the United States and the European Community over how deep the agriculture reform would be. There was a two-year stalemate owing to a change of presidential administrations from George H. W. Bush to Bill Clinton and to last-minute deals. Negotiators feared that regional trading agreements such as NAFTA would take preeminence over the GATT system.[61]

As the Cold War wound down, Eastern European economies in transition began to request that working parties be established on their accession in 1992, and the Russian Federation's working party was established in 1993. Other new states that had been part of the former USSR or Yugoslav Republic were granted observer status in the GATT council so that they could prepare for the possibility of applying to join the GATT at a later stage. Of the nine new CPs in 1993, seven were former colonies that acceded under Article 26:5(c), and similarly, of the nine new CPs in 1994, seven more acceded under Article 26:5(c).[62] China made a bid as well, hoping to become a charter member of the WTO. It was not successful, but did become a member in 2001. These applications meant that the GATT system would have nearly universal membership for the first time in its history.

The New Contours of Global Governance in Trade

For some, the conclusion of the Uruguay Round of multilateral trade negotiations has proven to be the end of the era of "big multilateralism," insofar as there has not been a major multilateral trade agreement since it was concluded.[63] After the establishment of the World Trade Organization, a large network of preferential trade agreements multiplied at the bilateral and regional levels. States could now seek to change policies in a variety of environments, in what some writers term the "spaghetti bowl of trade agreements."[64] For example, steel industry regulations could be discussed from one country to another, such as the United States and Japan, or the United States and Russia. A steel subsidies agreement is being negotiated within the OECD Steel Committee. A new GATT round, the Doha Round, commenced in 2001 but broke down. Nonetheless, the Doha Round negotiation group on WTO rules addresses subsidies and antidumping rules that affect steel, and several WTO dispute panels have ruled on steel policies.[65]

The World Trade Organization

As the Uruguay Round progressed, it became evident that some sort of multilateral trading organization would emerge from the round. Considerations for a multilateral trading organization evolved entirely differently from the other new areas of the Uruguay Round that had been agreed to in the Punta del Este declaration of 1986. The proposals for a WTO were different from trade-related intellectual property, trade-related investment measures, and services with respect both to when they emerged during the course of the negotiations and to how they emerged. That is, the idea for an international organization emerged relatively late in the negotiations, and it was not an agreed-on goal but a solution to the problem of how to implement the results of the round.

The Punta del Este Ministerial Declaration had given a negotiating group on the functioning of the GATT system a mandate to enhance the effectiveness of the GATT as an institution. The multilateral trading organization idea was initially floated within the group as a solution to the problem of how to implement the Uruguay Round. The idea for a formal international organization was slow to come to the fore because, even in 1991, academic commentators and others noted that it was possible that the Uruguay Round could be implemented and tied together without creating an international organization.

Italy's trade minister Renato Ruggiero had first suggested a new international organization in February 1990, and in April of the same year Canada submitted a formal proposal to correct the constitutional flaws of the GATT within the negotiating committee. The European Community likewise submitted a proposal.[66] Nonetheless, the 1990 Brussels Draft Final Act (a prospective conclusion to the Uruguay Round prepared for the Brussels ministerial meeting) did not contain an agreement regarding a new international trade organization. Although the European Community favored one, developing countries were hostile to the suggestion unless it would be instituted within the framework of the United Nations.[67] The United States was also ambivalent about a proposed organization, meaning that the question of whether one would be included in the Uruguay Round package remained an open question through December 1992. Technically, the GATT operated on the principle of one state, one vote. However, the CPs rarely voted. The United States was concerned that the decision-making system in the GATT could be dominated by smaller countries. It therefore sought a looser organization headed by a trade committee of ministers.[68] Despite American ambivalence, the first firm proposal for a new organization was eventually included in the 1991 Draft Final Act, or Dunkel Draft (another document attempting to conclude the talks).

Under the terms of the Uruguay Round, the WTO was established on January 1, 1995. Each prospective member must have accepted, or be about to accept, the provisions of the GATT 1947 and the GATT 1994 treaties by then.

The entire membership of the WTO heads the organization through a ministerial conference. Every two years, each government sends a delegation to this event, usually headed by a trade minister or equivalent. These events usually involve decisions on upcoming negotiating agendas, interim agreements, or other business before the forum. The conference appoints a director-general of the WTO secretariat in Geneva. The director-general is also in charge of the operations of the secretariat, such as translations, technical and legal research, and trade policy reviews. Relative to other IOs, the WTO's staff is small. It does not have policy-making authority.

Dispute settlement is the most visible work of the WTO. One country can file a case against another to challenge a policy or practice, usually on the basis of its incompatibility with the WTO system. If the panel rules against a specific policy, the country must change its practice in order to comply. Since the WTO was established, the dispute settlement process has been the most controversial component of the system.[69]

The Growth of Multilateral, Bilateral, and Preferential Trade Agreements

Although regional trading agreements posed departures from GATT principles, the CPs could sign regional trade agreements if they gave proper notification. Between 1948 and 1994, the GATT received 124 notifications of regional trade agreements relating to trade in goods. Between 1995 and 2017, the World Trade Organization has received notification of more than 400 additional agreements covering trade in goods or services.[70]

The increasing number of venues to discuss trade reinforces the advantages of wealthy states and disadvantages poorer states even further, since membership requirements and limited resources, particularly personnel, mean that poorer states cannot participate everywhere. Therefore, all states must make decisions about where to pursue their goals, even if they might achieve a better result somewhere else. Moreover, domestic politics influence the choice of forum. Interest groups within each state prefer the forum with the likelihood of the best outcome for the lowest transaction costs. Generally, bilateral or regional negotiations offer the best solutions. Some industries may find WTO negotiations or panels to be too slow as mechanisms to pursue for resolutions. Multinational corporations with longer time frames and multiple industries in the United States and Europe support preferential trade agreements and multilateral liberalization. However, they tend to put the most priority on the multilateral forum.[71]

Christina Davis argues that as the number of venues rises where a state can litigate issues related to trade, the possibility that rulings will differ rises as well. Some policies may be interpreted as acceptable to preferential trade area rules, but not those of the WTO. Or vice-versa. Thus, legitimate confusion can result about what the appropriate policy is. As a result, proliferating rules and rulings can contribute to further tensions over compliance. Thus, the relationship between preferential trade areas and the WTO with respect to further liberalization of the global economy is unclear — it could promote complementary commitments in each or undermine support when such commitments contradict each other. Or the ambiguity of new rules may push forward new attempts to negotiate new agreements.[72] The growth of so many overlapping institutions addressing trade policy means that every level of a trade negotiation must consider related institutions.

Conclusion

As the world economy approached the end of the twentieth century, developing countries forged new mechanisms of participation in multilateral forums at the regional and global levels. Multinational corporations emerged as important forces of economic integration through intrafirm production, undercutting traditional forms of interfirm trade across state borders. New domestic political constituencies both helped, and were hurt by, all of these new arrangements. Although the new mix of regional and global agreements has meant that industries have become more competitive and can provide a wide array of goods and services at reduced costs, benefits have not been evenly distributed within countries or across regions. We will see that despite the benefits of globalization, the domestic political effects of these and other changes to the world economy will become important components of broader movements against free trade and other forms of multilateral cooperation in the twenty-first century.

FIVE

The End of the Cold War and Changing Security Alignments

Despite the efforts of the World War II allies to preserve relations among themselves after the war, Cold War tensions shaped the way multilateralism developed in the following years, as well as the specific goals and outcomes in IOs. The Cold War was both a military and an economic rivalry; hence, it affected IOs across-the-board. During these years, the UN Security Council was deadlocked between the United States and the Soviet Union. NATO fostered a community within the West whereby the United States remained engaged in European security and opposed to the common Soviet threat. The GATT trading system and EEC deepened economic ties among capitalist states and fostered a sense of community among Western nations that rested on shared values of democracy, free-market capitalism, and a liberal order. Developing countries pressed for their own political and economic needs in the context of the rivalry between the communist and capitalist systems.

Not surprisingly, when the Cold War ended, the shape and agenda of multilateralism was redirected once again. New possibilities pushed a renewal of efforts at cooperation among former adversaries. Resistance from newly resurgent nationalisms pulled in the opposite direction. Previous alignments among states broke down and new ones formed. The thaw in relations between the United States and the Soviet Union brought new hope for the United Nations as a vehicle to resolve conflict. The Warsaw Pact disbanded. NATO took in new members. Yet it became tough to hold allies together with a sense of collective security when a clear, common military threat no longer existed. After a series of successive crises, the United States became more unilateral in its approach to intervention. And when the United States began to retreat from its role in world affairs, Russia began to reassert itself in Europe. In addition, transnational networks among criminals and terrorists sought to undermine the peaceful resolution of conflict and cooperation among states.

These multilateral politics played out across a span of more than twenty years. Kathleen Thelen argues that in domestic politics, political institutions reflect neither what their creators wanted nor who was in power when they were created. The coalitional base that supports them is constantly renegotiated across time. Eventually, institutions are transformed through the processes of layering, wherein new elements are grafted onto an otherwise stable institutional framework, and of conversion, wherein new goals or groups are brought into the coalitions on which the institutions are founded.[1] These same dynamics are at play in multilateral institutions. The end of the Cold War jump-started this process of renegotiation in international politics.

The history of multilateralism since the end of the Cold War shows that IOs have been part of the solution for some states seeking security from the military alliance of the West, yet part of the problem for states threatened by the expansion of that alliance. Some IOs have experienced new life, whereas others have been sidelined entirely. This chapter focuses on the security arrangements connected to the UN and NATO, with particular attention to the domestic politics of the two Cold War rivals and their postures toward multilateralism. But notions of security constantly change. Networks that have emerged outside the formal relations of governments and embassies promote values such as human rights and scientific exchange, yet other such nonstate networks threaten security. Therefore, subsequent chapters will explore the impact of the end of the Cold War on environmental, human rights, and economic concerns.

The End of the Cold War

The causes of the end of the end of the Cold War are widely debated. Arguments split between those that emphasize domestic politics and those that favor international politics. Explanations that emphasize the role of individuals explore the background and rise of Soviet leader Mikhail Gorbachev within the Soviet system as a reformer who refused to sit idly in the face of his country's economic problems, albeit he sought to shake up the communist system, not end it.[2] Explanations favoring the collapse of the Soviet domestic economic system point out that it lacked the capability to advance into the digital age without some relaxations on the country's repressive political system. For those explanations that look to the international system as a source, twentieth-century American foreign policy expert George Kennan had argued for a policy of containment of the Soviet Union on the grounds that the Soviet system would not be able to withstand the frustration of its inability to expand its global reach. Kennan's prophecy took on new meaning when the Reagan administration proposed a Strategic Defense Initiative, popularly called Star Wars, in 1983 that would defend against incoming missile attacks from the Soviet Union. The USSR lacked the capability to match the next round of the arms race and sought a new round of arms control agreements to mitigate the challenge it posed.

Regardless of the precise cause, Gorbachev's reform program contained four key features: *glasnost, perestroika, demokratizatsiya,* and "new political thinking." Glasnost, or openness, would ease censorship and bring apathetic individuals into the marketplace of ideas. Prominent dissenters and authors were released from jail and controversial writings published. Perestroika, or restructuring, would comprise reforms and improvements within the regime, even though many of the changes were small and mired in red tape. Demokratizatsiya, or democratization, was an attempt to put new life into Soviet council elections by allowing for multiple candidates, though not multiple political parties. New political thinking resulted in a pullback from the Soviet intervention in Afghanistan and initiated a round of arms control agreements, beginning with the Intermediate-Range Nuclear Forces Treaty of 1987, which eliminated an entire class of nuclear weapons from Europe, and the Strategic Arms Reduction Treaty of 1991. Although they were intended to shape a more modest communist Soviet state, the policies resulted in a dramatic reconfiguration of the Soviet Union's internal governance as well as its relations with the world, opening new possibilities for multilateral cooperation and rendering old strategies obsolete.[3]

The West therefore confronted the puzzle of how to resolve conflict in this new world order. The presidential administration of George H. W. Bush that followed the Reagan administration was significant in determining the shape of the solution because the United States held the world's remaining military arsenal. Moreover, it had been the major proponent of multilateralism as a bulwark of Western Europe against the communist threat during the Cold War. The Bush administration immediately confronted two key questions connected to these aspects of American power. The first was how to handle the future of NATO, particularly in light of the dissolution of the Warsaw Pact (the Eastern European collective self-defense pact) and the preponderance of American military strength in the new world order. The second question was how to conceive of the future of multilateralism in a world where it no longer served to unify the West against a common enemy.

Once the initial shape of global relations began to emerge, a series of successive crises solidified the direction of the turn in world affairs with respect to the Cold War and multilateralism as a mechanism to resolve conflict. For the George H. W. Bush and William J. Clinton administrations, an invigorated multilateral system of governance would cement US leadership, ensure that other countries would contribute to any efforts overseas, and allow the United States to address rising domestic political concerns simultaneously. Over time, the newfound emphasis on multilateral solutions was undercut by rising partisanship in domestic politics that challenged US contributions to the UN and American involvement across a spectrum of IOs. The disbanding of the Warsaw Pact and engagement of NATO outside its traditional European perimeter likewise gave rise to concern within the former Soviet Union about Russia's place in the world and the direction of multilateral cooperation as the new contours of the world order materialized.

NATO and the Foreign Policy of President George H. W. Bush

Just as the Cold War lacked an official starting point, it lacked an official end. Different countries perceived different threats in the new security environment that unfolded. George H. W. Bush was initially more reluctant than Ronald Reagan had been to trust Gorbachev's revolution. Many European countries feared a resurgent Germany. Poland, Hungary, and Czechoslovakia had withdrawn from the Warsaw Pact and sought to join NATO as a guard against future Soviet aggression, though the United States and its allies were reluctant to consider immediate expansion. Nonetheless, Gorbachev needed allies abroad. He could not lower the Soviet defense expenditures without getting some kind of economic benefit, or peace dividend, in return. He sought to declare an end to the confrontation and reshape the Soviet military-industrial complex.[4]

Events moved swiftly. In the summer of 1989, East Germans began to escape to the West when the Hungarian government began to allow them through its newly opened border with Austria. The Berlin Wall thus no longer provided the barrier to Western immigration that it once had. As more and more East Germans left through the Hungarian route, others sought asylum in the West German embassies in Prague and Warsaw. On November 9, 1989, the head of the East German communist party announced that citizens could emigrate freely to the West, and that very night, citizens began to chip away at the wall itself—physically eliminating one of the Cold War's most powerful symbols.

Therefore, in January 1990, Germany's former allies and enemies had to confront a new reality. The four occupying powers—British, French, Soviets, and Americans—retained legal control over the country, because no formal peace treaty ended World War II. The Americans were the most enthusiastic supporters of a unified Germany; however, they sought German membership in NATO as an "unequivocal prerequisite" to demonstrate that Germany would remain within the Western alliance.[5] As the four powers searched for an agreement, Iraq invaded Kuwait, and they had to confront a crisis in the Middle East.

Although the question of a unified Germany's membership in NATO was paramount, the future of the alliance was unclear. In the years preceding the fall of the Soviet Union, it had been strained by the revolution in Iran, the Soviet invasion of Afghanistan, and the suppression of the Solidarity movement in Poland. Each of these events had contributed to lively debates that went beyond the traditional disagreements over nuclear strategy.

Nonetheless, during these years, the members retained a common interest in deterring Soviet power in Europe.[6] Although the next generation did not have the memories that consumed the earlier one, most Europeans basically trusted the operation of nuclear deterrence as the lesser of many evils.[7] When the United States planned to deploy a new generation of short- and intermediate-range nuclear missiles, thousands marched against deployment in peaceful protests in 1981 and 1983. NATO was in jeopardy if the West Germans rejected American leadership and the reliance on nuclear weapons that came with it. Were Germany to withdraw from NATO, as France had withdrawn its force a generation earlier, the alliance could not survive. The United States would have no reason to remain in Europe.

In 1991, the Warsaw Pact and the COMECON, which tied the Soviet satellite economies together, self-liquidated. Germany reunified and the Communist regimes in Albania and Yugoslavia came down. Despite the initial reluctance of Western leaders to trust the credibility of this about-face in Soviet foreign policy, the country dismantled its autarkic approach to trade relations that was based on economic independence and self-sufficiency. Instead, it sought membership in the IMF, World Bank, and WTO in the years that followed. It courted foreign direct investment and rescheduled its debts. In 1997, it became a member of the Paris Club of public lenders and the London Club of private lenders.

Therefore, as Cold War tensions subsided and the allies lacked a common enemy, George H. W. Bush had to address questions on both sides of the Atlantic. A new generation in Europe did not see American militarism as helpful to the security dilemma on the continent. Nonetheless, the same problem existed as before: if Germany withdrew, the United States would have no reason to continue to play the same role in European security. If perestroika succeeded, the Soviets could dominate Europe, and/or the nationalisms of the past could resurface and provoke another war. Hence, Gorbachev's peace offensive posed a more immediate threat to NATO in 1989 than the collapse of the Soviet Empire. The fate of Germany became the top US priority.[8] The future of the alliance was cast further into doubt when Gorbachev survived a coup attempt in August 1991 and ultimately resigned on December 26 of that year. His replacement was Boris Yeltsin, who began as one of Gorbachev's supporters and later became an opponent. The Soviet Union dissolved, the former Soviet republics became independent states, and they created the Commonwealth of Independent States.

As these events unfolded, NATO leaders met and began to search for ways to adapt the alliance to the emerging security environment. In 1991, leaders issued a new Strategic Concept, or official document that outlines NATO's nature, purpose, and fundamental security tasks. Acknowledging that the threat that had concerned the alliance in its first forty years was gone, the leaders expressed trepidation over the adverse consequences of instabilities that could arise from outside powers or spill over into NATO countries.[9] This document reoriented NATO toward becoming an institution seeking collective security. The vagueness of the statement drove many leaders to seek a more tangible commitment from NATO. Eastern European states sought membership in all of the West's IOs, and among them, membership in NATO became a priority. NATO responded by forming institutional associations with these governments, establishing the North Atlantic Cooperation Council, which would connect them to the alliance.[10] In the years that followed, these countries continued to push for a more formal link.

The United Nations, the First American Gulf War, and Intervention in Somalia

Despite the primacy of the Bush administration's concerns with NATO as the USSR underwent such dramatic change, on August 2, 1990, the international community faced an immediate crisis in another part of the world when Iraq invaded its neighbor Kuwait. Attention thus shifted to the United Nations, where George H. W. Bush had previously served as US ambassador. Iraqi aggression was ostensibly in protest of Kuwaiti slant drilling, which Iraq alleged resulted in a theft of petroleum resources by Kuwait. In addition, Iraq owed Kuwait a substantial sum of money borrowed to pay for its previous war with Iran. Furthermore, the two countries disagreed about the amount of petroleum reserves the oil cartel OPEC (Organization of the Petroleum Exporting Countries) needed to keep on demand. When reserves were high, prices fell, and Iraqi oil revenues lowered, thus raising tensions with its neighbor and creditor.

Approximately one week after the invasion, President Bush declared his intention to remove Iraqi leader Saddam Hussein from Kuwait; however, he did not want the United States to appear to act alone. His administration believed that American voters would tolerate a longer deployment of troops if the actual period of combat was short, casualties were few, and a wide variety of countries supported the effort.[11] They shaped the conflict as "Iraq against the world."[12] The UN Security Council called for Kuwait's release five times in five weeks.

Outwardly, it appeared that Gorbachev supported Bush's effort to build an international coalition against Saddam Hussein. Yet despite the speeches of unity between Bush and Gorbachev, the Kremlin was less unified internally. Some believed that the USSR needed to cooperate with the West more than with the dictator Saddam Hussein. Others feared that immediately after the collapse of Eastern Europe, leaving Soviet allies in the developing world, such as Saddam Hussein, would signal an erosion of Soviet global influence. The Soviet Union had conceded on Germany and NATO. In exchange, it anticipated better relations with the West and received a promise of aid.[13] Despite the outward display of harmony with the West, therefore, substantive disagreements persisted within the Kremlin.

Once the Americans began the military campaign to remove Saddam Hussein from Kuwait, an aerial bombing operation continued for more than a month. Iraq retaliated with missile attacks in the region. A ground advance followed in Kuwait, and the coalition forces and Iraq engaged in massive tank battles. Behind the scenes, Gorbachev worked to broker a resolution between the USSR's former ally and the United States. When Iraqi forces fled Kuwait, US forces attacked Iraq directly. On February 28, 1991, Bush declared a cease-fire on his own, and in a move that has been widely debated, he ordered the troops not to continue to Baghdad, but merely to liberate Kuwait and remove Hussein from power.[14]

After the UN-authorized military action in Iraq appeared to have been successful, the Soviet Union dissolved, and the Cold War receded into the past, it appeared that the UN was reborn. It took on entirely different operations than it had in the past; from 1988 to 1992, it launched more operations than during all of the forty years before 1988. Many of these actions went beyond the truce monitoring of the UN's past. Peacekeeping operations monitored political reconciliation and elections. They assisted in nation-building, provided humanitarian relief, and helped to resolve civil conflicts. A new report, *An Agenda for Peace*, was released in 1992 by Boutros Boutros-Ghali, the UN secretary-general, which set out an expansive plan for preventative diplomacy, peacemaking, peacekeeping, and peacebuilding activities. Moreover, advocates of the UN began to float the idea of either creating a UN army or setting aside specific national military capabilities for UN operations.[15]

The George H. W. Bush administration remained committed to multilateralism as a solution to the world's problems, but multilateralism with the United States at its helm. The new activism extended beyond traditional strategic concerns and into humanitarian impulses, thus renegotiating the coalitional base that supported the institution. After his defeat in the November 1992 election, Bush determined that violence in Somalia had risen to the point where it posed a moral imperative for the world community. In a military action endorsed by the UN and European governments, the United States sent thirty thousand troops to Somalia in December 1992 to restore basic order and provide food and medical supplies.[16] Three months later, in February 1993, the United States began to withdraw most of its forces, and it eventually turned over operational control to the UN.

The mandate of the United Nations Operation in Somalia was to disarm all Somali factions and aid the process of reconciliation. Within weeks of UN control, however, the mission veered off course: it was characterized by combat rather than reconciliation. The remaining US combat troops in Somalia attempted to capture one of the Somali military commanders and political leaders, Mohamed Farah Aideed. The result was an escalation in American casualties, public unease, and congressional criticism.[17] Where the UN had initially been seen as a solution to many of the world's post–Cold War conflicts, it began to be seen as an impediment to decisive US military action.

The Clinton Administration and Rising Partisanship in US Foreign Policy

In January 1993, around the time the United States began to withdraw forces and begin to transfer control of the Somali operations to the UN, William J. Clinton took office. Clinton advanced the principle of assertive multilateralism, arguing that the United States should try to build a legitimate international order based on close cooperation with other countries, respect for international law, and strong IOs. At first, Clinton's policy was well received. Americans retained their new hope for the UN after the Cold War. Yet just as Woodrow Wilson's multilateral vision was challenged by an activist US Congress in the aftermath of World War I, so Clinton's would be as well.

The rise in partisanship is not surprising. The Clinton administration took office when the Soviet adversary had disappeared with the end of the Cold War and no other global antagonist was on the horizon. The new president had to balance the realities of fewer resources with his own insistence that the US government focus its primary attention on domestic concerns. The only way to reconcile the competing domestic and international demands on American resources was through multilateral cooperation. A stronger UN would serve to establish international order in an increasingly fragmented world. However, the administration faced challenges on the domestic front because Americans were still involved in the peacekeeping operation in Somalia, which was not progressing as planned. Critics claimed that the Clinton administration put UN interests above those of the United States and failed to advance US leadership.[18]

Most of the agencies of the federal government adhered to the Clinton administration's policy of assertive multilateralism. The military, however, was a notable exception. The Defense Department held the position that the primary mission of the armed forces is to fight and win wars, and not conduct peacekeeping, humanitarian relief, or disaster relief. Preferring to maintain a culture around the decisive use of force, the Department of Defense and Clinton administration notably clashed on the issue of creating a standing army—designating specific military units for short-notice deployment—for the UN Security Council. The result was that the administration pulled back from supporting any semblance of a UN army. Rather, it tried to increase the prestige, number, and resources of UN personnel dealing with peacekeeping and improve the UN's ability to meet the growing demand for such operations.[19]

Outside the military, the immediate detractors from Clinton's assertive multilateralism were in the Republican Party. These individuals had little personal experience in world affairs and viewed the United Nations with suspicion bordering on contempt.[20] Along with congressional criticism toward the Clinton administration's policy in Somalia, criticism also mounted within the Republican Party toward the administration's policy on multilateralism overall. This more general antimultilateralism argued that American national interests were being ignored in the conduct of foreign policy, particularly in making US foreign policy the servant of the UN.

After the Democratic Party suffered losses in the 1995 mid-term election, Republicans assumed control of Congress, and Senator Jesse Helms (R-NC) became chair of the Foreign Relations Committee. He pushed for cuts in US monetary contributions to the UN. He continued a long-standing practice of key members of Congress in using the US contribution to IOs to leverage reforms.[21] In addition, he proposed that the United States withdraw from the International Labour Organization and cut contributions to almost every other UN organization, with the exception of the United Nations Children's Fund. Boutros-Ghali attempted to reform the UN in response to US pressure. The UN adopted zero–real growth budgets between 1987 and 1995. In 1994, it created an Office of Internal Oversight Services in response to American calls for an inspector general to detect and eliminate waste, fraud, and abuse.[22]

In the years that followed, the US Congress, Clinton administration, and UN engaged in a protracted set of negotiations over American assessments to the overall UN budget as well as its arrears, or overdue amounts, on previous assessments. Some members of Congress began to pursue domestic, as well as international, issues through IOs. In 1997, Representative Chris Smith (R-NJ) attempted to attach an amendment to the State Department authorization bill that would require the UN and other IOs to respect the laws of countries that restrict abortion and refrain from lobbying governments in favor of loosening abortion policies. Eventually American arrears rose so high that UN regulations requiring that states owing an amount more than double their annual dues be stripped of their General Assembly voting rights loomed on the horizon. Congress and the president agreed to pay approximately three hundred million dollars in current dues to prevent the arrears from climbing to the point where the regulations would have kicked in.[23]

The UN, NATO, and Armed Conflict in the Former Yugoslavia

As problems with the UN rose in American politics, NATO's outlook improved. A series of armed conflicts in the former Yugoslavia broke out in the early 1990s and ultimately shaped the future of NATO and its operations. Yugoslavia had been a socialist country, established after World War II and a civil war. Six republics formed a federation among Serbs, Croats, Bosnian Muslims, Albanians, Slovenes, and others. President Tito suppressed tensions among these groups until his death in 1980. By the early 1990s, nationalist groups began to call for more independence, and the army, dominated by Serbs, responded in Slovenia and then Croatia. UN peacekeepers were largely unsuccessful in these conflicts, and as international peace efforts to stop them failed, the UN was humiliated.

Although the conflicts were on Europe's immediate periphery and all states agreed that they were serious, none equated them with direct threats to their vital interests and were thus unable to create a strategy for intervention. Moreover, NATO allies held different views of the source of each armed conflict. Whereas the European powers held the view that an end to the fighting could come only from a political settlement among Serbs, Croats, and Muslims, the Clinton administration blamed Serbian aggression more directly. For example, the United Nations had established a "safe area" under its protection in the town of Srebrenica in northeastern Bosnia; yet the UN's force there failed to prevent the town's capture and later massacre of more than eight thousand people, mostly men and boys, by forces under the command of the Bosnian Serb Army. In 1995, NATO's leaders responded to Serb actions against Muslims there by launching air attacks against them in Bosnia and Serbia. After the air campaign, the Western powers forced parties to attend peace talks in Dayton, Ohio. When the Dayton Peace Accords were signed in late 1995, NATO sent an implementation force to Bosnia for a year with sixty thousand troops.[24]

Although NATO did not pursue the prosecution of war criminals, its operations in Bosnia gave it renewed energy and purpose. Nonetheless, inter- and intrastate conflict in the Balkans persisted. Serbian leader Slobodan Milosevic continued to attack Muslims after the Dayton Accords, particularly the ethnic Albanians who comprise the overwhelming majority of the

Fig. 5.1. NATO Secretary-General Jaap de Hoop Scheffer visits Kosovo Force troops in Northern Kosovo, June 23, 2008. Courtesy of Kosovo Force, NATO, © KFOR.

population of Kosovo, a disputed territory in what was then Serbia. At this juncture, NATO leaders feared that the inaction in the early part of the decade would lead to a similar wave of human rights abuses and ethnic cleansing as before. In 1999, NATO launched a spring offensive against Serb forces in Kosovo.

Not every NATO ally shared the same degree of concern with the Kosovo intervention, however. Political divisions within NATO affected the military strategy and tactics. The Americans sought to intensify air attacks in and around the capital, Belgrade, whereas the Europeans wanted to limit the strikes to Serb forces attacking ethnic Albanians. NATO's command structure complicated tasks for the operation's commander, US general Wesley Clark.[25] Although the operation was successful in a limited sense, a NATO-led peacekeeping force remains in Kosovo to deter renewed hostility and threats, establish a secure environment, ensure public safety and order, support the international humanitarian effort, and support the international civil presence.

Thus, the result of NATO's changing mission in the 1990s was an alliance divided on its aims and purposes despite the outward signs of unity in the face of tensions in the Balkans. In the post–Cold War world, the United States retained its military superiority and sought to continue to play a leading role in global politics. Although most NATO members participated in the 1990–91 Iraq war, the United States planned and led it. The European powers preferred to stand back from the conflict in Somalia. It became apparent that global political and military engagement only occurred if the United States initiated action. The United States was willing to pay a disproportionate cost for leading multilateral interventions; however, the international community would be forced to allow the United States to conduct its foreign policy as it saw fit.[26]

The United States thus posed a particular paradox for multilateralism in the post–Cold War world. On one hand, it embarked on a unilateralist foreign policy underpinned by its position of preponderant power in economic and military affairs. On the other hand, it had supported international institutions including the UN, Bretton Woods institutions, and NATO from the end of World War II through the 1990s, despite frequently being at odds with these institutions. As the twenty-first century dawned, domestic support for multilateral institutions waned in American politics, undercutting the country's support for international agreements and treaties and eventually IOs.[27] Some of the direction of this drift can be explained by long-standing American tendencies toward isolationism throughout its history; other explanations focus on the rising partisanship in foreign policy and rise of the anti-internationalist wing of the Republican Party.

The UN and NATO were also in a state of flux. NATO survived the end of the Cold War with a much more ambiguous mission that went beyond European borders but with a much less clearly defined threat. Its treaty supports the UN Charter but does not fully trust the Security Council to provide for peace and security, thus leaving NATO politically autonomous in critical questions of war and peace. The UN emerged from the first intervention in Iraq as having authorized the war but without making reference to the articles in its charter that would have mandated the use of force to restore peace and security. Thus, the war was fought by the United States, which set up the coalition and remained in command throughout.[28]

Therefore, although the presidency of George W. Bush that followed the Clinton administration did not initiate the unilateralist American foreign policy, it did become more clearly aligned with it, as well as with its contradictions. For example, in May 2001, President Bush expressed outrage that the United States did not have a seat on the UN Human Rights Commission. Yet he did not press for ratification of the Kyoto Protocol on the environment or other international accords.[29]

The Terrorist Attacks on September 11, 2001

The unilateralist direction of US military intervention was secured following September 11, 2001, when the Islamic terrorist group al-Qaeda conducted four coordinated attacks on the United States. Al-Qaeda flew fuel-loaded, hijacked airplanes into targets and killed 2,977 people in New York City, in Washington, DC, and near Shanksville, Pennsylvania. Hundreds of victims were either nationals of other countries or held dual US citizenship. Although terrorism had existed for centuries, the scale of the attacks and targeting of civilians to such a large degree marked a turning point. Moreover, whereas previous global incidents had taken place primarily in Europe, Latin America, and Asia, 9/11 was the first major attack perpetrated by foreigners on American soil since Pearl Harbor.

The initial international response to the attacks was highly sympathetic to the United States. Both NATO and European Union (EU) ministers were called into emergency sessions. On September 12, NATO members invoked Article 5, the mutual defense clause of the treaty, which was the central pillar of the alliance's collective defense structure and thus mobilized NATO for war. Invocation was not a signal of symbolic unity but would lead the organization into new territory because it had not adopted specific guidelines regarding terrorism.[30] Although the vote to invoke Article 5 was unanimous, it was not without controversy. Some members feared that a positive vote would endorse any American military response. Others qualified their vote by preserving the right to act individually with respect to any US military operations. These public and private reservations within the alliance played into the American decisions to plan an independent campaign against al-Qaeda and the fundamentalist Islamists known as the Taliban in Afghanistan.

The debate among NATO members following the 9/11 attacks was a sign of disputes to come.[31] Although the allies had always had differences of opinion regarding how to operationalize their liberal values in IOs, as well as the substantive disagreements over policy that we have seen, they put many of these disputes aside during the Cold War. The events of 9/11 were a defining moment because the allies interpreted the events through different lenses. The United States, led by the George W. Bush administration, filtered the events through a lens of national security and the contest between good and evil. The administration linked terrorism and state sponsors of terrorism with the concept of war. Europe, however, Michael J. Williams argues, did not offer a corresponding narrative on the war on terror, having taken to the sidelines when major international crises occurred after the end of the Cold War. In its national security documents, Europe increasingly positioned itself in relation to the United States' answer to the crisis instead of offering its own response, perhaps because no consensus with respect to an answer exists. That is, the allies might agree that democracy is the best idea, yet Europeans argue that it cannot be imposed on existing political orders.[32]

The United Nations also reacted strongly to the attacks on 9/11. Security Council Resolution 1371 called on states to freeze terrorist financing, pass antiterrorism laws, prevent suspected terrorists from traveling across international borders, and order that asylum seekers be screened for possible terrorist ties. These dictates were passed under Chapter VII of the UN Charter, making them binding under international law. September 11 also changed the debate over American payment of UN dues. Even Republicans in Congress found it desirable to have a strong and cooperative UN in order to battle terrorism, among other goals. Within one month, the House approved legislation to pay the UN, and in an unprecedented action, media mogul Ted Turner contributed thirty-four million dollars as a private citizen. The United States also promised to pay another half a billion dollars for peacekeeping arrears, as well as its 2001 regular budget dues. In November 2002, the United States made a third and final payment of arrears to the UN and associated agencies, including the World Health Organization (WHO) and International Labour Organization.[33]

NATO and the Afghan War

In the immediate aftermath of 9/11, attention concentrated on Afghanistan because the hijackers were a part of al-Qaeda and some of them had trained there. Hence, the Bush administration sought to remove the Taliban from power in Afghanistan, where many of al-Qaeda's leaders were located, and ultimately dismantle the organization. The initial phase of the war that toppled the Taliban was relatively brief—approximately two months—and led to the second phase, from 2002 to 2008, when the United States continued to fight the Taliban militarily and rebuild the Afghan state. The international community was involved in this effort from the start. The Bonn Agreement that outlined the new government called for an international security force to support the Interim Authority and operate in the capital, Kabul, and its surrounding areas.[34] However, members of the Bush administration argued that NATO could not provide Washington with significant military force in the immediate Afghan campaign. The American planners limited NATO military support and deployments, confident that US precision bombing and missile strikes, together with special operations forces and limited US military units, would be sufficient to disengage the Taliban in Kabul and resistance in the outlying areas.

The NATO allies gave different reasons for the invocation of Article 5. Moreover, the American military put forth different explanations for the subsequent marginalization of the alliance by the American military. Because the mutual defense clause had never before been activated, NATO did not have a precedent to rely on.[35] Moreover, given the time frame, there was no plan for military action by NATO. Each ally would decide for itself how to contribute to the war, and they would have to consult again before committing NATO to any particular action.[36]

The NATO alliance thus suffered a major blow only weeks after its unified stand on behalf of the United States.[37] The war in Afghanistan was undertaken by a broad coalition of states organized by the United States under the banner of Operation Enduring Freedom, which NATO supported but did not participate in. NATO did contribute to the American war effort with naval forces that were deployed as an important part of burden sharing. NATO also deployed surveillance aircraft to the United States from October 2001 to April 2002, allowing the United States to send American airborne warning and control system units to support Operation Enduring Freedom. In addition, a number of European governments extended direct bilateral military assistance to the United States during the fall 2001 campaign in Afghanistan.[38] Nonetheless, neither NATO's decision-making body nor NATO's military command had any say in the Afghan campaign.[39]

As the years passed after the Taliban was removed from power in Afghanistan, the postwar occupation met many obstacles. Although NATO was divided on many political issues, its leadership understood the importance of the operation for the future of the alliance. It took command of the UN-sanctioned International Security Assistance Force in August 2003. Its primary mission was to facilitate the delivery of security, political support, and reconstruction assistance to the Afghan people. Its mission was comparable to UN nation-building efforts in the early 1990s; however, Afghanistan proved a difficult environment, having been the site of a civil war and resisting foreign occupiers for decades.[40]

By 2006, the insurgency that began in 2002–3 rose dramatically. Many on the ground pushed the alliance to become more strategic and attempt a more comprehensive approach to the situation. However, it needed an ally. The UN was present in Afghanistan through the UN Assistance Mission to Afghanistan but was reluctant to work too closely with NATO, even if the two organizations cooperated on the ground. Those inside the UN argued that they were a civilian organization, whereas NATO was a military one, despite the fact that the UN leads many military peacekeepers elsewhere.[41] When the war entered its third phase in 2008, the United States increased its troop presence and used its force to protect the population from Taliban attacks. The strategy included a timetable for the withdrawal of forces, beginning in 2011. By 2014, the United States and NATO combat missions formally ended, although the United States maintains a military presence there and the conflict continues.

The Second American Gulf War and the UN and NATO

As part of the so-called war on terrorism following the attacks of September 11, 2001, the George W. Bush administration turned to certain states that it believed might unite terrorist organizations into a deadly anti-US alliance.[42] No evidence linked Saddam Hussein to the September 11 attacks; however, some members of the Bush administration had been intent on reckoning with Saddam since taking office. The president believed that he was a ruthless dictator with a reputation for threatening the balance of power in the Middle East and the vital interests of the United States.[43]

Although many European allies were sympathetic to the United States after the attacks on 9/11, they were ambivalent about using force against Iraq. France, for example, did not want military action without a decision of the Security Council. German chancellor Gerhard Schröder would not lend support for a war on Iraq through NATO, even with the endorsement of the Security Council. Conversely, Tony Blair, the British prime minister, supported US policy.[44] Europeans, and many Americans, were more concerned with the Israeli-Palestinian peace process and argued that launching a war against Iraq would anger Muslims and lead to more terrorist attacks.[45]

When President Bush spoke to the UN General Assembly on September 12, 2002, he warned that the United States would enforce the UN's resolutions calling on Saddam Hussein to disarm and enforce an inspections regime on Iraq regardless of whether its allies would join in. When the UN inspectors returned and failed to report on the existence of facilities for chemical or biological production or storage, US officials argued that they had missed the obvious.[46] After many negotiations, the Security Council unanimously adopted Resolution 1441 on November 8, 2002. The resolution set forth a range of demands and created an inspection regime. It also indicated that noncooperation would lead to an armed response, but no indication was given as to how noncooperation would be measured or what timetables would be used. Next, the UN organized inspection teams, and US officials continued to plan for an invasion of Iraq.[47] The administration sought NATO support, but NATO was deadlocked. In February 2003, NATO shifted its decision-making authority to a committee in which France had no vote and agreed to dispatch military assistance to Turkey.

Other allies agreed on a statement that called for continuing efforts to resolve the Iraq conflict peacefully.[48]

In March 2003, the United States and a "coalition of the willing" launched a war on Iraq, despite overwhelming worldwide condemnation of the American defiance of the UN. As the war progressed, the United States concluded that it could not continue to pay the human and financial costs of going it alone. The administration offered a "mid-course correction," and Secretary of State Colin Powell stated that the president would pursue a strategy of partnership with NATO, the UN, and other allies that had existed for the previous fifty years. However, other countries continued to balk at participation without a UN commander and specific Security Council mandate. Donors demanded a greater say in Iraq policy and a fresh UN authorization. Support for the United States declined in Iraq, where resentment of the occupation was helping the guerrilla resistance to recruit new members.[49] Later evidence that the United States had abused and tortured Iraqi inmates at Abu Ghraib prison in Baghdad only increased the global questioning of the entire operation's legitimacy.

Eventually, the United States received a unanimous Security Council resolution that gave the new government legitimacy, spelled out its powers, and set the terms for ending the mandate of the coalition forces. Member states would contribute troops and resources voluntarily. Despite the UN's endorsement, no new offers of troops were forthcoming. The occupation ended formally on June 28, 2004, when sovereignty passed to a new Iraqi government. Coalition troops remained to maintain order while the country prepared for national elections.[50] As with the war in Afghanistan, the United States maintains a military presence in Iraq, with both troops and a large infrastructure to support personnel and equipment for missions there and in the region.[51]

Multilateralism and Conflicting Threats

The chain of events after 9/11 led to misunderstandings and provocations in the US-Russian relationship that were not necessarily intended, but they were nonetheless consequential. Russians had anticipated rewards from the

West for abandoning communist ideology, yet they did not see these rewards materialize. In the years that followed, the West perceived a halt in Russia's transition toward democracy and rising levels of corruption. In December 1999, Boris Yeltsin unexpectedly resigned the Russian presidency, with the position moving into the hands of his chosen successor, then prime minister Vladimir Putin. Putin offered the image of a strong leader who would restore the country to its prominent economic and political position on the world stage. Yet the continued existence and gradual expansion of NATO has contributed to rising animosity between Putin and the West.

Hence, multilateralism has both solved some security dilemmas and created others for countries both inside and outside NATO. Different members of the alliance perceive different external threats. They face varying kinds of domestic political opposition over how wars are waged when they are part of a coalition. These differences are particularly profound when individual countries engage in efforts that either distract from or undermine the overall effort.[52] Tension over the membership and operations of IOs therefore became its own challenge to further efforts at institutionalized multilateral cooperation.

The Progress of NATO Enlargement and Rising Tension with Russia

In the years following the collapse of the Soviet Union, the political leaders of the former Eastern Bloc made a case to the West that their governments were committed to transitioning to market economies. Most leaders saw Moscow as the major threat to the region's well-being, despite Boris Yeltsin's assurances that Russia was committed to democracy and free markets. When relations between the Yeltsin government and the West began to sour, Polish leader Lech Wałęsa and Czech leader Vaclav Havel met with President Clinton and requested that the United States support an expansion of NATO to the east. The administration was receptive, even though the military opposed it. Clinton advanced the cause and began the Partnership for Peace program in 1994 as a compromise measure to open the door to future enlargement. He advocated the program as one that would change the NATO dialogue so that it could eventually take in new members.[53]

Despite Russian objections, NATO offered formal membership to Poland, Hungary, and the Czech Republic in July 1997 on the assumption that these governments would comply with NATO's accession protocols and requirements. They would become full members by April 1999. At that time, the Clinton administration sought to expand NATO's mission to develop effective alliance programs to respond to threats from the proliferation of weapons of mass destruction and terrorism. Although some leaders were willing to discuss these issues, there was not a consensus about expanding NATO beyond the confines of the European region.[54]

Initially, the West feared chaos emanating from Russia as it transitioned. Civil wars, state failure, and collapse ensued in parts of the former Soviet Union. NATO was willing to add new members if they added to the security of the alliance. The immediate fear in Russia was that the country would be cut out of security decisions and isolated from the West. Were such isolation to occur, it would provide fuel for extreme nationalists inside the country.[55] Although NATO did not consider that Russian membership would contribute to the security of the alliance, the United States worked to create a role for Russia in the new order with respect to arms control and other issues. Russia was a part of NATO's Partnership for Peace institutions and joint training and planning exercises. The partnership was designed to lessen Russian concerns about NATO by creating channels for communication and providing an opening into understanding NATO operations. In 1997, both Russia and the West signed the NATO-Russia Founding Act that encouraged acceptance of the enlargement by giving Russia a consultative standing with NATO.

We saw that as NATO became more assertive in Bosnia, Russia initially approved action in the UN Security Council. As the intervention against Serbian paramilitaries increased, however, the Russians became less comfortable with the mission. When NATO intervened in Kosovo without the approval of the Security Council and in opposition to the Serbians, who were now considered Russia's allies, Russia participated in the postwar peace enforcement operation, but with a sense that the country's place in the world order was slipping. The later intervention in Iraq in 2003 without the Security Council's endorsement underscored Russia's sense of irrelevance.[56]

Table 5.1 NATO enlargement

Date	Members	Event
April 4, 1949	Belgium, Canada, Denmark, France, Iceland, Italy, Luxembourg, the Netherlands, Norway, Portugal, the United Kingdom, and the United States	North Atlantic Treaty Signed
February 18, 1952	Greece and Turkey	Accession
May 6, 1955	Federal Republic of Germany	Accession
May 30, 1982	Spain*	Joins NATO
October 1990	Germany unified and addition of new Länder	Join NATO
March 12, 1999	Czech Republic, Hungary, and Poland	Accession
March 29, 2004	Bulgaria, Estonia, Latvia, Lithuania, Romania, Slovakia, and Slovenia	Accession
April 1, 2009	Albania and Croatia	Accession
June 5, 2017	Montenegro	Accession

*Spain joined the integrated military structure in 1998

Source: "Enlargement," NATO, https://www.nato.int/cps/en/natohq/topics_49212.htm

As a candidate, George W. Bush had promised to continue the NATO enlargement policies of the Clinton administration. While the Putin regime shared some concerns with the Bush administration in the war on terrorism and supported the US-led war in Afghanistan, many in the Putin regime were uncomfortable with the American emphasis on preemption of threats. Over time, the Russian public came to view the enlargement of NATO as a source of humiliation. Nonetheless, new membership invitations were extended to the Vilnius Group of countries: Bulgaria, Romania, Slovakia, Slovenia, Latvia, Lithuania, and Estonia. After completing the accession protocols, these seven were formally admitted into the alliance at the June 2004 NATO summit in Istanbul, Turkey. Russia openly objected to the 2004 NATO expansion. However, domestic turmoil and economic considerations prevented Russia from acting to stop it.[57]

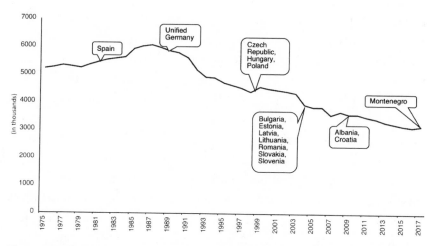

Fig. 5.2. Total NATO armed forces personnel strength as additional states join the alliance. Source: Compiled from NATO annual compendium of financial, personnel, and economic data for all member countries, https://www.nato.int/cps/ic/natohq/topics_49198.htm.

The perception of what security threat existed differed on many sides of the equation. By 2005, almost no Western military analyses viewed a Russian attack on a NATO member as a viable danger. Yet many of NATO's new members do have substantive concerns about Russia. In short: many of the "new members of NATO" are attracted to the alliance because it resembles the "old NATO."[58] How NATO would respond to these concerns is debatable. The total number of NATO armed forces personnel has declined, even in the years where the alliance's membership grew (fig. 5.2). Nonetheless, the Warsaw Pact is gone; NATO remains on Russia's borders. Many of the new members have sizable ethnic Russian populations within their borders who are unevenly integrated with other domestic populations.

External Problems with NATO: Russian Opposition

The seven Warsaw Pact countries outside the former Soviet Union have all joined NATO—Eastern Germany through its unification with West Germany, and the Czech and Slovak Republics as separate countries. Parts of the former Soviet Union itself joined NATO with the Vilnius Group in 2004. In the new European context, the Russian regime of Vladimir Putin perceives that the United States and its Western allies lack respect for Russia. The enlargement of NATO has left Russia nearly encircled and threatened. In addition, the United States and its allies have waged air strikes and wars beyond NATO's borders, bypassing the UN Security Council, where Russia could exercise its veto.[59] But Russia lacks the capability to mount a stronger offensive against NATO. In the interim, therefore, it voices strong disapproval of NATO activities where it perceives a threat and participates in coordinated efforts to pressure the alliance.[60]

The greatest direct crisis between Russia and the West occurred in Crimea in early 2014. Crimea is a peninsula in southern Ukraine on the Black Sea. The majority of people living there are ethnic Russians, yet the larger region has a majority of ethnic Ukrainians. Crimea has been a contested territory for many years. It was part of the Crimean War of 1853–56, when Britain and France invaded to check Russian ambitions in the Balkans as the Ottoman Empire's regional power receded. Russia lost that episode, but it nonetheless became the dominant power in the region. In 1954, Moscow transferred the region to Ukraine, itself then part of the Soviet Union. When Ukraine became independent in 1991, Crimea was transferred, too. In early 2014, troops loyal to Russia took control of the region, and the pro-Russian parliament voted to join the Russian Federation. A referendum was announced for March of that year, and when the vote was completed, Russia annexed Crimea, which it administers as two Russian federal subjects, the Republic of Crimea and the federal city of Sevastopol.[61]

The referendum and invasion have remained highly controversial because Ukraine and many world leaders consider these actions to have been a violation of international law and numerous agreements since the end of the Cold War. Putin justified the actions as defending the principle of self-determination for the Russians who live there. Nonetheless, since that time, Russia has engaged in ongoing military incursions in the Donbas region of eastern Ukraine. It has built up its naval presence in the Black Sea. Outside of Crimea, the Russian federation has intervened in Syria on behalf of a dictatorship.[62]

Russian leader Putin has used these recent actions to flaunt a more militarized country, characterized by anti-Western Russian nationalism. Nonetheless, he cannot confront NATO or the United States directly. In the interim, the regime has weaponized information in a campaign to sow doubt and division, weaken the cohesion of member states, create discord in domestic democratic politics, and blunt opposition to Russia. Although planting false stories in Western media is not a new tactic, contemporary disinformation is now considered a part of Russian military doctrine. NATO and the European Union have countered by establishing special offices to identify and refute the stories planted in Western media. Russian targets have ranged from the campaign over Malaysia Airlines Flight 17, shot down by insurgents using a missile Russia supplied, to anti-EU campaigns in favor of nationalistic themes and to interference in the 2016 US presidential election.[63] The goal of these campaigns is not to persuade anyone but to make the idea of truth irrelevant. Using social media keeps viewers hooked and distracted rather than attempting to provide a counternarrative to those of the West. These campaigns have found fertile ground in the West and particularly the United States, where antiestablishment movements likewise claim that all truth is relative.[64]

Western analysts debate Putin's ultimate goal. For some, Russia may seek to break up the NATO alliance altogether and regain lost territory. For others, the country may pursue regional dominance in Eurasia or restore Great Power status in the world. Yet other interpretations view Putin's aggression as reflecting the fear or paranoia of Western intentions to overthrow his regime.[65]

Internal Problems in NATO: US Leadership and the Military Capabilities Gap

As tensions with Russia have resurfaced, the internal cohesion of the NATO alliance continues to decline. Central and East European allies, including Poland and the Baltic states of Estonia, Latvia, and Lithuania, fear that US isolationism will leave them undefended against Russian aggression. Other NATO members have experienced losses in trade because of sanctions against Russia. Some far-right parties in France, Hungary, and the United Kingdom have been more open to cooperating with Putin.[66]

American participation has contributed to this sense of overall discontent. Members of NATO commit to spending 2 percent of their annual

GDP on defense. However, few meet this goal with the exception of the United States and United Kingdom. In 2015, members collectively spent more than $890 billion on defense, with the United States by some estimates spending more than 70 percent of this. During the Cold War, the United States spent approximately half.[67] Since the cost of deploying their respective armed forces is the primary financial contribution NATO members make to the alliance, this growing gap is a matter of concern.

Throughout the history of the NATO alliance, the United States always took a greater share of the responsibility for finance and troop deployments, despite calls for more burden sharing. The NATO allies have long debated military contributions. However, any gap that existed during the Cold War grew much wider in the 1990s. At the time, Washington sought to maintain its military superiority and spent vast new sums on defense. Europeans, lacking a military threat, spent far less on tanks, ships, and aircraft. Furthermore, American foreign policy, favoring the unilateralist approach, needed a strong military to be able to carry out its plans. Europeans relied more on multilateral solutions. By the turn of the twenty-first century, the gap between military capabilities on either side of the Atlantic undercut the capability of NATO to meet its collective security goals. Although members can defend their territories, no members except the United States, Great Britain, and France have the resources to engage in conflicts beyond their own territories.[68]

When President Barack Obama took office in January 2009, he had previously expressed opposition to the US war in Iraq and wanted to wind down US overseas commitments. Wishing to upgrade the American image abroad, Obama was both a realist and an isolationist insofar as he did not see that US military forces could change the situation on the ground in all cases.[69] As his presidency progressed, he increasingly believed that America's ability to direct global events was constrained. In a notable interview with Jeffrey Goldberg, Obama explained that his mission was intended to spur other countries to take action for themselves, rather than wait for the United States to lead.[70]

Therefore, the commitment of American presidents to champion the response to global events has waned in recent years. An advocate of multilateralism, Obama stated that he was focused on taking action with other countries where direct American interests were not at stake because "multi-lateralism regulates hubris."[71] Nonetheless, he expressed his frustration with American allies pushing the United States to act and then failing to show a willingness to do so. Thus, he perceived Europe and a number of Arabian Gulf countries to act as free riders who would lose interest once an effort was under way.[72] As we will see in chapter 9, the presidential election of 2016 changed the dynamic with NATO on the US side once again with the election of Donald Trump, who called NATO obsolete and argued that defense of individual members should be conditional on their contributions. The president's statements put Article 5 of the NATO Charter in jeopardy for the first time in the alliance's history.[73]

Despite these internal political challenges, renewed tensions with Russia have also contributed to a sense of an alliance revived with respect to its traditional military operations. After its 2014 Wales summit, NATO has reinforced its defenses in the East, expanded military exercises, and opened new command centers in Bulgaria, Estonia, Hungary, Latvia, Lithuania, Poland, Romania, and Slovakia. These centers could support a rapid reaction force of about twenty thousand, with the goal of assembling a force of about forty thousand in a major emergency. In 2016, allies agreed to rotate four battalions (about four thousand troops) through Poland and the Baltic states. NATO members have also increased air patrols over Poland and the Baltics. In 2015, NATO jets intercepted Russian warplanes approximately four hundred times. In 2016, that number doubled.[74]

Conclusion

Whereas the immediate end of the Cold War opened new possibilities for the UN Security Council to overcome its previous paralysis, the lack of a common military threat posed an existential test for NATO. In the years that followed, the United States became more unilateralist in its approach to action. The UN seemed to play less of a role in confirming actions of aggression and endorsing intervention. Although NATO survived the immediate challenges posed by the end of the Cold War, the nature of the institution seemed to change fundamentally. What began as an alliance based on a notion of collective defense was converted into an institution joining states against what threatens their territorial or political independence. In the contemporary era, the transformed institution with its new notion of collective security articulates not one specific threat but a group of threats. After 9/11, different perceptions of threats likewise informed varying views of multilateralism in the member states. A unilateralist United States considers its national interests to be threatened by terrorists. Europe does not perceive an external military threat for the first time in generations. New members of NATO perceive a threat from a resurgent Russia. Russia perceives a threat from the expanded NATO. Multilateralism thus became both part of the national security problem and/or part of its solution, depending on one's point of view.

SIX

Wellness of People and the Planet

We saw that the origins of nineteenth-century multilateralism were in the scientific progress of the Industrial Revolution and the need for politicians to tap the knowledge of experts to devise solutions to new social problems. In the second half of the twentieth century, scientific progress similarly revealed international problems that few even knew existed and raised questions about who would be able to benefit from solutions, once they were devised. The connections among these problems multiply their severity, and they are the most profound in the areas of medicine and environmental protection. In medicine, many diseases that threatened previous generations with premature death, long-term disability, and suffering can now be treated or cured. But these cures can be expensive. In ecology, the interactions among different parts of fragile global life systems with their physical surroundings can be measured and assessed. The results raise warning flags for human health and the long-term sustainability of the planet. But the states that pollute the most do not necessarily face the greatest consequences.

The forward momentum in science has exacerbated a range of North-South political tensions in both health and environmental politics and layered them onto the long-standing ones associated with debt, trade, and development. The spread of industrialization associated with development means that one segment of the world's population consumes larger amounts of energy, generates more waste, and has higher expectations for longevity and the environment around them than the segments of the world's population that lack access to these same advances. As the developing areas seek to catch up to the industrialized societies, their contribution to environmental degradation nonetheless threatens the global ecosystem. The environmental impacts of development in the global South are questioned in a way that they were not in earlier generations. Moreover, as with previous eras, underdeveloped national health-care systems may be fertile grounds for the spread of infectious diseases that ultimately threaten populations and health care in the industrialized world. All states do not set the same priorities for access to the kind of health care that others set for them. Some may target chronic conditions like hypertension, obesity, diabetes, and cardiovascular disease, and others may prioritize communicable diseases like malaria, tuberculosis, and HIV/AIDS. Hence, all people's lifestyles have ramifications for all. But all people within a state do not perceive their interests to be the same, nor do all states see their interests as the same.

In response, the existing multilateral framework has been forced to respond in ways that were unprecedented in the years before the mass production of goods and services, the advent of air travel, and eventually the digital revolution transformed people's lives. New institutions have formed. And older IOs, such as the World Bank and World Trade Organization, have taken important initiatives in these areas that are connected to, but not necessarily central to, their mandates in global economic governance. Private networks and foundations have again emerged as significant mechanisms to promote international cooperation. Alignments among countries within IOs have shifted according to state interests in energy production, geography, and where the environmental destruction has occurred; at times, action at the grassroots level has yielded more impressive results than efforts between states. The upshot is an even more densely connected network of public and private actors with overlapping agendas, funding constraints, and little real authority to act in a crisis—such as a natural disaster or an epidemic. It can appear that the more transnational activity takes place, the fewer the results.

Global Health Governance

Scientific investigations advance knowledge by generating hypotheses, or guesses, as to what is going on that can be tested and used to predict what will happen in the future after a variety of interventions. Scientists measure what they observe empirically so that new observations can either reinforce the previous findings and understandings or challenge them, if subsequent evidence calls them into question. In medicine, scientists constantly seek better understandings about disease in order to intervene and prevent or cure difficulties. Since the nineteenth century, the medical community has shared training in research procedures and data analyses relevant to patient outcomes, making it an inherently international endeavor reflecting our common humanity. Some diseases, such as smallpox, have been eradicated; treatments for others have improved to the point where they are diminished (such as tuberculosis) or become chronic but not necessarily life-threatening conditions (such as hypertension, diabetes, and obesity).

In the twenty-first century, medicine can do more, but it is not equipped to answer questions about how, or to whom, to distribute the benefits and burdens of advances. For example, the use of penicillin to treat infections opened the possibility of a cure for life-threatening bacterial infections. The mass production of antibiotics after World War II made it possible for ordinary people to receive the benefits of these drugs. Antiretroviral drugs can help AIDS/HIV patients live longer, better lives, but only if a patient has access to them. Action is still required to prevent the spread of some infectious diseases. Who will have access to the new medical advances? Who will pay for them? Should global health advocates focus on preventable disorders, chronic conditions, or infectious diseases? Furthermore, diseases related to lifestyles create different cultural challenges. Therefore, although the international exchange of knowledge in medicine has transformed the lives of large numbers of citizens in advanced, industrial countries who have gained access to higher education, better transportation, health care, and leisure time, it is not clear who will benefit the most from this progress, who will pay the costs for the underlying research and development that made them possible, and who will set the priorities for citizens in poor countries going forward.

Sophie Harman argues that in the present era "global health governance" refers to the agreements or initiatives between state and/or nonstate actors to control public health and infectious disease and to protect people from health risks or threats. It can involve public-private partnerships, multilateral and bilateral institutions, companies, celebrities, politicians, and civil society organizations. As the concept has grown to encompass even more arrangements, it has become grounded in notions of equality, rights, and the efficacy of development assistance.[1] The agenda for global health governance has been pushed and pulled by several factors since the nineteenth century: the appearance of disease, the religious and moral imperative to share knowledge concerning its treatment, broader advocacy for health and sanitation associated with development, and eventually the growing boundaries of what modern medicine can—and should—do for a population.

As we saw in chapter 1, the earliest calls for global health governance came from the appearance of cholera on trade routes and the necessity to protect a population from this disease. In the early twentieth century, private foundations pressed for improvements in health and sanitation. The Rockefeller Foundation established a division of medical education in 1910 to help strategically placed medical schools around the world—including England, France, Belgium, Brazil, Southeast Asia, Canada, and the South Pacific—to increase their resources and improve their teaching and research.[2] Private philanthropy continues to play a similar role. The 1918 influenza pandemic infected millions all over the world, making it one of the deadliest natural disasters in history. It is estimated that 500 million people, or one third of the world's population, were infected and approximately 50 million died, including approximately 675,000 in the United States (fig. 6.1).[3] National governments responded. In the present day, efforts to control the spread of avian flu or the Ebola virus from air travel continues in this tradition.

When colonies became independent states and joined IOs as members themselves, the international organizations included notions of health in broader development projects. Yet the needs of the state were overwhelming and ranged from basic health and sanitation to preventing the spread of infectious diseases to treating complex medical conditions. Eventually, IOs

Fig. 6.1. Clerks in New York at work with masks carefully tied about their faces for protection against influenza, October 16, 1918. American Unofficial Collection of World War I Photographs. Courtesy National Archives and Records Administration (45499337).

joined global advocacy efforts to eradicate preventable diseases, such as those associated with the use of tobacco products. And in the current efforts, the issues related to the global governance of health have broadened to cover those associated with the frontiers of Western medicine, where norms and ethics are still being worked out. In this new world, political tension has emerged not as much among states but among actors who disagree about who should set the agenda and how it should be pursued.

Formal Cooperation through International Organizations: The World Health Organization

We saw in chapter 1 that when countries first wished to cooperate on health issues, most states were driven by self-interest in protecting their citizens' health without threatening the progress of international trade and commerce. When governments held the first health-related conferences in the mid-nineteenth century, they were limited by uncertainty about the cause of many diseases and how to treat them. Thus, the system of health governance was fragmented and characterized by competition among units. World War II halted most of the existing arrangements.

Notable progress in public health nonetheless took place within countries, along with industrialization and the expansion of the welfare state. For example, at the end of the nineteenth century, Germany mandated vaccination and revaccination against smallpox, thus initiating a program of state-sponsored medical care for all German citizens. The government also imposed uniform entrance requirements and certification procedures on medical students. In 1876, all German industrial workers over sixteen years of age had to enroll in a medical plan unless they were otherwise covered.[4] As with the other international initiatives of the time, communicable diseases such as cholera, diphtheria, and typhus received priority over those associated with industrialization, such as cardiovascular disease and cancer. Public health in Germany was far from perfect after the introduction of these government initiatives, yet Germany's workers had better access to more capably trained physicians and broader financial aid than most other workers in history before that time.[5]

Other countries likewise attempted to solve health-care problems at the state level, with varying degrees of success. Uniform health care was more difficult to consolidate in France than Germany in the same years, due to the broader lag in provisions of the welfare state in general.[6] In England, health care had been a mixture of private, municipal, and charity systems. Yet after World War II, the Labour government established the National Health Service on the principle that health care would be free at the point of use, making it the oldest single-payer system in the world. France established state-planned and -operated health care in 1945. Chile's military government expanded health care, nutrition, safe water, and sanitation services in poor areas from 1974 to 1983.[7] Other governments, such as Taiwan and South Korea, implemented universal, redistributive, and publicly administered medical insurance programs in the late 1980s at the national level.[8] The United States did not support broad social insurance in the early twentieth century, and efforts to include health insurance in the New Deal reforms failed. Although some groups obtained insurance through government-sponsored programs for the elderly and the poor, the United States did not seek the goal of universal access until the twenty-first century.

When participants met in San Francisco to establish the United Nations, they called for a conference that would initiate a new health organization to work for international goals that would not be possible at the state level. Since countries had developed different ways of handling health at the domestic level, discrepancies existed from the start. Nonetheless, fifty-one UN members and ten nonmembers attended the 1946 conference held to establish a health organization. The Pan American Sanitary Bureau, Rockefeller Foundation, International Office of Public Hygiene, and Health Organization of the League of Nations were also represented.[9] The agency they established, the World Health Organization, came into being in 1948 as a specialized agency of the UN responsible for directing and coordinating authority for international public health. It was not necessary to be a UN member to join the WHO. Among other principles, the organization's constitution stated that it would seek to attain the highest possible level of health for all of its peoples. It also declared that the enjoyment of the highest attainable standard of health is a fundamental human right.[10]

The WHO is governed in a three-part structure comprising the World Health Assembly, the executive board, and a secretariat. The World Health Assembly is the most political layer, wherein delegates represent their states each year in Geneva. Delegates are usually from national health administrations; however, large states often also send diplomats familiar with foreign affairs. The executive board meets twice a year to consider the program and budget and to submit proposals for approval by the assembly. The thirty-four individuals are expected to work as experts on behalf of the whole conference and not as representatives of individual states. The secretariat carries out the WHO's programs and campaigns.[11]

Despite consistency in its governance structure, the global influence of the WHO has waxed and waned throughout its history, roughly corresponding to the changing membership of the United Nations, the North-South dialogue, and the progress of diseases and their treatments in the era that followed. As we saw in chapter 3, the NIEO forced a reconsideration of the role of multilateral cooperation throughout the system of IOs established in the postwar era. During the years when the NIEO was ascendant in the UN organizations, the WHO responded with a commitment to address the political, social, and economic causes of poor health. In so doing, it emphasized the question of equity and disparities in health between more and less advantaged groups. It prioritized universal access to essential health services that would be provided at the community level by nonprofessional workers trained for it. In a direct challenge to multinational corporations, the WHO criticized the unethical marketing of infant formula and inappropriate drugs. Its focus was on equity not between states but within them.[12] Furthermore, the rationing of radical and dramatic procedures (that are also quite sophisticated, complicated, and expensive) has been problematic.

The WHO's emphasis on primary, or basic, health care during these years was revolutionary because it sought to shift the concern from national governments with their own interests toward a community of democratic and communist states embracing a greater good for the international community as a whole. However, it did not garner the degree of support necessary in the WHO's membership, particularly with the United States. Many of its supporters were bureaucrats within either national health ministries or the WHO. Given the less prestigious nature of these ministries and the WHO's previous efforts to avoid political battles, the organization lacked the political influence to effect real change when it tried. After Danish physician Halfdan Mahler was replaced by Hiroshi Nakajima as director-general, the WHO lost its direction and failed to lead in responding to the world community's emerging health problems in the 1990s, such as population growth, the role of infectious disease pandemics, and addiction to drugs and alcohol.[13]

Nonetheless, the WHO remains the one organization with the authority to draft international treaties and agreements and submit them for ratification by member states. Later in the 1990s, it exercised that ability on the issue of tobacco control as a significant health issue that required international cooperation. The resulting Framework Convention on Tobacco Control demonstrated that the WHO could still exercise meaningful leadership on some international health concerns.[14] Among other things, the convention banned tobacco advertising, encouraged tobacco taxes, and called for control over tobacco use, such as health warnings on packages. Still, by the late 1990s, the WHO had few resources and little influence on its own health policies.[15]

AIDS and Health Efforts through the Multilateral System

The appearance of new global health threats such as HIV/AIDs and heightened concerns over epidemics of other communicable diseases shifted the work of other IOs within the global health governance system. As mentioned, the WHO experienced an internal leadership crisis with the end of Mahler's tenure as director-general. Moreover, the debt crisis of the 1980s challenged the ideological coherence of the North-South dialogue as different states sought diverse solutions to the new context for lending and development assistance, thus splitting the coalition in support of an NIEO. More important, however, the World Bank itself had rising influence due to its image as technocratic and nonpolitical at a time when the WHO appeared overtly political and sympathetic to socialism with its promotion of comprehensive primary health care. States such as the United States and other wealthy donors benefitted from preferential voting and greater say over policy in the World Bank. Thus, as with issues of debt, they preferred to work through the World Bank instead of other IOs where their influence was smaller. The result was that the World Bank had more money in the 1980s than the WHO, whose budget was static.[16]

The World Bank's entrance was surprising because it had played a minimal role in health issues for much of its history. When Robert McNamara became president in 1968, however, he broadened the notion of development to include such social factors as education, sanitation, and health. The initial focus was on family planning. Then, the bank partnered with the WHO to finance sanitation projects in developing countries. Later, the bank under McNamara led an effort to combat river blindness, a parasitic tropical disease, as another aspect of development. AIDS appeared in 1981. Because the early cases were in advanced, industrial democracies, the need for an international response was not apparent. The priority was to safeguard the blood supply and warn homosexuals of the risk factors of the new disease.[17] In 1986, the World Bank made an early loan to the government of Niger to screen blood for HIV as part of a larger loan.[18]

The World Bank's 1993 *World Development Report* marked a clear turning point. The report inserted the bank into the global health architecture by setting forth a new vision for its involvement in health issues and creating new forms of analysis for intervention. In the bank's view, government health-care spending should be directed where it can do the greatest good. To assess these areas, it introduced the concept of a disability-adjusted life year, or DALY. Put crudely, DALY is the sum of years of life lost and years lived with disability. An efficient healthy policy reduces the most DALYs for the greatest number of people. Treatment for tuberculosis and sexually transmitted disease costs little and benefits many, whereas cancer surgeries and heart transplants cost much more and benefit few.[19] The concept has been criticized. Wealthy individuals in poorer countries can travel to industrialized countries like the United States for complicated procedures if local access is limited, whereas poorer individuals cannot. Nonetheless, the concept of DALYs provided a guidepost for where governments would be urged to act.

Private Foundations and Global Health

The entrance of the World Bank was only one aspect of the broadened and changed system of global health governance in the early twenty-first century, where old actors were reformed and new ones joined the playing field of those seeking to effect change. The HIV/AIDs crisis presented a need for coordinated action, yet long-standing problems among IOs for funding, resources, and disagreements about tactics prevented one from emerging. Eventually, rather than using existing organizations, the spread of HIV/AIDS called for new solutions entirely. Two specific organizations formed: the Joint United Nations Program on HIV/AIDS and the Global Fund to Fight AIDS, Tuberculosis, and Malaria, or Global Fund. Born out of donor frustration with responding to requests from individual countries and agencies, the UN AIDS program would act as a catalyst and coordinator for UN-related agencies. The Global Fund would serve as an agent to *fund* the programs and interventions of other actors, apart from the existing United Nations or other bureaucratic infrastructure. New philanthropic organizations and new ways of conducting philanthropy also changed with the crisis.

As we have seen, private philanthropies have played a major role in global health governance since the late eighteenth century. Contemporary initiatives to fight specific diseases follow in this tradition; philanthropies support initiatives by funding specific health interventions, investment in research, development, and education, and collaborating with public bodies. Their motives vary along with the range of donors involved: personal compulsion, religious belief, tax avoidance, an interest in or retirement from political office, or the pursuit of medical knowledge. Most have not evaluated their own work.[20] Nonetheless, they remain significant in the evolution of multilateral cooperation because they work with and alongside governments, established IOs, and NGOs to provide resources for diseases that threaten millions of people each year, mostly in developing countries.

The Bill and Melinda Gates Foundation was one of the first new philanthropies to change the landscape of the governance of health. Founded in 2000 through the merger of existing foundations, the Gates Foundation provided 7 percent of total development assistance for health by 2010. In addition to its own initiatives, the Gates Foundation funds programs at the World Bank and is the largest single voluntary donor to the WHO, second only to the United States for total contributions to the institution.[21] The Gates Foundation is different from others in the field in that it stressed the notion of venture philanthropy early in its history, with an emphasis on results and the replication of successful models. These new approaches have obvious benefits in examples of projects where progress can be seen and monitored. However, they also run the risk of pushing aside health issues that do not demonstrate a return on the donor's investment, such as community home-based care, where the value is impossible to measure.[22]

In 2001, Bill Clinton left office and sought to create a nongovernmental organization that could leverage the distinctive capabilities of governments, partner organizations, and others to address rising inequalities in people's lives. A private foundation he established for this and other purposes, the Clinton Foundation, has focused largely on HIV/AIDS. The impetus for this work originated through personal contacts between President Bill Clinton and the prime minister of Saint Kitts and Nevis, who described his country's problems with health care at an international meeting in 2002. When the foundation looked into the problem, it learned that pharmaceutical companies were setting their pricing models on the number of buyers. Adjusting these models would reorient the market approach toward one in which, for certain payments, the companies would have an incentive structure to expand access to low-margin, yet high-volume drugs.[23] With the newer models, the Clinton Foundation does not purchase or collect money for drugs themselves but acts as an intermediary between manufacturer and purchaser to make the drugs accessible.

At the Group of Eight (G8) summit meeting of leaders from advanced industrial countries in July 2000, leaders agreed to create a fund for HIV/AIDS, tuberculosis, and malaria, three diseases that kill approximately six million people a year. By mid-2002, governments, charitable foundations, private citizens, and businesses had pledged two billion dollars to what became the Global Fund. Major contributors included the Bill and Melinda Gates Foundation.[24] Chevron, Coca-Cola, Ecobank, and other corporate sponsors and NGOs also joined the effort. The result has been a massive mobilization of resources and impressive number of programs that have saved millions of lives by expanding access to health care across the globe.

The entrance of the newer philanthropies, however, has met with some criticism. As with the Gates Foundation, the Clinton Foundation has been criticized for crowding out other voices and claiming credit for the work of smaller organizations. Conflicts of interest between the missions of these foundations and their funding sources are also apparent. For example, the Clinton Foundation has received donations from national governments and businesses whose interests may prevent access to antiretroviral drug therapy. Some of the companies where the Gates Foundation invests its endowment may cause the health problems the foundation seeks to alleviate. Their solutions and technologies may ignore local needs and technologies. Finally, these foundations exert disproportionate influence yet do not give the public an opportunity to express their opinions or concerns about their programs.

Yet, private foundations undeniably broaden the scope of available funds for health issues. They can also direct attention toward aspects of health care that would otherwise be neglected due to a lack of profit opportunity. Finally, their entrepreneurial approach can encourage flexibility and results in a way that the older international organizations did not. They can incentivize innovation for scientists and researchers to find new solutions and demonstrate to pharmaceutical companies that markets exist for treating these diseases.[25]

The Spatial Dimension of Global Health

The work of older, more established foundations in the field of global health, chiefly the Rockefeller Foundation, continues. At present, the Rockefeller Foundation advances a new interdisciplinary field called planetary health, which considers human health and the earth's natural systems as an interdependent whole. It also maintains its work on building health systems that can bend to stresses without breaking, such as in the 2014 Ebola outbreak.[26] The newly understood connections between human health and the earth's resources speak to what Kelley Lee terms the "spatial dimension" of global health, or the aspect of globalization that redefines the geographical boundaries that used to limit our interactions with one another. We have a common fate springing from forces that cross territory to affect all of our lives: flows of people, goods, services, knowledge, environmental change, and so on.[27] Lee argues that the spatial dimension comprises the global pharmaceutical, food, and tobacco industries with important ramifications for human health. But the globalization of human health issues has also resulted in new modes of health-care provision and ethical issues related to the practice of medicine, which are only beginning to be addressed by international conventions.

One of these new spatial issues related to health-care provision is the growth of medical tourism, in which individuals travel to another country for services that are unavailable, unaffordable, or illegal in their own country. In recent years, the direction of this travel is both from poor countries to wealthy ones (to obtain procedures that are not available) and from wealthy countries to poor ones (to obtain procedures that are less expensive or accessible in their own country). Major ethical and religious questions arise with respect to both medical tourism and the international trafficking in human organs.

When the medical community began to develop the capability to transplant human organs, procedures were limited geographically because a donor organ could only survive for a set period of time. Today, this limit no longer constrains many transplants. Even though the medical advances associated with transplants have saved many lives, the international community has struggled to keep pace. First of all, professional societies and governmental authorities have issued guidelines and rules for the international trafficking of deceased and living donor organs, particularly in countries with contiguous boundaries where one country is highly developed with sophisticated organ transplant centers and the other is relatively impoverished (for example, Mexico and the United States). The 2008 Declaration of Istanbul clarifies the issues of organ transplant tourism, trafficking, and commercialization and provides ethical guidelines for practice in organ donation and transplantation.[28] In 2017, the Council of Europe issued a framework for the prevention of and combatting against trafficking in human organs.[29] The medical and human rights communities have helped to shape, guide, and influence norms and approaches to transplantation.[30] Yet these issues are far from resolved. As noted, wealthier citizens in poorer countries can travel abroad for transplants, whereas others in these countries cannot, posing even more ethical questions about access to care.

Global Environmental Governance

As with medical science, environmental science proceeds through a laborious process of formulating hypotheses, gathering data, testing, and expanding knowledge from new findings that either reinforce or negate what was thought to be previously known. As with medicine, initiatives to control the use of the earth's resources have proceeded at the national and international levels, which complicates multilateral solutions along with the advance of knowledge. And as with medicine, the priorities of states are very different. Yet unlike world health, the UN's planners at the end of World War II did not understand the world's environment as a security or health threat, even though we now know that the environment, security, and health are clearly linked. At that time, natural resources in many parts of the world were still under colonial control. When the NIEO was negotiated across IOs, developing countries were far more concerned with exerting control over the distribution and price of primary commodities in the world economy than with the impact of their use on the ecosystem. As contemporary environmental problems *have* become understood, their very nature calls for more immediate, international attention. Yet the first major conference to be held specifically on environmental issues was not held for almost a century after the initial health initiatives of the nineteenth century.

Once scientific understandings of the problems increased and their connection to economic development become clear, global economic institutions became involved in endeavors to resolve them, much as they have in the area of global health. Ultimately, the severity of the situation and frustration with the lack of action at the national level in many countries has led to international networks of citizen action at the municipal and state levels, as well as the efforts of some industries to curtail further destruction through market and other mechanisms. Action in the contemporary world operates across formal international organizations and treaties, private networks, state and local initiatives, and business.

The Emergence of Scientific Understandings of a Global Ecosystem

The connections among health, wellness, and the use of the world's natural resources were not well understood in the nineteenth century when advances in medicine were made. Nonetheless, as with other networks of international activists in that era, the earliest solutions to the problems associated with resource domination and protection of the environment came from private organizations. Eighteenth- and nineteenth-century geographical societies, botanical gardens, and national scientific academies were spurred by the challenges imperial powers faced as they sought to understand and control colonial landscapes and ecosystems.[31] At the national level, conservationists created Yellowstone National Park in 1872 as the world's first national park. At the international level, bird-watching enthusiasts organized to protect species in a series of national efforts to address their migratory nature.[32]

However, many problems with industrialization were not immediately apparent to nineteenth-century wildlife observers. Perhaps most significantly, they did not understand the destruction that burning fossil fuels caused to the planet's atmosphere. Clearing land for commercial use has devastated forests and the world's diversity of plant and animal life. Although these human activities are not new, their effects have now accelerated to the point where they are discernible at the *earth system* level, meaning that they can be seen in all components of the environment: the oceans, coastal zone, atmosphere, and land. Action must be taken not only to minimize environmental harm but to stop interaction among the stressors that could threaten the viability of the ecosystem. How can the world minimize future destruction and distribute the burdens of adjustment among the people who caused it or who might damage it in the future?

When the scientific community began to warn of the dangers to the planet of overpopulation in the late 1960s, biologist Garrett Hardin argued that solutions to the problem were not technical in nature but moral. Making an analogy to common grazing land, Hardin pointed out that a pasture open to everyone works well if the populations of people and animals are relatively stable and below the carrying capacity of the land. However, when each herder increases his use without limit on a pasture that has limits, the pasture will not be able to sustain them. In his words, "Freedom in a commons brings ruin to all."[33] Applying the concept of the tragedy of the commons to the problem of pollution, Hardin argues that the social arrangements that make people responsible also coerce them to do what they might not otherwise do. Coercion is a dirty word to those used to the freedom to pollute as they please.[34] For example, if society sought to address the problem of overpopulation, people would lose privileges that they currently enjoy.

In the years since Hardin initially presented the concept of the tragedy of the commons, scientific knowledge of the causes of the range of environmental problems has both broadened and deepened, as has the conundrum posed by the necessity of coercion to resolve them. Kate O'Neill defines global environmental governance as efforts by the international community to manage and solve shared environmental problems.[35] These problems include those associated with climate change, ozone depletion, air pollution, biodiversity loss, conservation, deforestation, desertification, pollutants and other harmful chemicals, hazardous waste trading, whaling, and degradation of rivers and lakes, marine environments, and other natural resources.[36] These problems are not new. Yet their acceleration has increased their severity and the threats they pose to the quality and duration of human life.

Comprehensive attempts to address these problems began with national efforts. For example, in the United States, the first Earth Day was held on April 22, 1970, at a time when air pollution was commonly accepted and students were protesting the war in Vietnam. Those seeking to protect the environment first had to form a wider consciousness of the links among the environment, pollution, and public health. Earth Day founder Senator Gaylord Nelson (D-WI) hoped to marshal the energy of the anti–Vietnam War movement in order to force environmental protection onto the American political agenda after a 1969 oil spill devastated marine life along the California coast (fig. 6.2).

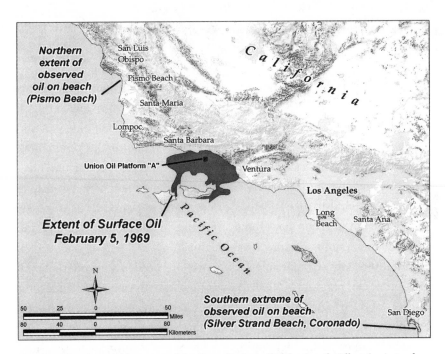

Fig. 6.2. Map showing the extent of the Santa Barbara, California, oil spill, 1969. Antandrus at English Wikipedia, CC BY-SA 3.0, https://commons.wikimedia.org/w/index.php?curid=16365110.

Together with House member Pete McCloskey (R-CA), Nelson and other Earth Day organizers promoted national events to demonstrate against oil spills, polluting factories and power plants, raw sewage, toxic dumps, pesticides, freeways, the loss of wilderness, and the extinction of wildlife. The event united a disparate group of activists, who worked to create the United States Environmental Protection Agency and pass landmark legislation, including the Clean Air Act, Clean Water Act, and Endangered Species Act.[37]

Scientists concerned with overpopulation, pollution, and the use of the world's resources called for an international conference to address environmental issues. Some participants were motivated by a mercury poisoning incident in Japan that had affected water and fish, others by a similar groundwater contamination incident in Sweden. Human technology seemed to be running out of control.[38] The result was the first major conference on specifically environmental issues, the United Nations Conference on the Human Environment, held in Stockholm, June 5–16, 1972.

Formal Cooperation through Treaties and International Organizations

The global environmental movement was forged among many disparate actors and interests, and deep internal divisions were inevitable. The initial rift at the international level reflected the North-South divide of the 1970s and issues related to who would benefit from primary commodity production. Developing countries faced an entirely different set of environmental challenges related to their level of industrialization, and many of the initiatives in the more industrialized regions of the world appeared to be a loosely veiled attempt to retain power and influence over national resources and sabotage their efforts at future development.[39]

The Stockholm Conference set important precedents for international environmental politics to follow. It was one of the first major global forums outside of UNCTAD in which the South negotiated collectively and adopted many of the strategies that became the hallmark of the NIEO.[40] Stockholm allowed the developing countries an opportunity to present a Southern position on the environment. Although the Soviet Union boycotted the conference in protest of the voting status of East Germany, NGOs were invited and participated, albeit at a forum that was separate from the intergovernmental negotiating process. In the years that followed Stockholm, the United Nations has worked on behalf of the protection of the global environment by holding major international conferences to discuss emerging issues. The conferences do not necessarily create new institutional structures or binding law; however, they often result in resolutions and action plans that lead to the creation of structures necessary to oversee them.[41]

The first of these institutions came from the Stockholm Conference itself, which passed a resolution recommending the creation of several pieces of UN environmental machinery. As a result, the General Assembly created the United Nations Environment Programme (UNEP) and selected Nairobi, Kenya, as its headquarters. Although many applauded the UNEP's location in a developing country, it has caused operational difficulties. Nairobi is geographically distant from most international meetings and secretariats; therefore, UNEP officials and environmental diplomats must spend significant time and money on travel. In addition, the infrastructure in Nairobi has been costly and unreliable. Finally, UNEP has faced challenges attracting qualified staff to work there, given concerns about security and personal safety.[42] The number of bilateral environmental agreements did not grow noticeably in the first ten years after Stockholm. Participants at the conference envisioned multilateral cooperation as consisting of development assistance, information exchanges, and capacity building, not negotiating additional regulatory treaties.[43]

As the world's understanding of the causes of environmental problems and their interconnection grew, particularly with respect to the atmosphere, the goals and strategies of the movement changed, too. In the late 1970s and early 1980s, the science of ozone depletion was uncertain. Although some countries sought to ban the use of chlorofluorocarbons (CFCs), others objected either because they rejected the principle of regulation in general or because they succumbed to industry pressure. In the mid-1980s, the scientific certainty about the problem solidified, and it appeared to be far more severe than had been previously understood. Eventually, the United States supported a binding treaty to ban the use of CFCs and encouraged Japan and the European Community to either cut or freeze their use. In September 1987, delegates met in Montreal to seek an agreement that mandated a freeze in the production of the most common CFCs by 1989, with further cuts to follow. The Montreal Protocol established a fund to pay for transitions in developing countries. It holds the distinction of becoming the first UN treaty that every single member ratified.[44]

Why did action on ozone succeed so spectacularly? The main reason, some authors argue, was that it required only a small number of similar industrialized countries to agree. The cost of including developing countries was low, and it was paid by the wealthier nations. Another reason was that solving the problem did not require broad or deep domestic adjustments. The United States was the largest producer and had enacted ambitious regulations before the global discussion even began. Although the chemicals are useful, they are not essential to industrial economies, and substitutes existed. Every serious cost-benefit analysis of eliminating them demonstrated far greater health gains than costs. Finally, the regime was neither fragmented nor deadlocked as later ones would be.[45] The success in creating an ozone regime and scientific progress set a path that later efforts would follow for better or for worse. Global regulatory treaty negotiations became the go-to solution to the problem of multilateral cooperation in this area.

In addition, the progress of understanding the planet as an integrated, dynamic ecosystem at risk of disruption from human activities resulted in the new, unifying concept of sustainable development. The idea was to allow for action on the environment without threatening the strategic priorities of powerful economic actors or upsetting the existing UN landscape.[46] Developing countries were skeptical of the notion of sustainable development when it was introduced in the report of the World Commission on Environment and Development. Yet they gradually accepted it because it addressed the concern that they could not develop by using the same resources as those countries before them had without endangering the ability of the planet to sustain life.

During the same years, the science of climate change continued to advance. In 1988, the Intergovernmental Panel on Climate Change (IPCC) was established under the auspices of the UNEP and the World Meteoro-

logical Association to assess the scientific, technical, and sociological information relevant for understanding the risk of human-induced climate
change. The IPCC does not carry out new research or monitor climate
data. It assesses published and peer-reviewed scientific technical literature
with the goal of informing international policy and negotiations on these issues. Thus, the IPCC has become a vehicle for climate experts to synthesize
their findings and present them to the world's political leaders. As their ability to measure the effects of climate change has improved, scientists agree
that climate change is occurring and that human activities are responsible
for most of what has come about since the 1970s. Chief among the causes
are carbon dioxide (CO_2) emissions from burning coal, oil, and gas. Further
accumulation of greenhouse gas emissions would risk many human and
natural life systems.[47]

The scientific evidence for climate change mounted as the UN began to
plan for the next major environmental conference, the United Nations
Conference on Environment and Development, or the Earth Summit, in
Rio de Janeiro, Brazil, in 1992. The political actors involved, including the
developing countries, reached consensus on the need to accept the notion
of sustainable development. The conference afforded an opportunity to
highlight the primacy of their developmental aspirations. Moreover, in the
intervening years, Southern professionals' mindsets were increasingly
shaped by Northern universities, environmental NGOs, and thinly veiled
advocacy for the environment. They were thus less likely to question the legitimacy of the discourse on the environment because their own training
and professional interests became tied to it.[48]

Preparation for the Earth Summit aimed to achieve international accords on specific issues—such as climate, ozone, forests, or arid lands—that
would regulate the entire system.[49] In so doing, the Earth Summit attempted
to integrate a network of treaties and agreements that could manage international environmental problems. In this regard, the Earth Summit was a
success. Participants reached three major Rio agreements on climate and
biodiversity: the United Nations Framework Convention on Climate
Change (UNFCCC), the UN Convention on Biological Diversity, and the
UN Convention to Combat Desertification. The three are linked through a

joint liaison group that was set up to boost cooperation among them. It now also includes the Ramsar Convention on Wetlands.

In the area of climate change, the UNFCCC is a framework or umbrella treaty. The distinction means that the countries signing it established an objective and general obligations. Further agreements, or subsidiary agreements, would work gradually toward achieving that objective. Hence, the UNFCCC did not state when, or at what levels, stabilization of greenhouse gas emissions should occur.[50] Parties to the UNFCCC meet each year in an attempt to produce a global plan to reduce emissions.

The first subsidiary agreement to the UNFCCC was the Kyoto Protocol, which commits its parties by setting internationally binding emission reduction targets. In 1997, the signatories to the Kyoto Protocol agreed to cut carbon emissions to 5.2 percent below 1990 levels. The Kyoto Protocol did not include developing countries in those obligated to lower emissions because the parties recognized that developed countries are principally responsible for the current high levels of greenhouse gas emissions in the atmosphere after their more than 150-year head start. This approach, termed the common but differentiated responsibilities principle, places a heavier burden on developed countries.

The United States played a role in negotiating the Kyoto Protocol, and the Clinton administration signed the treaty. Yet the administration never attempted to gain ratification. First of all, critics argued that the distinction between industrialized and developing countries could not be sustained in the twenty-first century. Most scientists and governments agree that achieving the UNFCCC's objective requires that all major emitting countries abate their greenhouse gas emissions. Second, many in the United States also feared that the Kyoto Protocol would adversely affect economic competitiveness if some countries reduced their emissions and others did not.

Although Kyoto entered into force in 2005, it was set to expire at the end of 2012. Countries began negotiations on a new treaty in 2007, culminating with the Copenhagen Conference in 2009. Approximately 115 world leaders attended the high-level segment of the Copenhagen Climate Change Conference, making it one of the largest gatherings outside the UN headquarters in New York. They negotiated the Copenhagen Accord, which included the goal of limiting the maximum global average temperature increase to no more than 2 degrees Celsius above preindustrial levels, subject to a review in 2015. The global financial crisis and national interests prevented a comprehensive deal. Hence, the Copenhagen Conference did not result in an agreement on exactly how to limit global average temperature increases or produce a legally binding agreement.

Nonetheless, Copenhagen was an advance because major developing countries were included in the distribution of responsibilities. Although they are still formally part of the group of developing countries and identify with it, ministers from Brazil, South Africa, India, and China (BASIC) issued statements after quarterly meetings to discuss strategies and common positions on climate change. They agreed that developed countries have a greater obligation for action because they have a greater historical responsibility in terms of their contribution to the average global temperature increase. Even so, in coordinating their positions, the BASIC countries made the first promises to reduce the pace of the rise of their greenhouse gas emissions along with the developed countries. The system thus shifted from a system with a basic distinction between North and South toward a system with at least three categories of states: the developed North, the developing South, and the emerging powers somewhere in between.[51]

In the next major attempt at a United Nations climate agreement, negotiators met in Paris in 2015 with the goal of working through voluntary pledges that countries make to reduce CO_2 and other gases, and not through standards and targets set internationally, which states must implement. The result of the conference, the Paris Agreement, is the second major subsidiary agreement to the UNFCCC. Unlike the first subsidiary agreement, the Kyoto Protocol, the Paris Agreement emphasizes consensus building in voluntary and nationally determined targets. It encourages countries politically and does not have the same legally binding nature as a treaty. The Paris Agreement is only sixteen pages long, and some question whether it represents significant change, given its mostly procedural nature and lack of binding quantitative greenhouse gas obligations.

The Paris Agreement requires parties to undertake nationally determined contributions to mitigate emissions, participate in a transparency framework that includes communicating their greenhouse gas inventories, and be subject to international review of their implementation.[52] Executive branch officials in the Obama administration stated that since the Paris Agreement is not a treaty that requires Senate advice and consent to ratification, Senate approval would not be necessary. President Obama signed an instrument of acceptance without submitting it to Congress and deposited it with UN Secretary-General Ban Ki-moon.[53] The major UN environmental accords are summarized in table 6.1.

Environmental Efforts through the Broader Multilateral System

The impact of these agreements on the environment is not entirely clear. The UNFCCC has a near-universal membership, with 198 parties.[54] The UN Convention on Biological Diversity and UN Convention to Combat Desertification each have 196 parties.[55] These numbers are impressive. Nonetheless, the three Rio conventions have also locked the UN into a framework that is grounded in the pillars of development and international law in the area of environmental issues. As such, it cannot engage some of the more recent challenges posed by the global environment, such as those related to human rights and conflict resolution.

As we saw with global health concerns, later activities have moved to agencies outside the UN. Thus, in recent years, the UN has tended to be marginalized on environmental issues.[56] New IOs are created, but others have also been grafted onto existing organizations. Although the older organizations have been important sources of expertise and funds, they have also contributed to the tendency for environmental concerns to be fragmented across the patchwork of multilateral society. Among the most significant of these are the World Bank and the World Trade Organization.[57]

As we saw in chapter 6, the World Bank encouraged and funded large-scale infrastructure and development projects in the 1950s. Yet it was not until the 1980s that transnational environmental activist coalitions began to target the World Bank on the premise that these development projects had no regard for their environmental costs. The most notable was activism associated with the Sardar Sarovar Dam project on the Narmada River in

Table 6.1 Summary of major UN environmental action

Place, year	Activity	Results
Stockholm, 1972	UN Conference on the Human Environment	Created UNEP in Nairobi as the leading environmental authority that sets the agenda, provides implementation of agreements, and serves as an advocate for the environment within the UN system.
1983–87	The World Commission on Environment and Development	The commission, led by Gro Harlem Brundtland, prepares and releases its report, *Our Common Future*. It defines and popularizes the term "sustainable development."
Montreal, 1987	Montreal Protocol on Substances that Deplete the Ozone Layer is signed	The treaty phases out the production of substances that are responsible for ozone depletion. It is considered a milestone of environmental cooperation.
1988	Creation of IPCC	UNEP and the World Meteorological Association create the IPCC to synthesize scientific findings on climate change and present them to the world's political bodies.
Rio de Janeiro, 1992	UN Conference on Environment and Development, or Earth Summit	Three new agreements are reached on climate change (the UNFCCC), biological diversity, and deforestation. Delegates establish the Commission on Sustainable Development to ensure compliance.
Kyoto, 1997	Kyoto Protocol is signed	The first subsidiary agreement to the UNFCCC commits its parties by setting internationally binding emission reduction targets to fight global warming.
Copenhagen, 2009	United Nations Climate Change Conference	The Copenhagen Accord is perceived to fall short of doing enough to prevent dangerous climate change. BASIC countries work to devise strategies and common positions on the issue.
Paris, 2015	United Nations Climate Change Conference	The second major subsidiary agreement, the Paris Agreement to the UNFCCC, unlike the first, contains voluntary, nationally determined targets to fight global warming.

India. The controversy surrounding the dam centered around the human and environmental costs of disrupting so many lives in the region. Yet the argument in favor of the project was that the benefits outweighed the costs. Not building it would also pressure the environment if the water from the river continued to flow into the sea unused. After construction began in 1987, the bank set up an environment department and later created the Morse Commission in 1992, which criticized the dam project. Since then, all World Bank projects must submit an environmental impact assessment.

Although protests were successful in pushing the environment onto the bank's agenda, later examples have shown that even if a damaging project is cancelled at the World Bank, *the government* does not necessarily cancel it as well. In one notable example from the 1990s, China's Three Gorges Dam on the Yangtze River went ahead with bilateral and private-sector alternative funding over environmental protests. Governments can be less transparent than the World Bank and have fewer opportunities for international review. Thus, the effect of the World Bank on the environment is not clear. As a partner with others, it can force an examination of environmental concerns in the planning stages and have an impact beyond its financial contribution. Yet if it goes too far, the partners can choose to go it alone and ignore environmental concerns outright.

Another existing economic IO that has taken on environmental concerns is the World Trade Organization. Ignoring environmental guidelines could give some countries an advantage over others in trade. Thus, as with the World Bank, the WTO's effects on the environment are not clear. For example, the WTO created a committee on trade and the environment in 1994, with a mandate to study the impact of environmental policies on trade. However, the committee is a consulting forum and not a regulatory body; that is, it is not a rule-making component of the trading order. Moreover, the GATT/WTO's influence on national regulations can be either direct—wherein the GATT/WTO can overrule national standards if they are deemed to be a nontariff barrier to trade—or indirect—wherein the GATT/WTO can shape the development and implementation of the national environmental regulation. With respect to indirect influence on national regulations, higher environmental regulations raise the costs of production for the average firm, leading to a race to the bottom of national regulations in countries where governments want to attract investment.[58]

Transnational Environmental Efforts at the Grassroots Level

Activism in recent years has also taken place outside the framework of states, as well as IOs, and at times has exceeded the efforts of each. In 2009, political economist Elinor Ostrom won the Nobel Prize in Economics for her seminal book *Governing the Commons*.[59] In it, she took on the notion of the tragedy of the commons and argued in favor of solutions that can rise from the bottom up. According to Ostrom, common problems can, in some cases, be better solved by voluntary organizations than by a coercive government.

Where frustration has built at worldwide inaction on climate change, several American states and Canadian provinces have enacted regulations similar to those imposed by Kyoto. Some countries, such as Canada, that ratified the Kyoto Protocol did not meet their targets and withdrew. Some US states have pursued aggressive goals. Given the size of some state economies such as California, these policies can add up to serious reductions in greenhouse gas emissions if fully implemented, even without ratification at the federal level.[60] In addition, mayors of megacities across the globe convened the C40 Large Cities Climate Leadership Group to promote solutions. The initiative shares data and takes actions to reduce global greenhouse gas emissions to constrain global temperatures to rise no more than 1.5 degrees Celsius above the preindustrial average levels.

In sum, the global environment, and the area of climate change in particular, is regulated by a diversity of actors, including nongovernmental organizations (NGOs), firms, transnational networks, and others exercising varying degrees of authority. As Jessica F. Green notes, these actors can range from giant multinationals like Walmart—when it takes steps to achieve sustainability goals—to NGOs—when they monitor wildlife trade.[61] Some firms have taken measures to reduce emissions so that they can save money and prepare for the future, albeit considerable opposition in the public and private sector remains.[62] In China, experimentation has occurred at the national and regional levels. Private initiatives have emerged within NGOs.[63]

Conclusion

Scientific progress has created entirely new problems that require multilateral cooperation to resolve. However, the way these issues are framed, how their agendas are set, and their connections to one another have important implications for how they will be handled within the existing system of IOs. For example, the connections between war and the environment, and war and medicine, have been self-evident since the nineteenth century. Armies destroyed livestock and forests. They spread disease and left unexploded devices behind. It has always been apparent that it is difficult to farm a battlefield for many years after a war has ended or that battlefield medical efforts have driven many advances in surgical techniques. However, the contemporary persistence of war in some regions of the world has created an impasse for sustainable development to occur. Conflict enhances vulnerability, marginalization, and the risks associated with disasters and extreme events. Natural resources can be a key element in sustained or recurrent episodes of violent conflict.[64]

The result is that the connections among the issues themselves and preexisting boundaries in IOs have created entirely new problems and complicated easy solutions. For example, the connection between the degradation of the environment from industrialization and human health has become even more apparent with advances in our understanding of the causes of disease and how they are spread. In addition, cancer clusters can indicate exposure to toxic chemicals associated with manufacturing or consumer products. The lack of trees and flowers in cities can contribute to the development of allergies in children who are not exposed to microbes at an early age. The framing of environmental issues as a matter of international law and economic development makes it easier to keep questions of climate change, water deprivation, or human insecurity out of the UN Security Council or Human Rights Council. Other UN organs with environmental expertise cannot move into activities in the peace and security or human rights spheres.[65]

SEVEN

Global Justice and Human Rights

Multilateralism embodies principles shared among states. Yet as we have seen, principles are constantly debated, and states emphasize some to the detriment of others. Notions of global justice and human rights are no different. They have been constantly subject to interpretation and reinterpretation. International humanitarian law in the nineteenth century addressed issues of the treatment of soldiers, the wounded, prisoners of war, and noncombatants, yet these topics were framed within discussions of the obligations of the rights and responsibilities of states. The atrocities of World War II in the twentieth century led countries to attempt to codify the rights and responsibilities of humans that are intrinsic to their nature, and not attached to any specific state or official office. In the second half of the twentieth century, abstract ideas about *individual people* and their place in global society emerged as part of what has come to be called the legalization of global politics across issue areas, wherein states take on obligations to honor rules or commitments embedded in international (and many times domestic) law. With the proliferation of international organizations, these rules have become increasingly precise, and they are interpreted or implemented by third parties. Ultimately, the third party may resolve disputes among states and even create new rules altogether.[1] In time, multilateral mechanisms began to enforce these ideals and even punish individuals who violate the rights of others under specific circumstances.

This chapter explores how the advance of notions of global justice and human rights has taken place at the same time as the scientific progress and globalization of the post–World War II era. These concepts have become embedded in international law associated with the United Nations, multilateral treaties, and other IOs, and they have been promoted by nongovernmental organizations on the ground. This dialogue on rights and justice, however, has been contested every step of the way. The language of rights transfers responsibility for certain categories of behavior from the polity to the world community, yet it leaves unanswered the question of who has the responsibility for acting on behalf of, and paying for, human rights. In the twenty-first century, the debates have come full circle, wherein some view the discourse as suffused with cultural imperialism and representing a hypocritical imposition of Western values where they are not appropriate.

The consequence is that, as the depth and passion of the philosophical debate over justice and rights would imply, the introduction of moral purposes into the work of multilateral organizations can also leave them open to charges of hypocrisy, cultural imperialism, and their own form of immorality when crimes against humanity are allegedly committed by officials acting in official roles on their behalf. The architecture of governance in this area is thus challenged by issues and debates as ancient as Greek democracy and as new as videos of terrorist executions. Moreover, the material resources needed to address problems such as the global refugee crisis are accompanied by the difficulty of determining a universal understanding of who is responsible for punishment of crimes and what rights the individual can claim as a citizen of global society.

Notions of Justice, Courts, and International Humanitarian Law

Early ideas about justice and respect for the dignity of human life are embedded in international humanitarian law. International law comprises treaties, customs, reasons, and principles of law. Broader definitions include judicial decisions and the writings of authorities on the topic. The absence of a legislature, judiciary, or executive makes comparisons between international and domestic law problematic. Yet even though international law has not been applicable in controlling aggression, conflict, and war, it has shaped the character of international society by developing a system of rules and procedures covering almost every aspect of interstate relations.[2] International humanitarian law connects the concepts of international law with individual people by attempting to prohibit superfluous injury and unnecessary suffering during a war. All human beings must be treated with respect for their inherent dignity. Parties to a conflict cannot kill and maim at random, cleanse ethnic populations, forcibly displace civilians, burn religious monuments, torture, use sexual violence as a weapon, or use cruel, inhumane, or degrading treatment of any kind against any human being. Although this branch of international law recognizes that combatants will be killed in armed conflict, it prohibits inhumane and painful ways of doing so, such as drowning or torture. Hence, some weapons are outlawed as they cause needless injury and unnecessary suffering, such as chemical, biological, and poisonous weapons, exploding bullets, and weapons causing injury by nondetectable fragments.[3] Since 1977, activists have sought to respond to developments in the field of modern weaponry and outlaw certain weapons, such as antipersonnel land mines. The contradictions remain. Although initiatives to negotiate a treaty banning the use of nuclear weapons have been made, none have been successful.[4]

Early International Courts and Arbitration Panels

In order to ensure fairness in the distribution of benefits and burdens, to resolve disputes, and to allow for punishment of wrongdoers, international organizations need a mechanism with the authority to administer justice according to mutually agreed rules of behavior. Courts perform these functions in the domestic sphere, and so it is not surprising that a nascent system of international tribunals and arbitration panels arose alongside multilateralism in order to perform these tasks for disputes among states. As we saw in chapter 1, the first major international court, the Permanent Court of Arbitration, was established in 1899 and still exists. Arbitration differs from adjudication, however, insofar as courts are permanent and arbitration panels are ad hoc, or created on a case-by-case basis. Whereas courts have a permanent composition and fixed procedures, arbitration procedures and panels are determined by the parties for each case. Arbitration is thus much more flexible than a court proceeding; courts are usually concerned with developing consistent, coherent international law, whereas arbitration seeks to settle a specific dispute. Courts can thus have more systemic impact.[5]

Despite the development of international humanitarian law, there were no true international courts or bodies specifically charged with ensuring compliance for much of human history. This duty is still left primarily to states themselves. That is, states have a duty to try and punish individuals alleged to have committed war crimes. International humanitarian law does provide a special status and role for a humanitarian organization: the International Committee of the Red Cross. The 1949 Geneva Conventions instruct the Red Cross to encourage compliance with international humanitarian law, and the treaty gives the organization the authority to visit prisoners, organize relief operations, reunite separated families, and carry out other humanitarian activities during armed conflict. As a result, many states consider the International Committee of the Red Cross to have a legal personality, and they give it privileges and immunities under their domestic laws.[6]

States established the first permanent international tribunal, the Permanent Court of International Justice, after World War I. Provided for in the Covenant of the League of Nations, the court's jurisdiction was technically limited to disputes between states. It did, however, accept disputes that derived from an individual if a state brought the individual's case to the court; then, for purposes of the court, such a case became one between two states.[7] During the years of its existence, the Permanent Court clarified a number of aspects of international law. It was dissolved in 1946 and replaced with the International Court of Justice as the principal judicial organ of the UN system. The International Court's role is to settle legal disputes submitted to it by states in accordance with international law and to give advisory opinions on legal questions authorized by UN organs and specialized agencies. Therefore, if the conflict is international in nature, and if both parties accept the voluntary jurisdiction of the court, one of the state parties can bring a case to the International Court of Justice.[8]

Philosophical Debates over International Law, Justice, and the Power Politics of States

In the interwar period, the connections among international law, society, peace, and justice concerned many prominent thinkers. Christian theologian Reinhold Niebuhr argued that humans cannot create ideal societies in which there will be peace without coercion and perfect justice. But they can create a society where there will be enough justice and where coercion will be nonviolent enough that the common enterprise will not sink into a complete disaster.[9] In a civilized society, the vices of individuals are delegated to larger and larger communities without eradicating conflict. People have the illusion that they are moral, but the illusion does not last.[10] Therefore, for Niebuhr, group relations can never be as ethical as individual ones.[11]

During the same years, E. H. Carr argued that law provides the machinery for settling disputes about legal rights. He pointed to the nascent machinery of international dispute settlement in the Permanent Court of Arbitration and Permanent Court of International Justice; however, he saw the key distinction between the national and international to be that national courts have compulsory jurisdiction, a legal term meaning that a state has agreed to accept jurisdiction in certain prescribed matters, whereas international law does not recognize this concept.[12] Carr argued that law is a function of political society and dependent on that society for its development. It is conditioned by society's political presuppositions. Hence, the decision that a given issue is suitable for treatment by legal methods is political, and its character is likely to be determined by the political development of the international community—or political relations between the countries concerned. The upshot for Carr is that it is necessary to develop political cooperation before the international machinery can be perfected.[13]

Why preserve the distinction between the legal and the political? Because when a dispute enters a court, differences in power between countries do not matter. Yet in politics, power is an essential factor in every dispute.[14] Nonetheless, Carr's work opened the door to more legal solutions. Every government needs power as the basis of its authority, but it also needs the moral basis of the consent of the governed. In the long run, people will always revolt against raw power. At the same time, there will never be a political order in which the grievances of the weak and few receive the same attention as those of the strong and many. Power creates the morality convenient to itself, and coercion is a fruitful source of consent. But to build a new international order and a new international harmony, transnational society needs to be accepted as tolerant and unoppressive, or at least preferable to any practicable alternative.[15] When the issue of power is settled, morality resumes its role.

The cataclysmic events of World War II forced many to rethink existing conceptions of international humanitarian law, particularly with respect to civilians, and to attempt to introduce notions of morality into the international order that followed. Although a considerable portion of this law provided rules that regulate how states conduct war once it has begun, and other rules concerned the means and methods of warfare as well as treatment of prisoners of war, there were no rules regarding civilians. The aerial bombing technology in World War II made it possible to target thousands of miles of territories, thus killing more civilians than soldiers. The treatment of individuals in concentration camps by the Nazis revealed additional gaps in the law. Thus, the four Geneva Conventions of 1949 set out explicit rules for civilian protection.[16] Taken together, the Hague Regulations (on weapons and targeting during war), Geneva Conventions, and two amendment protocols of 1977 (on the protection of civilians and those no longer able to fight) currently form the major body of international humanitarian law.

Human Rights and International Law

Once the atomic bomb had been detonated and its destructive capacity understood, people realized that if they didn't prevent total war, the human race could be annihilated.[17] The world's major religions—Hinduism, Christianity, Judaism, Islam, and Buddhism—teach a profound respect for the life of each person.[18] The universality of respect for human life leads to the notion that all human beings possess human rights simply by existing. Yet as human rights became understood after the war, they moved beyond the confines of war and began to represent the bare minimum that is required for a person to live a human existence. A conception of these rights is not about taking care of others; it is about creating conditions so that people can take care of themselves if they are able.[19]

Therefore, for much of world history, nation-states retained jurisdiction and concern over the rights of people. States remain the main protectors of individual rights. There have always been notions of protecting special groups in other countries, such as diplomatic representatives, consular personnel, and aliens (foreign-born residents). Yet the creation of the United Nations was an important first step in acknowledging a role for international society in protecting the rights that all humans possess just because they are human. As with other disagreements reinforced by the Cold War, a fundamental contradiction existed immediately among states both with respect to the nature of the rights to be protected and the priorities among them.

Despite the ongoing debates, UN treaties and agencies added to an expanding machinery in international law through which to assert and protect human rights. Seven references to human rights are in the UN Charter itself. Articles 55 and 56 put obligations on member states to promote universal respect for and promotion of human rights, albeit these responsibilities are contradicted in Article 2(7), which provides that nothing contained in the Charter shall authorize the UN to intervene in matters that are in the domestic jurisdiction of any state.[20] The Universal Declaration of Human Rights of December 1948 attempted to codify them. Later conventions and agreements extended and refined the notion to include other groups into the common view of what these rights are. As the UN's machinery for human rights has continued to evolve, NGOs have made human rights a reality by naming and shaming perpetrators and assisting victims.

In the same way that the notion of human rights has become more widely accepted, it has reshaped important aspects of multilateralism and international relations more broadly. Rights are an important part of the language of morals, but they are unique within that language. That is, when an individual person claims rights, he or she is not begging or pleading. When individuals exercise rights, they do not offer gratitude. Rights are insisted on as part of one's status as a person. Therefore, rights are not invoked where people are at the mercy of others or out of pity. They are a weapon of the weak against the strong. The idea of rights is thus closely connected to that of political individualism. Society comprises independent, rational beings who decide what is best for themselves. Provision of rights provides for political order.[21]

The Universal Declaration of Human Rights

The Universal Declaration of Human Rights served as the foundation for much of the codification of human rights that followed and has been considered the Magna Carta for all the people of the planet.[22] The evolution and development of the declaration have deep roots in the domestic politics of sovereign states. Although the Holocaust represents the most brutal abuse of human rights at the state level in this era and was a motivating factor behind the need to enumerate specific human rights, US race relations, too, were troubled. During Franklin Roosevelt's first five years in office, eighty-three African Americans, or roughly seventeen a year, were lynched.[23] The administration did not promote antilynching legislation because Roosevelt feared that the southerners who occupied strategic positions in Congress would block the rest of his agenda.[24] First Lady Eleanor Roosevelt's views tended to be more liberal. For example, though she tempered her public criticism of the Japanese internment camps that became administration policy, she privately complained to her friends that the internment of US citizens was another reason to hate war.[25] The contradiction between what the United States promoted internationally and how it acted domestically would become a stumbling block in early UN human rights work.

By the end of 1940, Franklin Roosevelt began to think about ways to encourage global cooperation, and he unveiled his ideas in his four freedoms speech of 1941. As we saw in chapter 2, Roosevelt and Winston Churchill discussed a new organization based on these principles during the Atlantic Conference in the summer of 1941.[26] The world would be based on four essential human freedoms committed to the individual: freedom of speech and expression, freedom to worship God in one's own way, freedom from want, and freedom from fear. After Roosevelt died, President Harry Truman asked Eleanor Roosevelt to join the US delegation to the United Nations in order to tie himself to the previous administration. She traveled to London for the UN's first meeting.

On the way, Republican senator Arthur Vandenberg, an isolationist and opponent of Roosevelt's policies, asked Eleanor to serve on the UN's Third Committee, which dealt with humanitarian, educational, and cultural questions.[27] The fate of European refugees was one of the first issues on the committee's agenda. This issue posed a problem between the United States and the Soviet Union because many refugees refused to return to the Soviet Union under communism. The head of the Soviet delegation argued that anyone who refused to return home was a traitor. Yet many Jewish survivors wanted to emigrate to the United States, despite the State Department's immigration policies. Some who returned to Europe were attacked by the local population who refused to give up property seized during the war. Others were Zionists who wanted to establish a home in Palestine.[28] Eleanor Roosevelt defended them all. In addition, she was determined to meet some of the 250,000 Jewish survivors and former Nazi slave laborers among the 2 million war refugees.[29]

Although the UN Charter referred to human rights, it did not enumerate them. The representatives thus sought to establish a universal declaration to define these rights. The UN's Economic and Social Council established the Commission on Human Rights with eighteen members from different nationalities and charged them with preparing an international bill of rights. The commission, in turn, established a drafting committee to write the declaration and selected Eleanor Roosevelt as chair. The commission met in two sessions over two years.

The first question the commission addressed was whether the rights of society or the individual should be paramount. To resolve it, the commission reviewed many constitutions and legal treaties.[30] Questions of US race relations plagued the commission's work. African American activist W. E. B. Du Bois submitted a brief to the human rights division in 1947 titled "An Appeal to the World: A Statement of Denial of Human Rights to Minorities in the Case of Citizens of Negro Descent in the United States of America and an Appeal to the United Nations for Redress."[31] Although Eleanor Roosevelt had warned against the hypocrisy of condemning the Nazis for their racial policies while permitting white supremacy in many areas of the United States, Du Bois put her in a tough position. She was sympathetic to

Fig. 7.1. Eleanor Roosevelt holding the Declaration of Human Rights poster in Spanish text at Lake Success. Courtesy of the Franklin D. Roosevelt Presidential Library and Museum, Hyde Park, New York.

the sentiment in the brief but did not support the commission's receiving petitions from anyone but member states.[32] Later debates sought to protect social and economic rights.

Despite the difficulties inherent in drafting a universal document, Eleanor Roosevelt presided over the adoption of the Universal Declaration of Human Rights in 1948, a document that reflects the UN's determination to stem international conflicts by overcoming differences among cultures and countries (fig. 7.1).[33] Franklin Roosevelt's four freedoms were captured in the preamble to the Universal Declaration. Nonetheless, the divisions over how to define human rights persisted. As the Cold War deepened and African and Asian states joined the UN, the composition and focus of human rights organs changed and the universality of the concept was again questioned. Human rights became a wedge between East and West, North and South.[34]

Different groups used concepts of human rights differently. In East-West relations during the Cold War, equality opposed liberty, group rights opposed individual rights, economic and social rights opposed civil and political rights. The East claimed that it put a priority on economic and social rights, such as the right to work and the right to an adequate standard of living, whereas the West claimed to do better on individual freedom, civil liberties, and other values of an open society.[35] The origins of the dispute reflected differing notions of the derivation of the concept of human rights. In Marxist-Leninist doctrine, rights come from the law, which comes from government, which reflects the underlying economic relations of society. In a capitalist society, human rights will be defined by the interests of the capitalist class. There cannot be true human rights until all are free in a socialist society. Therefore, it is not surprising that in a socialist society, the primary liberty is the freedom from exploitation.[36] During the same years, East-West debates about human rights were mirrored in North-South deliberations. In its most radical statements, the global South nations argued at the United Nations and elsewhere that all economic and social rights are a prerequisite for the exercise of all other human rights and fundamental freedoms.[37]

Human Rights Machinery in the United Nations

The Universal Declaration was a landmark event in the promotion of human rights. In order for its ideals to become a reality, however, additional UN instruments and mechanisms were needed. The Universal Declaration, while the foundational document of international human rights law, is a resolution of the UN General Assembly and not itself directly binding. In 1966, two International Human Rights Covenants on economic, social, and cultural rights and on civil and political rights gave the Universal Declaration the force of treaty law, although they were not immediately operative.[38] Other single-issue treaties have expanded on particular rights since then.[39]

The initial machinery was thus in place with the Commission on Human Rights that had drafted the Universal Declaration itself. Under the authority of the ECOSOC, the commission established the Sub-Commission on the Promotion and Protection of Human Rights. The commission was to set standards for human rights worldwide, and the subcommission was to undertake studies and make recommendations to the commission concerning the prevention of discrimination of any kind relating to human rights and fundamental freedoms.[40] Hence, from the time of its creation in 1946 until it was replaced by the UN Human Rights Council in 2006, the Human Rights Commission was the UN's principal mechanism and international forum concerned with the promotion and protection of human rights.

As international human rights law has grown increasingly complex, a number of bodies have been established: some are based in the UN Charter, others are political bodies consisting of state representatives with mandates established by the Charter, and still others are treaty-based committees with independent experts set up by human rights treaties and mandated to monitor state parties' compliance with their treaty obligations. Human rights treaties have come to exist on topics ranging from race discrimination to the rights of migrants. Each has its own compliance and oversight mechanism; some allow individuals to raise concerns, others only states.[41] According to contemporary understandings, though a country may not be a state party to an individual human rights convention, lack of membership does not mean that individuals in that country do not possess those rights. It just means that these rights will have to be protected through domestic means alone.[42]

As would be expected, given the diverse notions of the definition of human rights, the varying priorities attached to each right, and the differing power relations of each state within the international community, establishing an enduring machinery in this area has proven to be a difficult undertaking. At first, the commission's work focused on promoting human rights more broadly and helping to conclude specific treaties, but with the utmost respect for the sovereignty of the UN member states. After 1967, the commission became more active. In 1993, the World Conference on Human Rights in Vienna adopted a declaration to better integrate the human rights work of governmental organizations and NGOs. Participants called for a more proactive effort in condemning human rights abuses and for a new interpretation of national sovereignty.[43] The result was the creation of the

Table 7.1 Human rights treaty bodies that monitor implementation
of the core international human rights treaties

Human Rights Committee
Committee on Economic, Social and Cultural Rights
Committee on the Elimination of Racial Discrimination
Committee on the Elimination of Discrimination against Women
Committee against Torture
Subcommittee on Prevention of Torture
Committee on the Rights of the Child
Committee on Migrant Workers
Committee on the Rights of Persons with Disabilities
Committee on Enforced Disappearances

Source: "Treaty-Based Bodies," OHCHR, http://www.ohchr.org/EN/HRBodies/Pages
/HumanRightsBodies.aspx

Office of the High Commissioner for Human Rights, which currently leads
the UN's human rights efforts.

Ten human rights treaty bodies monitor implementation of the core international human rights treaties (table 7.1). Since the adoption of the Universal Declaration, all UN member states have ratified at least one core
international human rights treaty, and 80 percent have ratified four or more.
The treaty bodies are created in accordance with provisions of the treaty that
they monitor.[44] The Office of the High Commissioner supports their work
and assists them in harmonizing their working methods and reporting requirements through their secretariats. In addition to this work, the Office of
the High Commissioner operates through three other divisions that cover
this complexity: research, field operations, and the Human Rights Council.

Thus, in the years following the UN's founding, the Commission on Human Rights was the key intergovernmental body in this area. Yet the commission was plagued by problems caused by the fundamental contradictions
between the activities of its members and its purported purpose. Seats on
the commission were allocated according to the UN's regional group system, with no regard for the human rights record of those selected to serve
on it or those elected to chair it. At the same time, the commission did not

always appear to keep its focus on human rights issues. Rather, it appeared to be a forum for other political issues, such as the status of Israel or US foreign policy.

In 2006, the United Nations Human Rights Council replaced the Commission on Human Rights. Unlike its predecessor, the Human Rights Council consists of members elected by the UN General Assembly. It considers the candidate's contribution to the promotion and protection of human rights, as well as its voluntary pledges and commitments in this regard. The seats are still distributed among the UN's regional groups, but the General Assembly retains the ability to suspend the rights and privileges of any council member that it determines to have persistently committed gross and systematic violations of human rights during its term of membership. Terms are for three years, and no state can serve more than two consecutive terms. The Special Procedures Division of the Office of the High Commissioner for Human Rights provides substantive and organizational support to the council, yet is separate from it.

In the interim, state members of the UN have continued to negotiate new treaties with additional human rights obligations. For example, the Convention on the Rights of the Child defines who is or is not a child and sets out the civil, political, economic, social, health, and cultural rights of children; every member of the United Nations except the United States has ratified it. The first human rights treaty of the third millennium, the Convention on the Rights of Persons with Disabilities, intends to protect the rights and dignity of persons with disabilities. Adopted by the UN General Assembly on December 13, 2006, it came into force on May 3, 2008. Parties agree to promote, protect, and ensure the full human rights of persons with disabilities and that they enjoy full equality under the law. As the treaty has been negotiated, it has changed people's perceptions of those with disabilities from being objects of charity to being full and equal members of society. A December 2012 vote in the US Senate on the Convention on the Rights of Persons with Disabilities was six votes short of the two-thirds required for ratification.

Other issues promoted by human rights organizations have not reached the treaty stage but have nonetheless advanced within the UN machinery. For example, from its founding until 2006, the UN political bodies had not discussed lesbian, gay, bisexual, and transgender (LGBT) rights. In December 2006, Norway presented a joint statement on human rights violations based on sexual orientation and gender identification on behalf of fifty-four states to the Commission on Human Rights. Later in 2008, Argentina presented a joint statement at the General Assembly on behalf of sixty-six states. An Arab League statement opposed the latter statement. In 2017, both statements were open for signature, yet neither was officially adopted by the General Assembly.

Nonetheless, activists persist in this area. On June 17, 2011, South Africa led a resolution at the UN Human Rights Council requesting that the High Commissioner for Human Rights draft a report documenting discriminatory laws and practices and acts of violence against individuals based on their sexual orientation and gender identity. The resolution passed. The report came out in December 2011 and documented violations, including hate crimes, criminalization of homosexuality, and discrimination. In July 2014, the UN agreed to extend equal benefits to its employees who had entered into same-sex unions in jurisdictions where they were legal. In a stronger statement in 2016, the UN Human Rights Council agreed to appoint an independent expert to find the causes of violence and discrimination against people due to their gender identity and sexual orientation. In that same year, the Security Council condemned the 2016 nightclub shooting in Orlando, Florida, marking the first time that body used language recognizing violence targeting the LGBT community.

Human Rights Machinery and Nongovernmental Organizations

When states adopted the Universal Declaration and other international human rights instruments, they did so with the understanding that states would also enforce them. Therefore, from the end of World War II to the end of the Cold War, states established human rights bodies such as the UN Human Rights Commission without any sense that they were relinquishing sovereignty. No UN body believed itself competent to enforce standards, and even the Human Rights Commission took the position that it had no power to act. Pressure to change the UN machinery and conclude new declarations, conventions, and in effect redefine sovereignty came from actors outside the formal apparatus of the UN and enmeshed in a nascent global civil society. The evolution of the protection of human rights on the world scene has thus occurred in tandem with the growth and development of human rights NGOs that have come to occupy a new space among IOs, states, and people. Two major actors in this area have been Amnesty International and Human Rights Watch.

Amnesty International was founded in London in 1961 as a volunteer movement. Volunteers and staff operate under an ethos stressing volunteerism, individualism, practicality, self-discipline, and moral import.[45] The founders of Amnesty sought to mobilize world opinion against abusers of human rights until they could no longer be flouted. To achieve this goal, the organization had to work along with the system of sovereign nation-states even if it embodied a movement legitimized by universal principles. Yet the movement is embedded in the system of states. Members work in national sections with their own constitutions that submit resolutions to international meetings, such as Amnesty International Peru, Amnesty International Senegal, and so on. They conduct their own media and fund-raising. This form of organization has been compared to the Red Cross, which must have seemed natural in the 1960s.[46]

The early 1960s were a time when European churches no longer held a preeminent role in defining morality for society at large, traditional Protestant church attendance declined, and churches did not fulfill their role of integrating society. Moreover, mainstream churches no longer held a monopoly on morality, sharing it with functional specializations such as medicine, education, technology, and business.[47] In this environment, Amnesty was successful in encompassing both ecumenical Christianity and those on the left who formed new social movements.[48] In some ways, Amnesty is a secular religion, with its volunteers and staff using religious language and ideology even if they are not themselves religious people.[49] Amnesty's morality is thus detached, objective, and universal. It expresses no opinion on the argument but stands for the principle that no one should be imprisoned, tortured, or killed just for engaging in the argument.[50]

Early in its history, Amnesty worked by collecting and collating prisoner cases and sending material to groups that raised money to send as relief to their families.[51] Newspapers picked up coverage of the early campaigns to seek the release of prisoners of conscience and improve their situation once they were released. By prohibiting a country's Amnesty organization from involving itself in the release of prisoners of conscience within its own nation, the organization adhered to a nonpartisan stance. Hence, it had a humanitarian purpose, insofar as it acted in the name of humanity itself.[52] As the organization grew, researchers investigated the cases for adoption, briefed mission delegates, and then undertook missions themselves. Researchers needed a high level of expertise.[53] In the 1970s, Amnesty International grew into an organization whose members sought not only to preserve hope for prisoners of conscience but to work against prison torture and disappearances—situations where someone is abducted or imprisoned and the responsible state or political authority refuses to acknowledge the person's fate or whereabouts so that they are not protected by the law.

As Amnesty's vision of human rights expanded, criticism of its activities did, too. When its agenda broadened to include the challenges from globalization, refugees, and women's reproductive rights, its authority to fix the meaning of universal rights also came under attack. In addition, many of the rights added in recent years involve questions of social identity, thus blurring the clarity and universality of its message. For example, in the United States, the movement includes gay rights. A prisoner of conscience can be imprisoned for their sexual orientation or for advocating for gay rights. Are these two issues one and the same? Early in the 1970s, sexual orientation was not in its mandate, and such questions did not arise.[54]

In addition, as Amnesty evolved, other groups entered the human rights space, adding another dimension to the direction of the overall agenda. Human Rights Watch originated with Helsinki Watch, a group founded in 1979 to monitor compliance with the 1975 Helsinki Accords. Helsinki Watch aimed to support citizens' groups in the Soviet Bloc in monitoring government compliance. By naming and shaming abusive governments through media coverage and exchanges with policy makers, the group advanced a new methodology of action. In 1981, Americas Watch was founded in response to the civil wars in Central America. Americas Watch not only addressed government abuses but also applied international humanitarian law to investigate war crimes by rebel groups. It also raised concerns about the role played by foreign governments, such as the United States, in providing military and political support to abusive regimes. Quickly thereafter, new Watch Committees were added in Asia (1985), Africa (1988), and the Middle East (1989). In 1988, the organization adopted the name Human Rights Watch as an umbrella.[55]

Based in New York, Human Rights Watch sought to build a membership base by researching and writing reports on a wide range of human rights concerns. It reported on the 1991 Persian Gulf War and addressed violations of the laws of war in bombing campaigns. However, the ethnic cleansing and genocide in Rwanda in 1994 and in the Balkans in the 1990s prompted the need for both real-time reporting of atrocities and in-depth documentation of cases to press for international prosecutions. Later, Human Rights Watch included work on the rights of women, children, refugees, and migrant workers into its operations. Human Rights Watch included gay rights, women's rights, children's rights, and others earlier in its history than Amnesty did, and it was quicker to respond to the media-driven agenda of the 1990s.[56]

With the growth of Human Rights Watch, competition grew in the environment for human rights NGOs. When other human rights groups, journalists, and entities began to provide information about human rights, they often could do it faster and in greater depth than more conventional organizations. The new reality came to a head in Rwanda, where the killings were no secret. Instead of performing its traditional role in documenting the human rights abuses, Amnesty needed to mobilize its membership to pressure to stop the killing.[57]

The end of the Cold War further changed the picture for human rights. Technological advances in communication, enhanced mobility, and better networking and training permitted human rights advocates to draw attention to abuses with greater skill and impact than ever before. They found new ways to use the treaty bodies, monitor, and use individual complaint mechanisms when available. Eventually, the role of the UN Security Council as a target for human rights lobbying grew to the point where it began to issue resolutions creating international criminal courts to hear cases against alleged war criminals, condemning the use of child soldiers, and promising action in a host of human rights cases.[58]

In more recent times, human rights organizations have faced an even more existential challenge. Most of the world's great powers have promoted the protection of human rights. The work of organizations like Amnesty has thus been used to justify wars that some — who do not promote such rights — consider imperialist. There is no real defense for these charges: human rights embody a very Western view of the world and of human rights, one that is specifically linked to the United Nations. Some would argue that American hegemony is the biggest global threat to human rights, even as the US government uses the language of human rights itself.[59] Other dilemmas emanate from the local human rights concerns of minority populations in advanced industrial states. For example, London society is far more multicultural than the staff of Amnesty International working there. Amnesty engages international audiences and relations among states. The country-based organization reinforces this orientation: local human rights abuses inhabit the political world of social justice. Hence, a prominent political activist treated badly in Chile figures more prominently in the work of the NGO than, for example, a woman in southeast London whose husband beats her every night. The battering is not considered a human rights violation, but the political persecution is.[60] Theories of human rights are color blind, yet however principled the ethos and culture of human rights are, they operate in a world that is not.

Enforcement of Human Rights in the Domestic and International Arenas: The International Criminal Court

The establishment and growth of the UN and an international human rights machinery changed notions of sovereignty in the late twentieth century. By that time, justification for foreign intervention ranged from peace enforcement to peacekeeping and to humanitarian intervention. Rather than seeing the protection of universal values as being the responsibility of each state and its own citizens, human rights came to be understood as the international responsibility of *all* states.[61] Whereas human rights law imposes obligations on states with respect to their treatment of individuals, international *criminal* law imposes obligations on individuals themselves.[62] Therefore, once a notion of universal human rights spread, even if it was contested, the next step was to hold individuals accountable for violating the rights of others. This step occurred regardless of that person's position in the state apparatus. Offenders could then be punished for their acts, if a court rendered judgment on behalf of the international community.

The establishment of the International Criminal Court (ICC) distinct from the United Nations thus represented an important step toward the goal of holding individuals accountable for their actions, even if the ICC was associated with various UN organs. For Kathryn Sikkink, the "justice cascade" refers to a trend in world politics where individual criminal accountability for human rights violations has become a legitimate norm in world politics and where criminal prosecutions on behalf of that norm have grown. The term does not mean that perfect justice has, or will, be done or that most perpetrators of human rights violations will be held criminally accountable.[63] Justice here refers to legal accountability for crimes. The norm of individual criminal accountability is powerful because it is connected to ideas about justice. What is new is that justice is now discussed in the international as well as domestic context.[64] There are three underpinnings to the justice norm. First of all, the most basic violations of human rights cannot be legitimate acts of state and must be seen as crimes committed by individuals. Second, individuals who commit these crimes should be prosecuted. Third, the accused bear rights and deserve to have those rights protected in a fair trial.[65]

Origins of the International Criminal Court

Before World War II, states operated according to the impunity model, the idea that neither states nor state officials should be held accountable for past human rights violations. Foreign national courts were not allowed to judge individuals who had acted as state representatives. State officials could be judged only by their own courts to ensure that foreign states did not interfere in the sovereign authority of others. The impunity model eroded after the war when the world community learned of the atrocities of the Holocaust. After World War II, France, the United Kingdom, the United States, and

Fig. 7.2. Top Nazi Leaders on trial at Nuremberg, November 22, 1945. Hermann Göring (front row left in the box) takes notes, and Rudolph Hess (second from left) watches the proceedings intently. Next to Hess is former foreign minister Joachim von Ribbentrop. Left to right in the back row are Admirals Karl Dönitz and Erich Raeder. United States Army Signal Corps. Harry S. Truman Library & Museum Accession Number 2004-440.

the USSR signed the Charter of the International Military Tribunal at Nuremberg, thus establishing the Nuremberg Tribunal under the principle that individuals acting on behalf of, and with the protection of, their state can be held personally accountable for crimes committed in violation of international law.[66] Similarly, the International Military Tribunal for the Far East, also known as the Tokyo Trial or the Tokyo War Crimes Tribunal, was established to try the leaders of the Empire of Japan. The Nuremberg prosecution charged twenty-four individuals, acquitted three on all counts, and found the others guilty on at least one count. The Nuremberg Tribunal famously asserted that individuals have international duties that transcend the national obligations of obedience imposed by the state.[67] Yet the Nuremberg and Tokyo trials occurred in the cases of complete defeat in war. In the mid-1970s, a newly democratic government in Greece resurrected the idea that individuals could be held accountable when it put its own past state officials on trial for torture and murder.

When the former Yugoslavia broke up in the 1990s, mass atrocities took place in Croatia and Bosnia and Herzegovina. Thousands of civilians were killed and wounded, tortured and sexually abused in detention camps. Hundreds of thousands of others were expelled from their homes. To address the horrendous crimes, the UN Security Council established the International Criminal Tribunal for the Former Yugoslavia (ICTY) at The Hague in 1993. Eleven judges from several countries worked with a chief prosecutor and deputy prosecutor in 1995. It indicted seventy-four individuals, despite the notable lack of resources needed to manage its work.[68] It was the first international war crimes tribunal since Nuremberg and Tokyo. In creating the ICTY and bringing the perpetrators to trial, the UN hoped to deter future crimes and bring lasting peace to the former Yugoslavia.

Not long after, the genocide in Rwanda posed a conundrum for IOs and human rights groups alike. In this episode, Rwandan president Juvénal Habyarimana's death in an airplane crash triggered chaos. A UN peacekeeping mission was already on the ground in Rwanda with a mandate to oversee the implementation of a peace agreement connected to an ongoing civil war. Cables from the mission to the Department of Peacekeeping Operations in New York warned of imminent atrocities. Those in Rwanda sought permission to undertake military operations. Yet the Secretariat had not informed the Security Council of this news and ordered the peacekeepers to remain neutral.[69] Therefore, when mass killings later took place that were directed at both ethnic and political groups, the UN mission was a bystander to the genocide because its mandate made it powerless to intervene militarily.

In his powerful indictment of the UN in Rwanda, Michael Barnett concludes that the UN's culture influenced how its bureaucrats looked at and acted during the mass killings. The bureaucratic culture situated and defined their knowledge, informed their behavior, distinguished acceptable from unacceptable consequences, and helped them to determine right from wrong. In Rwanda the UN produced powerful, autonomous bureaucrats who could be spiritless and driven only by impersonal rules and procedures.

These bureaucrats appeared to have little regard for the people they were expected to serve.[70] Barnett acknowledges that the UN was highly dependent on the Great Powers and forced to choose among competing obligations. Yet he and other observers of the genocide ask whether the institutionalization of ethics can lead individuals to substitute bureaucratically laced moralities for private moralities. The hope is for a Nuremberg principle in IOs: that individuals are accountable for their actions even if those actions are not consistent with the letter of their official responsibilities.[71]

In the months following the killings, the Security Council established the International Criminal Tribunal for Rwanda (ICTR) to prosecute persons responsible for the genocide and other serious violations of international humanitarian law committed in 1994. This situation was more complex and on a larger scale than that of the former Yugoslavia. The ICTR needed not only to bring justice to the perpetrators of the genocide but also to address the continuing assaults on refugees and displaced persons. A UN Human Rights Force that functioned with the UN High Commissioner for Refugees thus became linked to the Rwandan tribunal. The Human Rights Force assisted the tribunal by identifying those connected with the genocide. By 1997, the force had more than 130 human rights observers in Rwanda.[72]

In short, states drafted the Universal Declaration of Human Rights and other treaties after World War II. NGOs, the UN, or foreign governments issued reports documenting human rights violations and called on countries to improve their record. Sometimes states could cut military or economic aid to pressure violators. Yet individuals were mostly beyond reach.[73] By the 1980s and 1990s, human rights violations appeared to get worse, not better. The ICTY and the ICTR set the stage to establish a permanent International Criminal Court to enshrine the norm that states no longer enjoy the exclusive right to punish crimes, but that right can be exercised at the international level on behalf of the international community as a whole. Although states can, and still do, prosecute and punish individuals, the exercise of national criminal jurisdiction can be described as one performed for the international community, and not just as an exercise of sovereign power.[74] In 1998, a conference was convened in Rome to give reality to a global Nuremberg principle. A permanent International Criminal Court would try and punish individuals accused of atrocities and genocide, no matter what safeguards their official positions provided.

As with many other efforts to advance multilateralism, the United States played a contradictory role. When the Clinton administration took office in 1993, Madeleine Albright became the US ambassador to the United Nations. Albright had a commitment to human rights and had been a tireless supporter of the court. When the Security Council voted to establish the Yugoslav Tribunal, she declared that the Nuremberg principles were reaffirmed.[75] The United States thus appeared mildly favorable at first because a court might be useful in cases of Somali crimes or against the Libyan terrorists who had downed Pan Am Flight 103 over Scotland in 1988.[76] Presidential administrations at the time would have preferred regime change and criminal prosecution of the leadership, were these options available, as opposed to the military engagement they did use.[77]

As the Rome Conference went on, controversies arose over the issues of jurisdiction and accountability. The United States sought to rein in the proposed court's broad powers of prosecution, particularly with respect to its power to charge and prosecute US soldiers, sailors, and air personnel who served overseas and might be accused of war crimes. Together with China, India, and Israel, the United States wanted the Security Council to have veto power over prosecutions. In addition, the United States sought an independent prosecutor for the court to initiate its own prosecutions.[78] One third of participants at the Rome Conference, including Canada and many US-based NGOs and human rights associations, took the other side and argued for an unrestricted court. When the conference ended, NGOs engaged in a campaign for universal ratification that transcended the North-South divide. Northern NGOs provided resources, and Southern NGOs provided local knowledge.[79] However, the United States did not participate, severely curtailing the jurisdiction of the ICC when it became a reality.

The International Criminal Court in Operation

The ICC was created on July 1, 2002, after sixty states had ratified the conference document, the Rome Statute of the International Criminal Court of 1998. With the new model of the ICC, domestic courts still have priority in criminal prosecutions. But if domestic courts are unable or unwilling to prosecute, the ICC can exercise jurisdiction. Thus, the ICC is a backup institution in a global system of accountability.[80] Its organizational structure follows the ICTY and ICTR, and its mandate is likewise to try individuals, as opposed to states, and to hold them accountable for the most serious crimes of concern to the international community: genocide (killing or causing serious harm with the intent of destroying a whole or part of an ethnic, racial, or religious group), war crimes (as detailed in the Geneva Conventions), crimes against humanity (such as enslavement, torture, rape, forced pregnancy, and persecution on political, racial, national, ethnic, cultural, religious, or gender grounds), and the crime of aggression. The final crime proved to be the most difficult to define because the drafters of the statute could not agree on its definition.[81] The ICC is separate from the United Nations and is funded by voluntary and assessed contributions made by state parties to the statute.[82]

Having been denied veto powers, the United States did not join.[83] President Bill Clinton signed the Rome Statute in the final days of his presidency in 2000, but the treaty was never submitted to the Senate for ratification. In May 2002, the United States withdrew its signature from the treaty. After that time, the United States further expressed its opposition by declaring its intention to punish countries that attempted to try its nationals. It sought bilateral agreements that would pledge countries to provide immunity from ICC prosecution to Americans abroad.[84] Six other countries voted against the statute: China, Iraq, Israel, Libya, Qatar, and Yemen.

However, in the first decade since its creation, other criticisms of the ICC have emerged outside the United States and within states that had initially supported the court. International tribunals can make local peoples feel that Western values, procedures, and priorities are forced on them. This problem has been particularly acute in Africa because the cases tried in the first decade were exclusively from that continent.[85] At the same time, the ICC is a court of last resort. Many African cases have been filed because they could not be resolved in African judicial systems as currently constituted.[86] Burundi, South Africa, and Gambia have announced their intention to leave the court. Kenya, South Africa, Uganda, and Zimbabwe have also initiated a campaign for all African Union members to leave it. A summit meeting of the African Union in 2016 did not call for mass withdrawal under pressure from opponents, led by Botswana. However, an African Union interministerial committee is debating the issue and will present reform demands at future meetings of ICC members.[87]

The ICC has also been criticized in more general terms. The paucity of its convictions calls its effectiveness into question. Any perception of bias with respect to a given conflict can undermine its deterrent effect. In addition, as with all international criminal tribunals, the complexity of undertaking an international trial can result in a gross mismatch between victims' expectations and what can actually be accomplished. While trials drag on, victims live in deprivation. Defendants are in relatively more comfortable prison surroundings in The Hague. A comparison between local criminals and international ones is even starker. Ordinary criminals can die locally, whereas those committing war crimes and tried in an international setting do not die from their prison conditions. In addition, the ICC is limited in that it takes on the worst cases, making it difficult to measure its effects overall. And finally, on a fundamental level, it is unable to address the root causes of conflict. True justice may require a redistribution of wealth or power in society, and that is simply outside the realm of the ICC's capacity.[88]

Despite these limitations, the ICC has become involved in many ongoing conflicts, such as the Syrian civil war. It may prove more successful in the future. The mere existence of an ICC may indicate that an effort to promote justice will follow the conflict. Yet its involvement may also create tension with humanitarian organizations working on the ground when asked to share information with the ICC. If they comply, they could be seen as enemies by some and denied access to vulnerable populations; if they do not, they could be considered to promote impunity.[89] Other results of the ICC are also too early to judge. Although amnesties have been granted in order to end conflicts for much of world history, the trend now is to limit any grant of amnesty so that the worst offenders in a conflict are still seen as violating international law and subject to prosecution.[90] Thus, the ICC and rise of international criminal prosecutions could mean that conflicts are extended because amnesty is not as readily available, or they could serve as a check on human atrocity during the conflict itself because it is apparent that the international community has taken an early interest.

Conclusion

Postwar multilateralism reconfigured the connection between the individual and international society, beginning with Franklin Roosevelt's four freedoms speech and the Atlantic Charter. After the war, human rights became enshrined in the UN Charter and Universal Declaration of Human Rights. At the dawn of the twenty-first century, international law is not just about states but applies to individuals when states fail to respect rights. Individuals can petition international bodies and are seen as having standing. Political leaders can be held responsible for their actions in international society. More specific identities have since joined the initial codification of human rights, including refugees, children, and people with disabilities. The process of promoting universal human rights continues to be pushed and pulled by technological advance. At first, NGOs advanced it with campaigns that exposed egregious violations and sought to aid victims and their families. More recently, their work has been challenged by new forms of media that have ended NGOs' monopoly on research and reporting of abuses.

Although the machinery of international humanitarian law is relatively recent, the origins of the debate over justice and human rights lie deep in philosophical thought, which questions whether morality can ever exist in international society. For some, justice is intrinsic to a good political order. A good society and a just society are one and the same. For others, justice is a particular feature of society, wherein individuals receive the treatment that is proper or fitting for them, in terms of either what benefits they should receive or what punishment should be theirs.[91] For some, human rights in the modern day are what John Locke and others conceived of as part of God's natural law in earlier times. Political communities are established to protect these rights. For these scholars, modern-day declarations of rights, notably the United Nations Declaration of Human Rights and subsequent covenants and conventions, are the loose equivalent of the eighteenth- and nineteenth-century declarations of natural rights. Others reject the notion of human rights altogether, either out of a broader rejection of the concept of rights or out of a need to take into consideration the details and complexities of social life that do not make any right inviolable. According to this latter critique, government is about securing balances and compromises among competing goods and evils.[92] Therefore, the old debates occur in a constantly changing new architecture. Globalization threatens NGOs like Amnesty International because they are moral authorities in an era where all authority is under scrutiny.

EIGHT

Money and Finance in the New Global Economy

In the forty years following World War II, a newly integrated world economy took shape, connected by transnational production, commercial air travel, and digital communications. As we saw in chapters 3 and 4, the Bretton Woods conference in the areas of finance, development, and trade grounded this new economy in a set of international organizations that brought binding legal instruments and laws to bear on states, even if they were not the type of formal governing bodies national governments employed. Over the years, the work mandates of the International Monetary Fund, World Bank, and World Trade Organization were restyled. The original institutions—and the World Bank in particular—took on new initiatives in areas that cross the frontiers of their original domains, such as environmental concerns and health governance. The ongoing integration of production, trade, and eventually finance further blurs the boundaries around the work that these formal IOs do and contributes to new types of multilateral cooperation. As industrialization has progressed in the world economy, therefore, money and financial flows have facilitated it and served as their own objects of multilateral concern.

We will see that the substance of multilateralism in the governance of finance has taken one of two paths. On one path, international financial regulation has departed from traditional modes of international organization into what scholars term "soft law." Unlike the "hard law" terrain of, for example, trade and the WTO, soft law tends to be dominated by regulatory agencies and officials, and it is far more fragmented among IOs. It follows informal bylaws, agreements, and declarations with no determined sense of international obligation.[1] Hence, new forums can be created or refocused in finance, just as responsibilities can be shared or moved among them. On the other path, international financial regulation has become so much more formal that it arguably involves the surrender of a degree of state sovereignty. The forward march of European integration has resulted in a common currency, the euro, and elements of a banking union with a Single Supervisory Mechanism for financial institutions and a common authority to close banks and share the costs of doing so among members.

Multilateralism in the area of money and finance has not progressed without its detractors. It is conducted by a small circle of bankers and policy makers possessing high levels of technical expertise. To outsiders, both the formal and informal institutions appear opaque and disconnected from democratic institutions more broadly conceived. In due course, IOs in this area can look like both the cause of and the solution to many of the world's financial problems. When crises occur and banks and other institutions must be bailed out, they become targets for global anger.

The Postwar Global Financial System and the IMF, OECD, and BIS

Money is something that serves as a medium of exchange in a market. It comes in the form of coins, notes, or other items that are accepted as payment, usually in a given country or group of countries. Trade is the exchange of goods and services across countries. Hence, money and trade are tied together because the exchange of money allows buyers and sellers to conduct their transactions in currencies that each can use to purchase food, pay rent, and buy other items in the country or group of countries where they live, even if their customers are overseas. A national banking system channels money among people and companies operating in an economy by connecting savers and spenders, buyers and sellers.

The banking system's function in providing a payment mechanism for a national economy usually makes it one of the most regulated national industries. When banks fail, national governments generally bail them out at a high cost to taxpayers because if they all fail at the same time, citizens cannot pay their bills and the entire economy could collapse. Most banking systems have a central bank, which is a national bank that provides financial and banking services for its country's government and banking system, implements the government's monetary policy, and issues currency. Central banks also usually serve as lenders of last resort so that all banks do not fail simultaneously in a country. In this role, central banks continue to lend funds to keep the others operating when no other bank will. In addition, if a bank becomes insolvent, the national government usually replaces the depositors' funds through some deposit insurance program in order to keep overall confidence in the system high. In recent times, the increasing magnitude of cross-border banking operations has driven the need for greater international cooperation. In that way, banks outside the country in question do not undercut this confidence by posing risks to taxpayers who will have to pay the costs of a bailout outside their own national system.

The three major postwar international institutions that initially attempted to achieve cooperation in the area of money and finance were the IMF, Organization for European Economic Cooperation, and Bank for International Settlements. However, the OEEC declined in importance after 1952 when the Marshall Plan ended, and the North Atlantic Treaty Organization emerged as the preferred vehicle for US economic aid to Europe.[2] The BIS had a checkered history with Germany during the war and would not recover from these associations until later in the century. Among the three, the IMF immediately emerged as the most significant IO addressing money and finance in the postwar era, although its role has changed constantly in response to changes in the global financial system.

The IMF and International Finance

Before World War I, countries allowed money to flow freely across borders. Most had a central bank that exchanged a national currency for gold or silver through the gold standard system. The metal could then be exchanged for a local currency in another country. After World War II and the rise of multilateralism through formal IOs, countries adopted a system of exchange rates that was fixed to the U.S. dollar, and to gold, under the auspices of the IMF. Countries could control the rate of exchange of their currency because an IO governed exchange rates with an attached permanent international institution and legal framework. The IMF resolved many policy dilemmas because with a formal framework, governments could manipulate economic policy in the pursuit of multiple goals such as full employment.[3] Ngaire Woods argues that the postwar settlement reflects more than a compromise between the two most influential states at the time: the United States and the United Kingdom. The Bretton Woods negotiations embraced large-scale new ideas about international economic governance at a time when individual politicians and the war-weary public agreed that such governance was necessary.[4]

Whereas currencies make it possible to conduct trade, manufacturing and the development of entire economies require international finance—or flows of money around the world—to provide the investment capital in large volume. Since fluctuations in exchange rates among currencies affect the value of foreign investments, money and finance are difficult to separate within the interrelated elements of the global economy.[5] The terms can be confusing because many writers use them interchangeably. We saw in chapter 4 that the international trading system rebounded from World War II and was aided in this effort through a series of successive GATT rounds of multilateral trade negotiations, which lowered tariffs and other barriers to trade. Even though the IMF provided governance for exchange rates among currencies, the international financial system was slower to recover from the ravages of the war than the trading system was. Immediately after the war ended, governments played a heavy hand in what monies came into and exited their domestic economies by imposing capital controls. With flows of money around the world restricted, there was no real international financial system.

The freeze began to thaw in the 1950s, when a period of bank consolidation and mergers occurred in the United States. The entities that emerged from these mergers constituted a core group of money center banks that began to focus their efforts on lending to governments, large corporations, and other banks despite their initial reluctance to lend outside the United

States.[6] In the years that followed, these banks expanded the number of their overseas branches to provide services to multinational corporations doing business there. As foreign direct investment grew, the banks' operations grew with it.[7] Thus, they rebuilt a network that had existed in the 1920s and collapsed in the Great Depression.[8]

Rebuilding the network put pressure on the IMF's adjustable fixed/pegged rate system in which rates were linked to both gold and dollars. Early signs of stress appeared in the 1960s. In late 1960, foreign monetary authorities bought about two billion dollars in gold from the United States, making the price of gold in the London market shoot up in October.[9] The incoming administration of John F. Kennedy was concerned that Americans were buying more from overseas than they were selling, causing problems with the US balance of payments situation. Later in the decade, bankers in the City of London began to take deposits in a small number of accounts that were denominated in currencies other than the country's national currency, the pound sterling. When these so-called Eurocurrency accounts initially formed, they were small in volume. International movements of capital were limited, so they did not have much of a destabilizing effect on the exchange rate system or contribute to large payment imbalances.[10] Their appearance thus was insignificant at first.

The United States allowed dollars to flow out and into the world economy; in this way, the system had enough dollars that were needed. The United States also converted dollars into gold at a fixed rate, so participants were confident that the system would survive. Nonetheless, the American supply of gold was limited. At some point, the foreign dollar holdings would be greater than the gold the United States had on reserve to cover it. The United States could not manage the system alone indefinitely. At the time, however, this threat was not imminent.

Realizing that a crisis could occur, a group of the ten leading industrial economies, the Group of Ten (G10), formed to augment the IMF's resources. By then, the same individuals usually represented their countries across international monetary forums and retained their position for several years. Moreover, these individuals met frequently. The overlapping duties and connections were important because they each remained an employee of their own bureaucracy, and this fact allowed them to influence policy outcomes at home more strongly than those representatives of countries who worked permanently at IO headquarters such as Washington, DC, Paris, or Basel, Switzerland.[11] In addition, many friendships and personal relationships developed among influential policy makers from several countries.[12] As academic studies at the time recognized, the work of IOs, particularly in finance, is deeply enmeshed in the web of personal relationships that operate across institutional boundaries.[13]

As the G10 began to meet more regularly, different IOs addressed varying tasks depending on what powerful states within the G10 wanted and which states needed to be involved. Representatives from the G10 tried to find an IO to study issues relevant to the world economy, such as the US balance of payments difficulties in the 1960s. Among the existing IOs, they chose the BIS to take on new issues and report back to the relevant ministers from these countries in an informal, flexible manner. Over time, the informal grouping of states began to reinforce the segmentation of members of IOs into camps of wealthier and poorer countries based on their shared perceptions of common problems and potential solutions.

The BIS began to assert itself within the system on behalf of wealthier countries. Established before the IMF, the bank was supposed to manage reparations payments and promote central bank cooperation. It was not intended to govern finance. Because many individuals at the BIS had collaborated with the Nazi regime during the war, the bank had been a target for American and Norwegian negotiators at Bretton Woods.[14] The conference agreed to a recommendation to liquidate it and included this in its final act.[15] The BIS most likely did not shut down because those who wanted to close it were divided about how, and when, to do so. Its supporters—mostly central bankers—advocated for it; in addition, Swiss corporate law and international treaty protected it.[16]

Given this wartime and postwar history, the BIS appeared to be a more European institution, whereas the IMF was a more global one. Nonetheless, the same individuals continued the pattern of crossing boundaries among institutions by attending meetings elsewhere as formal representatives. For example, the Bretton Woods institutions conducted early technical cooperation with the BIS. Representatives of the IMF and IBRD attended annual meetings of the BIS, and representatives of the BIS did likewise at the Bretton Woods institutions.[17] While the Federal Reserve participated in the BIS's activities, it remained an informal member for reasons dating to the interwar period and US opposition to German reparations. It therefore did not take up the seats on the board that it was entitled to under the original subscription. The Federal Reserve Bank of New York, one of the twelve regional reserve banks that the Federal Reserve System comprises, remained the BIS's correspondent for the American market through the 1950s, 1960s, and 1970s.[18]

The United States Closes the Gold Window

As the American balance of payments situation worsened and problems appeared on the financial horizon, the domestic economy experienced setbacks that provoked political problems. Prices rose faster than wages. Foreign governments could redeem dollars for gold under the IMF agreement, and they began to do so more frequently, eventually threatening American gold holdings. In the summer of 1971, some members of Congress issued a report arguing that the dollar needed to be devalued (or its exchange rate against foreign currencies needed to be lowered so that foreign goods cost more) and the IMF pressured other countries to revalue (or their rates needed to be raised so that what they sold Americans cost more). Others stated that the United States needed to float the dollar within limits (meaning that the United States would not adhere to a fixed rate but would let the market set it).[19] Dollars continued to flow out of the US economy, and the crisis climaxed the weekend of August 15, when President Richard Nixon ended the convertibility of dollars for gold, officially closing the gold window. The United States devalued the dollar in 1971 and again in 1973.

The action angered the country's allies. The G10 attempted to respond to the crisis, but the United States did not want the group to conduct surveillance of its members' policies, given that it was heavily European.[20] In the years that followed, the informal groupings of states that coordinated the industrialized countries' response changed constantly. In 1973, a less formal

Fig. 8.1. President Gerald R. Ford meeting with foreign heads of state in the Salle des Marbres in the Château de Rambouillet at the International Economic Summit Conference (at that time the G6) in Rambouillet, France, November 15, 1975. Courtesy of Gerald R. Ford White House Photographs, White House Office Photographic Collection (12/6/73–1/20/77). National Archives Identifier (7518995).

group of finance ministers from the United States, the United Kingdom, West Germany, Japan, and France, accompanied by their senior officials, or deputies, formed at the White House. This group came to be called the Library Group. Japan's finance minister invited these same finance ministers to dinner when the IMF held its annual meeting six months later in Nairobi, Kenya. In time, the Group of Five (G5) represented the top five world economies in terms of GDP. Italy and Canada were added in 1975 and 1976, respectively, forming the Group of Seven (G7). Thus, as with the G10 earlier, the combinations continued to form and reform, based on personal networks and shared understandings of approaches to problems. Heads of state and government, finance ministries, and central bank governors attended the groupings.[21]

Even after the IMF's original fixed exchange rate regime ended, domestic American problems persisted. An American banking regulation, Regulation Q, limited the amount financial institutions could pay in interest. Western European and other international banks took increasing numbers of Eurocurrency deposits in the 1970s as compared with the 1960s, particularly in dollars. These deposits were not subject to Regulation Q because they were held outside the territorial United States, even though they were still in (mostly) American banks. The Eurocurrency or Eurodollar accounts therefore multiplied. Other sources of deposits denominated in currencies other than that of the host country bank grew. The Soviet Union put hard currency deposits in European banks. When the price of oil shot up later in the decade, so-called petrodollar markets developed as offshore centers where dollars earned by the oil producers could be deposited and saved outside the domestic American regulations. Eventually, the growth of these markets made it impossible for the United States to guarantee the value of the dollar in the fixed rate system that remained.[22] After a series of interim measures, the United States eventually abandoned efforts to maintain it, and the dollar's exchange rate came to be set in private markets determined by supply and demand, or float.

Bank Herstatt, Franklin National, and the Formation of the Basel Committee

When exchange rates were set by international agreement, there was no risk that exchange rates would change and that foreign goods would cost dramatically more or less. The new financial environment, in which exchange rates floated, thus brought along exchange risk. In turn, the new risk carried novel opportunities and rewards. It likewise put new regulatory stress on the bankers, particularly those in the United States, where banking laws are fragmented among federal and state authorities. As Joan Spero points out, the complexity of the situation required cooperation but created opportunities if the differences remained, given the varying standards for evaluating a bank's condition and those required for it to engage in international finance.[23]

Early in the 1970s, two banks failed, prompting calls for coordinated, international action: the German Bankhaus Herstatt and the American Franklin National Bank. Bank Herstatt's troubles began with its large foreign exchange business. It lost four times its capital in September 1973, when the dollar's value shot up unexpectedly. It lost even more when the dollar's direction changed again in January 1974.[24] The twentieth largest bank in the

United States at the time, Franklin National also had problems with foreign exchange trading activities during 1974. The bank's traders used foreign exchange trading to compensate for losses experienced in other divisions. They speculated in volatile markets where they lacked experience, and management did not control them.[25]

As the two banking crises of 1974 persisted, leaders looked to the BIS as an organization of central bankers that could help them manage the new environment. The head of the New York Federal Reserve informed other major central bankers of Franklin Nation's foreign exchange problems so that they would be able to react quickly and understand why the Federal Reserve might have to intervene to support the dollar. Foreign central banks likewise cooperated during the crisis by helping the search for a bank to purchase Franklin National. Meeting in Basel in July 1974, less than two weeks after Bank Herstatt collapsed and as the Franklin National crisis unfolded, the central bankers committed to a degree of cooperation without specifying what conditions would be needed for assistance. The Bank of England wanted international rules that would limit its responsibility as a lender of last resort and tried to persuade others to take the same position.[26]

Eventually, the bankers began to believe that they would have to come up with some way of coordinating their supervisory practices and international regulation. The British again took the lead with the G10, which had been working on assigned topics through its committees of experts. Governor Gordon Richardson of the Bank of England proposed that the G10 governors establish a standing committee on regulatory and supervisory practices that would improve regulation and create an international early warning system.[27] The Basel Committee on Banking Supervision (BCBS) was established in the fall of 1974 with its own secretariat at the BIS, although it would operate only in a consultative capacity. Although the group reached an agreement, the Concordat, in 1975, it did not release it publicly for five years. The statement on bank supervision in the document was vague, and thus of limited value, because it did not attempt to establish standards for the quality of the supervision. Moreover, the agreement was not precise enough to eliminate confusion among supervisors and banks regarding where responsibility rested. Finally, the Concordat lacked any

Fig. 8.2. Headquarters of the BIS and the BCBS in Basel, Switzerland. The headquarters also hosts the FSB, International Association of Insurance Supervisors, and the International Association of Deposit Insurers Secretariats. Courtesy of Kathryn Lavelle.

enforcement mechanism to guarantee that supervisory authorities would comply with its provisions. The 1983 Revised Concordat attempted to address these weaknesses.[28]

The two initial financial crises after the collapse of fixed parity thus provoked central bankers to attempt to cooperate in banking regulations in order to prevent future instability. Yet the BCBS lacks an extensive formal mandate, a constitution, or bylaws. It is an informal committee set up by, and answering to, the G10 governors. Its membership is drawn from nationally established regulatory and supervisory authorities, not central banks. The greatest constraint on the BCBS is not that it must answer to a superior body but that each member is a separate sovereign state that must implement its proposals in its own law.[29]

The Latin American Debt Crises of the 1980s

Another new kind of financial crisis emerged with the Latin American sovereign debt emergencies of the 1980s. As we saw in chapter 4, these crises changed the nature of the relation of developing countries to IOs in terms of how they aligned themselves within IOs. As we will see here, the series of crises that began with Mexico in 1982 also changed the international financial system in terms of how the banking system interacted with investors and IOs. The crises of the 1970s originated with the supervisory and regulatory practices in industrialized countries. Those in the 1980s threatened the banking system of the industrialized core of the world economy yet began in the developing world. Neither the IMF nor the nascent Basel committee was equipped to handle the situation. Over time, the nature of both institutions changed to meet the challenges of the new international environment for lending, as well as the new atmosphere for the work of the World Bank, UN, and other development IOs.

Large commercial banks began lending to some developing states on a large scale in the 1970s because they were overflowing with cash deposited by oil exporters benefitting from the oil price boom during those years. Whereas countries previously obtained loans from a given set of lenders, new procedures like credit syndication (meaning that groups of lenders worked together on a given loan) and floating rates (meaning that the rate of interest changes in response to some economic indicator) raised the number of willing lenders.[30] This private debt was heavily concentrated in a few Latin American and Asian countries. At the end of the 1970s, the boom in prices of primary commodities ended just as the second oil shock hit and interest rates rose. This combination of events meant that the countries selling primary commodities to make payments on those loans had less money coming in even as the higher interest rates increased the payments required. To make matters worse, the world recession of 1981–82 reduced world trade, commodity prices, and export earnings. When Argentina invaded the Falkland Islands, Britain froze the London-based assets of Argentina, which, though directed at Latin America specifically, added to the general mood of financial uncertainty.

Mexico approached default on its sovereign debt in August 1982. The potential default alarmed the international banking system because so many of the Mexican loans were now syndicated. Syndication meant that a group of lenders had collaborated to provide funds for the borrower. A collapse of one lender would threaten the others. When Jesús Silva Herzog, Mexico's secretary of finance, informed Jacques de Larosière, managing director of the IMF, that Mexico could not pay, Larosière responded that the fund would help but that Mexico would have to avoid default.[31]

The problem the IMF confronted with Mexico was that the international banks needed to *increase* their exposure, or lend more, to a country to avoid its default at a time when they were particularly loath to do so. Herzog was willing to work with the banks and the IMF.[32] The United States preferred to work with an established IO than directly with the country because a bilateral bailout would anger US taxpayers, who would see it as a use of their money to save a foreign entity.[33] Thus, a bailout could have been arranged without the IMF, but at a higher cost to all of these parties. The banks needed the IMF's country analysis and leverage in dealing with governments. The IMF needed the banks' resources. Mexico needed both the IMF's analysis and money and the banks' money. Mexico signed an agreement with the IMF in November 1982. The banks provided new loans and agreed to extend the moratorium on payments of the loans' principal.[34]

The crisis, however, did not stay confined to Mexico. Once it hit, investors began to pull up their short-term Brazilian loans. As successive rounds of sovereign debt crises arose in other Latin American countries, the Mexican negotiations served as a template for later negotiations. A separate bank committee of twelve to fourteen banks was formed for each country, and these banks would negotiate a new schedule of payments. Each bank on the committee would keep the other creditor banks in its country or region informed and under pressure to agree.[35] However, by 1987, participants wanted to separate the IMF's strategy from the interests of commercial banks and reduce the overall levels of debt significantly.

Ultimately, the separation of the interests between commercial banks and IOs transformed the nature of the international banking system itself. Banks reduced the large volume of loans to these countries by converting the loans into bonds (which are essentially IOUs), selling them to investors, and thus removing them from their books. Mexico was the first to negotiate terms under the Brady Plan of 1989 (named after US Treasury Secretary Nicholas Brady) that allowed for this kind of debt restructuring to developing countries in so-called Brady bonds. The bonds were attractive to investors because US Treasury securities guaranteed part of their interest and principal payments.[36] Mexico converted $43 billion into Brady bonds; Venezuela converted $9 billion into the bonds.[37] Settlements with Argentina and Brazil followed in 1992.

As a result, Latin American debt changed from being owed to commercial banks to being owed to bondholders. The trend continues into the current era, where some developing countries can issue bonds directly in global capital markets, and the variety of debt instruments and derivatives (or financial products whose value is derived from another instrument) used has also grown. The trend undercut the very system of money center banks that had reknit the global financial system together after the war. A broad set of financial institutions became more powerful in their wake, giving different countries, types of banks, and investors varying (and often conflicting) interests in outcomes during crises to come.

At the same time, NGOs began to take an interest in debt relief issues for poor countries. Although the movement did not take off at first, a wide-ranging activist network eventually grew up in this area comprising religious organizations, poverty activists, academics, and others questioning the terms of the original loans.[38] The Jubilee 2000 campaign led to the cancellation of more than $100 billion of debt owed by thirty-five of the poorest countries.[39] A joint IMF–World Bank approach to debt reduction packages under the Heavily Indebted Poor Countries initiative provided for $76 billion in debt-service relief over time in thirty-six countries.[40]

The European Central Bank and the Euro

The end of fixed parity in the IMF ushered in new instability, risk, and rewards to the global economy. Ongoing financial crises led countries to seek multilateral solutions on a continuum that ranged from less formal, such as the BCBS after the Franklin and Herstatt episodes, to more formal, such as the newly assertive IMF after the Latin American crises, to even more formal institutional arrangements as we will see occurred among members of the European Economic Community throughout these years.

During these years, Europeans confronted a different economic environment than Americans did because trade constituted a greater percentage of their economies. They were thus more vulnerable to exchange rate fluctuations and different rates of inflation than Americans were, and they responded in a correspondingly different way. Their financial governance grew far more formal and ultimately converged to the point where some states surrendered a degree of their monetary sovereignty to the European Central Bank (ECB), which sets monetary policy and has taken on some regulatory functions for national banking systems. Nonetheless, the process of European monetary and regulatory integration has been part and parcel of the same global currents as those that propelled the formation of the less formal BCBS and renewed IMF. And it has been facilitated by similar networks of bankers, central bank governors, and transnational authorities working together based on shared technocratic expertise, yet largely insulated from mainstream politics.

Europeans recognized the advantages of a common currency for decades before one came to fruition. Immediately after the collapse of fixed parity in the IMF, the six countries of the EEC attempted to mitigate a degree of risk among themselves by establishing a narrower range within which their currencies would fluctuate against one another. Other countries joined the group, although the arrangement was plagued with crises. In 1979, the European Monetary System (EMS) became operational among the EEC's members and sought to create a "zone of monetary stability." It created a European Currency Unit, which was a basket of the currencies of the EMS member states used as the unit of account. Hence, the rates were not fixed, but adjusted on the basis of agreement among representatives of the governments.[41] In the 1970s atmosphere of exchange rate fluctuations and inflation in the United States, however, Germany and France sought more than a simple joint float against the US dollar. They wanted greater overall economic and political integration.[42]

Internal European integration thus continued alongside monetary integration. Signed by members in 1986, the Single European Act was the first revision of the Treaty of Rome, committing members to formal, political cooperation within the EEC. Cooperation would comprise the free movement of goods, services, capital, and people by the end of 1992, as well as monetary policy. Some believed that a common European currency was necessary to lock exchange rates together and prevent countries from destabilizing devaluations against one another. By that time, the step to monetary union did not seem as improbable as it once had, since the countries in the Exchange Rate Mechanism (with the exception of Germany) had already given up a high degree of their own ability to set monetary policy in the EMS.[43] Moreover, the same antagonisms that accompanied the original efforts at forming the European Coal and Steel Community persisted. As it functioned in the early 1980s, the EMS operated with Germany at the center, and the other currencies pegged to the German national currency, the deutsche mark. Other countries resented the arrangement.[44] As calls for a monetary union increased, proponents argued that the ending of French and German rivalry would contribute to the sense that the Western European states would no longer wage wars among each other.[45] In addition, monetary union would provide a means of competing with the economic hegemony of the United States.

In 1988 and 1989, the work of the Committee for the Study of Economic and Monetary Union, chaired by Jacques Delors, opened the possibility of replacing national currencies with a single one in three discrete, but evolutionary, stages. The first stage outlined in the Delors Report (the report of the committee) would abolish exchange controls and open up capital movement within the EEC. Next, the participants would create a European Monetary Institute and coordinate monetary policies. Finally, they would fix their rate of conversion and introduce the common currency, the euro. Monetary policy would thenceforth be conducted by a European System of Central Banks, and a Stability and Growth Pact would come into effect to coordinate fiscal policies among members.[46]

Along the way in 1989, the Cold War ended, and Germany unified. East-West German monetary unification powered an economic expansion.[47]

The EMS as it was then constructed collapsed in 1992. While no single cause explains the breakdown, the reunification of Germany certainly contributed to it. The German government did not raise taxes to pay for unification, and the Bundesbank (the German central bank) raised interest rates to safeguard the national currency. Other countries followed suit, and the rate of exchange of a number of currencies was therefore not aligned with the degree of economic activity that was taking place among them—destabilizing the rates. Although the early version of the EMS ended, the European Currency Unit basket of currencies used among them survived. In addition, the crisis taught the Europeans a lesson. Later efforts would need strict criteria for government spending among them.[48]

Despite these difficulties, European leaders pressed forward with their plans for a deeper level of integration with the Maastricht Treaty in 1992, which agreed to create a single currency by January 1999, albeit without the UK's participation. The Maastricht Treaty, or Treaty on European Union, contained three pillars that would together form a European Union (EU) out of the European Economic Communities: a European Monetary Union, common foreign defense policy, and internal cooperation. It set targets for inflation interest rates, exchange rate stability, and fiscal stability for countries that sought to participate in the monetary union. The fiscal criteria—a budget deficit of no more than 3 percent of GDP and a public debt of not more than 60 percent—would be difficult to achieve. Yet the fiscal criteria would filter out countries that lacked the stability culture. Countries used various indicators to meet the targets and thus could claim that they met them. Decision making by consensus made it difficult to single out members in questionable circumstances. Major decisions required unanimity among EU members; countries not participating could thus obstruct progress elsewhere. The monetary union that eventually resulted was larger than originally anticipated.[49]

As envisioned by the Delors Report and Maastricht Treaty, the stages would progress toward monetary union. An interim European Monetary Institute was established to prepare for a common monetary policy. A Stability Pact provided for oversight of national budgets. Countries agreed to lock their exchange rates as of January 1999 and switch over to the policy direction of the European Central Bank, which would now direct monetary policy. Such a monetary union was unprecedented. The coordination of monetary policy on this scale was a major advance. The ECB went beyond pegging exchange rates among the eleven continental European states that created it by replacing their national currencies on January 1, 1999, with the euro.[50] The new central bank in Frankfurt sets short-term interest rates and seeks to establish price stability; it does not, however, have a mandate to fight unemployment, as does the US Federal Reserve. Although the Stability Pact was repeatedly broken, the Maastricht Treaty did not make a provision for leaving the euro.

The 1997 Asian Financial Crisis

As the world's financial system continued its recovery from the instability of the end of the Bretton Woods fixed exchange rate system and the Cold War, investors directed larger and larger flows of capital toward Asia. The region was attractive because many states there had high growth rates. Many global investors also looked to Asia because interest rates were low in major financial centers and the yield was higher in emerging markets. As we saw, exchange rates were fixed in the Bretton Woods era, and countries put controls on the amount of money entering and exiting their national economies. When the Bretton Woods fixed system ended, developed countries eventually allowed their exchange rates to float and removed controls. The result is that in advanced industrial economies, private market participants, and not public ones, now have exchange risk that comes with floating rates because rates can change. Asian governments, by contrast, were loath to discourage foreign investment and allow their exchange rates to float similarly when Bretton Woods ended.[51] Many Asian countries continued to peg their rates to the dollar after the era ended, and they eventually liberalized their capital markets, meaning that they took away restrictions on the flows of money across their borders, but kept the attendant exchange risk. Because many Asian currencies remained fixed, or pegged to the dollar, any profits realized by private investors were unlikely to be wiped out by exchange rate movements as they could be in developed countries.

The combination of exchange rates pegged to the dollar and liberalized capital accounts posed a problem. When its capital account is liberalized, a country is more integrated with the global economy. Foreigners can buy major assets in the country without worrying that if they sell them, their money will have to remain there. Yet a country with a liberalized capital account is also left open to the possibility that investors will do just that—sell large assets and take the proceeds out of the country, jeopardizing the country's banking system if it is fragile. Countries that liberalize their capital account and keep their exchange rates fixed are thus vulnerable to pressure on those rates, because if capital flows out, the government must provide the foreign exchange to investors selling assets, withdrawing from bank accounts, or cashing in securities and wanting to take their money out of the local currency. At a certain point, the government might not have enough foreign exchange to cover these withdrawals. If the exchange rate were flexible (as they are in the advanced industrial economies), it would change according to market demand and ameliorate the problem. Asian countries therefore faced considerable risk. Yet extensive government involvement in their banking systems seemed to ensure that governments would not allow these banks to fail.

Thailand was the first country stricken when global circumstances changed. Money flowed into Thailand as foreign investors purchased real estate, driving up prices. Yet many of the new high-rises in the capital, Bangkok, lacked residents. The Bangkok Bank of Commerce collapsed in mid-1996, the Thai baht collapsed July 2, 1997, and the crisis spread to other countries in the region. An election in South Korea made investors uneasy, and a broader crisis was averted when the new government committed itself to maintaining debt service and implementing the IMF's recommendations. However, the government of Indonesia's actions did not reassure investors, and a run on banks ensued, eventually shutting down the entire banking and financial system.[52] The crisis later spread to Russia and Latin America.

The IMF's response was similar in each country. It provided large sums of money for the countries to maintain their exchange rates. The sums came with conditions that usually included higher interest rates, cuts in government spending, and increases in taxes. The IMF assigned these conditions because these spending patterns were assumed to lie behind the problems. When the reforms failed to produce their intended results, countries and the IMF debated whether the packages induced the problems or the governments did so in failing to take the reforms seriously. In short, was the IMF part of the problem or the solution?[53] The debate continued in the years following the crisis. Some analysts argued that the IMF's policies had not only made the downturns worse but contributed to the onset of the crises themselves by promoting rapid financial and capital market liberalization.[54]

Moreover, the IMF's responses to each country followed a problematic pattern. It provided money for countries to sustain their exchange rates so that investors would stop attacking the currency. However, the money also allowed countries to provide dollars to firms that had borrowed from Western bankers to repay the loans. It thus bailed out the international banks at the same time it bailed out the countries. Lenders did not suffer the consequences of the bad loans they made, and a problem of moral hazard ensued, in which lenders did not guard against risk because they were protected. When the IMF imposed conditions on the countries that borrowed, it forced the states to surrender significant aspects of their economic sovereignty. These policies undermined democracy and did not necessarily restore economic health because some of the conditions had nothing to do with the problems that had caused them in the first place.[55]

In 1999, the G7 (which became the Group of Eight, or G8, after Russia began to participate in the meetings) recommended the establishment of two entities to address some of the systemic roots of the crisis. One of these was a Group of Twenty (G20) to promote open and constructive discussion among industrial and emerging-market countries on key issues related to global economic stability. As with the other groupings, there were no formal criteria for membership. However, the formation of the G20 acknowledged that jurisdictions outside the advanced industrial economies could threaten the global economy.[56] The other entity was the Financial Stability Forum (FSF), which drew on senior representatives of national financial authorities, international financial institutions, standard-setting bodies, and committees of central bank experts from the G7. The FSF created working groups to study systemic risks and publish best practices. As with the informality of the G20, however, the FSF lacked any powers or ability to mandate standards, even voluntary ones.[57]

Immediately after the 1997 financial crisis, Asian countries developed self-insurance systems to guard against future balance-of-payments difficulties. Moreover, the Association of Southeast Asian Nations plus three (China, Japan, and South Korea) established regional financial incentives to strengthen the region's ability to address a crisis. The most famous of these is the Chiang Mai Initiative, which created a network of bilateral currency swap arrangements among the member countries. In May 2007, the finance ministers from these states agreed to pool a part of their foreign exchange reserves in order to multilateralize the initiative without having to rely on the IMF.[58]

The response, therefore, was not a rejection of multilateralism itself but a rejection of the IMF. In response, the IMF instituted a significant number of internal reforms. It raised the significance of its financial sector surveillance program and integrated it with its work on macroeconomic analysis. In addition, the IMF commenced more regional and multilateral analysis in order to capture trends and actual and potential spillovers from financial market developments. The IMF also assessed its tools for crisis prevention and sought to improve country ownership of its programs. Finally, the IMF worked on a program of reform of its own governance to increase the voice of emerging markets in its processes.[59]

The 2008 Financial Crisis

Approximately ten years after the Asian crisis, another major international financial crisis challenged the global economy. Originating in markets for US housing finance, it spread throughout the broader US and international economies before it morphed into a crisis in European sovereign debt markets. Early on, the severity of the downturn prompted British prime minister Gordon Brown to call for a "New Bretton Woods." During a press conference, Brown cited wartime leaders Franklin D. Roosevelt and Winston Churchill, who envisioned a framework for the future while the battles raged on: "With the same courage and foresight of [these] founders, we must now reform the international financial system around the agreed principles of transparency, integrity, responsibility, good housekeeping and cooperation across borders."[60] Brown sought a reformed IMF that could act as a central bank for the world. It could monitor the international economy and financial system, possibly including global rules to prevent conflicts of interest and raise the level of transparency overall. At the November 2008 and April 2009 meetings of the G20, leaders all felt threatened simultaneously. They agreed to joint monetary and fiscal expansion, increased funding for the IMF, and new rules for financial institutions.

The 2008 financial crisis did usher in a new era of relevance for the IOs attached to the global governance of finance. Despite their popularity, however, most of Brown's proposals were not enacted. The crisis receded in some countries faster than others. Some suffered more damage than others. The crisis thus furthered the path of divergence between the trends toward hard and soft law responses. The more traditional IMF and World Bank restored a degree of their footing lost after the 2007 Asian financial crisis, yet the newer, looser governance arrangements such as the BCBS, G20, and new combinations among them, such as the FSF, grew in prominence as well.

The Housing Crisis in the United States

American financial institutions lent large sums to high-risk borrowers in the lax regulatory environment for housing finance at the close of the twentieth century. These borrowers had poor track records paying their bills but paid a higher rate of interest to compensate for it. Thus, in the low interest rate environment that preceded the crisis, they were seen as a group of borrowers that could provide higher returns if the likelihood that they would not pay could be spread out over a group. A series of financial institutions that held the packages of debt of these borrowers failed in succession in the years that followed. The events reached a climax in September 2008 when the US investment bank Lehman Brothers declared bankruptcy. Although a buyer was found for Lehman's North American holdings immediately, it took longer to find one for its European and Middle East investment banking operations, pushing already distressed global financial markets further into turmoil. Stock markets worldwide collapsed and the value of retirement plans, government pension funds, and numerous other investment portfolios fell with them. When Congress failed to pass its first attempt at a bailout bill, stock prices plummeted further.[61]

The speed and magnitude of the crisis made clear that existing markets and institutions were not prepared for such systemic failure. Governments in advanced industrial countries were forced to bail out their financial sectors with taxpayer money. To many, it seemed as if citizens in these countries experienced capitalism on the way up and socialism on the way down.[62] The US domestic response came immediately from the Federal Reserve System. The Treasury Department placed the two housing finance giants Fannie Mae and Freddie Mac into conservatorship and managed them, having guaranteed their debt.[63] Congress later enacted legislation in the form of the Troubled Asset Relief Program to attempt to purchase the toxic financial products that fed the crisis. Other reform programs were initiated throughout the country's fragmented banking system, with varying degrees of success.

The international dimensions to the crisis were more thorny, due to the volume of funds needed to resolve it and the inadequacy of the IMF's resources to handle them. At the time, the IMF's total resources were $352 billion, of which $257 billion were usable. The most the IMF had ever lent in one year was $30 billion.[64] It had been holding discussions about how to assert itself in a world that didn't seem to need it. Yet after the crisis commenced, it reemerged as a crisis fighter. Although many states did not want to approach the IMF because they perceived a stigma attached to borrowing there after the 1997 crisis, the IMF created a new three-month, short-term lending facility aimed at middle-income countries. In 2009, IMF first managing director John Lipsky proposed doubling the lending resources of the IMF.[65] Although Congress eventually passed a measure for increased funding, it came after a considerable struggle over provisions for workers' rights and funding for the US war in Iraq.[66]

The world's leaders also looked to the less formal arrangements that had been organized after the Asian financial crisis for solutions to the problems of systemic crisis. The FSF was transformed into a Financial Stability Board (FSB) with a broad mandate to assess and improve the financial system. Its regulatory focus shifted from individual firms or sectors onto the entire system of regulation. It began to operate more as a clearinghouse for information sharing and contingency planning. It also created a supervisory college to monitor large financial services firms. All members of the G20 joined the newly empowered FSB. Its permanent secretariat was also enlarged at the BIS, where it is located; however, the FSB does not have direct reporting links to the BIS.[67]

The European Sovereign Debt Crisis

European decision makers had already responded to the immediate financial crisis in 2008 when José Manuel Barroso, the president of the European Commission, formed the High-Level Group on Financial Supervision in the EU in order to make recommendations on a range of problems—one of which was stronger coordination of bank supervision.[68] The group's final report, published in 2009, contained a proposal to establish a new European Systemic Risk Council under the auspices of the ECB, where central bankers would play a more active role in warning about risks to the financial system and try to ensure better transfers of information among supervisors.[69]

Although the global situation was now reasonably stable, a new flashpoint occurred with the Greek elections of 2009. The recently elected government took power, and it announced that the Greek budget deficit was considerably higher than previously stated. Investors doubted that the government could make payments on its sovereign debt. Since monetary integration had leveled the terrain among European financial institutions, the Greek crisis was not confined to Greece. A troika of IOs intervened, with the coordinated efforts of the IMF, European Commission, and ECB.

The Greek crisis exposed the reality that higher government spending and debt burdens increased sovereign debt in some parts of the eurozone but not others. Ireland and Portugal experienced sovereign debt crises of their own. Domestic banks held higher amounts of the sovereign debt because foreign investors were both less willing to buy it and more interested in selling it. Hence, when the agencies that rate debt downgraded sovereign debt (indicating that they thought it was riskier), domestic banks held more, and their own governments were less able to bail them out because these governments held higher amounts of debt. The United Kingdom (among some other EU members) had remained outside the euro area. Although the Bank of England provided some relief by purchasing large sums of sovereign debt, the ECB could not provide the same level of support to euro area members because it was prohibited from purchasing bonds directly from member governments.

When the ECB did begin to provide relief to European governments, it did so by buying sovereign debt on private bond markets, and not from central banks. This strategy was highly controversial because such purchases are only permitted to pursue monetary, and not fiscal, policy according to the terms set when the euro was created. However, it is not always easy to separate the two policies, and the true intent of the ECB in this case was not clear. The two initial candidates to replace Jean-Claude Trichet as ECB head when his term ended in October 2011 were Mario Draghi—then the head of the Financial Stability Board—and Axel Weber—then head of the Bundesbank.[70]

Draghi had been a director of the World Bank and had spent ten years as head of the Italian treasury and two years at Goldman Sachs before becoming head of the Italian central bank. A former economics professor, Weber clashed on policy with other eurozone central bankers by criticizing the ECB's decision to buy government bonds. In February 2011, Weber abruptly took himself out of the running for the ECB position in protest of the bailouts, eventually taking a job at the private bank UBS.[71] He and others maintained that the central bank was falling under the sway of politicians.[72] Draghi became the next president of the ECB, and on July 26, 2012, he famously stated that the ECB was willing to do whatever it took to preserve the euro.[73] In later interviews, Italian prime minister Mario Monti, who had participated in the EU leaders' summit, told an interviewer that Draghi could say what he had, and follow through by buying large quantities of sovereign bonds of fragile governments, because the leaders gave him political support that June.[74]

Fig. 8.3. Mario Draghi at the World Economic Forum Annual Meeting in Davos, Switzerland, January 27, 2012. Copyright by World Economic Forum. Swiss=image.ch/Photo by Monika Flueckiger.

Conclusion

The financial crisis originating in US financial markets in 2008 was only the latest in a series of postwar financial crises that reshaped the direction of the multilateral governance of finance in the postwar era. The multilateral framework for finance, initially constructed on a foundation of three related IOs—the BIS, the IMF, and G10 deputies—fragmented into more and less formal hard law and soft law arrangements. After the collapse of fixed parity in the IMF in 1971, the BCBS and other combinations of central banks from industrial states began to appear on an ad hoc basis. European states responded by tying their monetary systems together more closely, ultimately creating a common currency. As the financial crises of the 1980s and 1990s progressed, the BCBS became a more permanent entity, and the IMF reemerged as a venue to resolve sovereign debt. Eventually, the G20 and Financial Stability Forum (now the FSB) have come to the fore, but without substantive enforcement capability.

Excitement and euphoria accompanied the introduction of European currency notes in 2002. Yet roughly ten years later, citizens blamed the same currency for exacerbating the hardships of the global financial crisis.[75] While currency unions pose one kind of problem for economics, they pose another for national politics when institutions such as the ECB are not embedded in domestic political authority, as are national banking regulators. Although the multilateral response among IOs may have prevented a global meltdown in 2008 on the scale of the Great Depression of the 1930s, their response nonetheless engendered serious resentment of the globalization project both in advanced industrial democracies and elsewhere. Moreover, we will see that the controversies over the response to the financial crisis have been directed across the range of hard and soft law institutions by populist movements on both sides of the Atlantic.

NINE

Dissent on Globalization

Multilateralism has been driven by the forward march of industrialization, which has both deepened technological, productive, social, and governmental relations and driven peoples and governments to construct cooperative ventures that allow for ongoing progress. Industrialization has thus gone hand in hand with globalization. As used here, "globalization" refers to the process of international integration resulting in the exchange of worldviews, products, and culture. In the twenty-first century, the continuing innovations of the Industrial Revolution have accelerated these two complementary processes through advances in travel technologies and digital communications, such as the jet engine, high-speed data transmission, and mobile phones that perform as computers. We have seen that, for some segments of the population, industrialization and globalization have meant advances in medicine, access to better, cheaper goods and services, a cleaner, safer environment, and the possibility of justice against the domestic abuse of power. However, they have left other segments of the population disenfranchised, poorer, and even *more* subject to environmental disaster than before. The pace and depth of globalization mean that the same economic, social, and political forces that knit the world community together on one level also feed nationalist forces on another, particularly in Western democracies. Nationalist forces thus reassert a cultural, economic, and ideological role for the state and a rejection of multilateralism in many forms.

Whereas critics of multilateralism have always existed, the location and dynamics of their attacks changed with the dawn of the twenty-first century. In the 1960s, multinational corporations and international lenders like the IMF and World Bank were viewed as postcolonial intrusions. In the Asian financial crisis of the 1990s, many viewed the Bretton Woods institutions as contributing to instability instead of resolving it. As trade balances continued to shift after 2000, critics' voices grew louder in labor sectors where job losses were the most profound, culminating with dramatic moves against immigration and membership in IOs like the European Union and WTO. The aftermath of the global financial crisis of 2008 fueled the censure of IOs because taxpayers in advanced industrial economies were forced to bail out financial institutions that had operated without boundaries or constraints. Hence, a vigorous debate between globalizers and nationalists has emerged in the national elections of countries that had previously championed integration and, by extension, the public and private efforts at multilateralism that foster it.[1] Within this debate, protestors target the postwar IOs, regardless of whether they caused globalization or are merely artifacts of larger processes.

This chapter focuses on three sources of the early twenty-first century pushback against multilateralism that built in sequence: job loss, terrorist attacks, and a massive global refugee crisis. Ultimately, these forces converged in opposition to new forms of trade liberalization, immigration, and the European Union. International organizations became potent symbols of the forces of globalization, despite the fact that these characterizations may grossly overstate the power that they actually wield. The antiglobalization movement is as rife with contradictions as the concept of globalization itself. Yet it is also a movement that has mobilized constituencies—as seen in the British referendum to leave the European Union—and posed real challenges to future efforts at multilateral solutions to the world's problems—as with the US absence from the Asian Infrastructure Investment Bank. Even so, these challenges have always existed and have not yet reached their logical conclusion. Hegemonic war, the ultimate challenge to multilateralism, remains a distant prospect. The domestic effects of antiglobalization policies have yet to be felt in many parts of the world. Nonetheless, the contest has strong countervailing forces on each side.

The Antiglobalization Movement Takes Shape
in Western Democracies

Controversy over the work of IOs is not new. Overt resistance to the IMF and World Bank has existed in developing countries since the imposition of austerity measures following the debt crises of the 1980s. Some people protested the international financial institutions' influence and lack of democratic mechanisms. Others questioned governance issues associated with weighted voting, the IMF and World Bank's management of capital movements and crisis prevention, and their provision of global public goods.[2] However, the expansion of late twentieth-century globalization did not just bring about trade imbalances in poor countries. It also eventually brought about job loss and changes in working conditions in developed countries. In the 1990s, widespread protests against Nike and other multinationals occurred in the West and circled back to target the Bretton Woods institutions.[3] Hence, they were under fire from citizens in developed and developing countries alike.

Citizen Activism in the Global Economy

In the previous chapters, we have seen growing efforts at citizen activism on a global scale across a range of issues. Between the 1950s and 1990s, the number, size, and density of advocacy networks grew exponentially, particularly in the areas of human rights, women's rights, the environment, and development.[4] In domestic politics, the causes for the explosion of interest group activity are varied. In the United States, the political activity of groups expanded at a time when the congressional committees grew less powerful and political parties grew more powerful. Special citizens' groups mobilized members, donors, and activists around interests, giving individuals the choice to support issues they cared most about and not have them packaged by a political party.[5] In the aftermath of the US war in Vietnam, many involved in the peace movement turned to human rights causes, raising the number of groups active on global issues.[6] Outside the United States, the end of the Cold War amplified their number again as the cessation of ideological and social orthodoxy allowed many diplomats and UN practitioners to interact with nongovernmental organizations more freely.[7] New technol-

ogies made barriers to information obsolete, and NGOs had increasing resources and professionalism. Governments around the world began to
channel resources through NGOs, in no small part because they were perceived to be cost-effective.

The expansion of the activities of NGOs initially appeared to be a positive development because it allowed a greater percentage of the world community to participate in global affairs. NGOs could bypass recalcitrant
national governments and provide information to international organizations. They could marshal powerful allies to bring pressure on a government to change its domestic practices, particularly in areas such as the
environmental and human rights issues of the 1970s and 1980s. Later, they
took on problems associated with global debt. Eventually in the 1990s,
groups of NGOs, IOs, and scholars working on debt issues were effective in
transforming the governance of debt into debt forgiveness for the most heavily indebted countries.[8]

Ultimately, this expansion of activity would lead NGOs from providing
straightforward support for the work of IOs to seeking a stronger voice in
policy discussions. When a state changes its behavior in response to international pressures, it has a new relationship with its citizens and international
actors.[9] The activities of NGOs thus challenged the sovereignty of many
state members of international institutions. The more that NGOs in the developing world participated in the work of states and IOs, the less they
seemed to be truly independent actors.

In advanced industrial democracies, the growth of citizens' groups had
the effect of changing democratic politics by increasing the number of con-
stituents who need to be satisfied in order to advance a piece of legislation
or enact a policy.[10] Business groups had always had some kind of representation. But the Jimmy Carter administration made human rights a cornerstone of US foreign policy; activists sought to limit US contributions to
development projects in IOs that might benefit human rights offenders,
thus connecting Cold War adversaries to the questions of human rights.[11]
NGOs and other interest groups would continue to tie issues together in domestic politics in later presidential administrations, further complicating
American support for IOs across the political spectrum.

Antiglobalization Protests and the Bretton Woods Institutions

Capitalism itself changed during these years. Brands, lifestyles, and even the news began to be marketed globally. For example, the American basketball player Michael Jordan become a star worldwide due to the strength of his own talent and personality, marketing campaigns that emphasized an American lifestyle, satellite technology that made sports all-encompassing and instantaneous, together with multinational corporations. That is, when Jordan scored during a basketball game, fans in ninety-three countries could see it in real time with direct satellite. Products associated with Jordan were likewise sold everywhere. Walter LaFeber argues that transnational corporations produced and distributed goods globally, backed by advertising that sold them not only as products but as lifestyles—in this case with the Nike slogan "Just Do It!" The athletic equipment illustrated the freedom that seemed to come with it.[12] Of the fifteen largest advertising agencies in the world at the time, twelve were American.[13] During these years, media companies that promoted global brands such as Nike, Wheaties, Coca-Cola, and Gatorade featured the world's most recognized athlete.[14] CNN did not use the word "foreign" in its broadcasts because the interconnected world was no longer "foreign" to Americans. Eventually, the negative effects of the promotion of global brands were transmitted through the media as well. Reports of poor treatment of workers in Nike's factories in Vietnam resulted in protests and lower sneaker profits in the late 1990s.[15]

Antiglobalization protestors initially fell into several groups that shared some, but not all, characteristics. One group comprised individuals who opposed capitalism and corporations in general.[16] Another group viewed globalization as the cause of a range of social ills, including poverty in poor countries, deterioration of the environment, and job loss. Others resented the rise of the United States. For these individuals, the collapse of communism may have been celebrated, but the loss of the Soviet Union as a countervailing superpower was more problematic. Antiglobalization could also be considered anti-Americanism.[17]

On November 30, 1999, some forty to fifty thousand protesters converged on the WTO meeting in Seattle, Washington, at times disrupting the conference, and later rioting. The Seattle police chief resigned after the debacle. Although labor unions and environmentalists dominated, the protests also attracted a visible anarchist element. The surprising aspect of the WTO protests was not the opposition to trade liberalization but the opposition to the WTO itself. At once, the WTO seemed to symbolize the frustrations of all of the new and disparate issues in global governance. With these issues, multilateralism had either emerged later in the postwar era or had been so decentralized that there was no clear target for the protestors to attack. For example, protestors claimed that the WTO trampled labor and human rights, killed people by denying medicines to AIDS victims, and destroyed the environment.[18] The irony of the Seattle protests was that the meeting would have been considered a failure even without them. The ministers lacked consensus on an agenda for a possible new round of negotiations.[19] Nonetheless, the disruptions shocked a world community that had grown complacent with the liberalization agenda.

After Seattle, the antiglobalization movement grew stronger and protested every major meeting of the IMF, the World Bank, and the WTO. The next major clash occurred at the Group of Eight summit meeting in Genoa, Italy, in July 2001. One group of protestors threw bottles and firebombs at a jail. Others smashed computers. The Italian authorities assembled twenty thousand police and troops to confront the conflict. One demonstrator was killed after being shot in the head by an Italian trooper during the riots.[20] In recalling the protestor's death, UN Secretary-General Kofi Annan remarked, "I recall the meeting in Genoa, where these leaders, we had to go into a meeting where you are almost in a fortress, barricaded away from the people. You have no idea what is going on outside, and suddenly we were told that somebody has been killed in the demonstration and [Italian] Prime Minister [Silvio] Berlusconi said that what we are doing there is not going to count. Nobody is going to cover it; they will focus on the dead man. Another leader says: 'But what are these people about? Why are they shouting? We are the decision-makers. What authority do they have?' and the next leader said: 'Be careful, they vote for us. They put us in; we cannot ignore them.' "[21]

As Annan's recollection indicates, the relationship between citizens in democratic states and decision makers in multilateral forums is complex.

Influencing policy outcomes and the selection of those who hold positions in responsive governing institutions constitute the essence of political participation at the domestic level. By definition, states mediate the same activities at the international level. Participation therefore poses a challenge for IOs because states, and not individuals, have historically been the primary participants. Moreover, more powerful states have generally determined most outcomes. However, we have seen that new links formed between the activities of individuals and groups within democratic states and outcomes in international organizations; moreover, the activities of individuals and groups acting outside states can influence both policy outcomes and broader multilateral arrangements.[22]

In the debate that followed the Seattle and Genoa protests, contradictions in both the pro- and antiglobalization movements multiplied. It is not easy to generalize about the effects of globalization in the developing world where everyone did not share the protesters' sentiments. For some, globalization reduced isolation. Others gained access to knowledge that would have been beyond the reach of the wealthiest people in the world a century earlier. Cheaper sources of food may harm some farmers, but they also give poor people access to food they may not have been able to afford previously. The same digital communications that underpin globalization enable links among antiglobalization protestors.[23]

The Bretton Woods institutions remained a target of the antiglobalization movement even after the initial protests subsided. For Joseph Stiglitz, the IMF's policies exacerbated the conditions in Indonesia and Thailand in the 1997 Asian crisis. Market reforms in Latin America have produced irregular results. Therefore, around the time of the protests, Stiglitz argued that it was the more narrowly defined economic aspects of the project that were the subject of controversy. In particular, he pointed to the international institutions that wrote the rules that mandate policies like the liberalization of capital markets, albeit for Stiglitz, the globalization project should be repaired and not terminated.[24] The World Bank, IMF, and WTO became what Richard Peet termed an "unholy trinity" of a failed religion called neoliberalism.[25]

The Bretton Woods institutions were also criticized for internal operations that favor wealthy countries. For example, Stiglitz criticizes the IMF and WTO for being dominated by wealthy, industrial countries and, more precisely, by the commercial and financial interests within these nations. Thus, the policies of the institutions naturally reflect this dominance both in their representatives—IMF finance ministers at the IMF and trade ministers at the WTO—and in the leaders that head them. To make matters worse, the leaders are chosen behind closed doors. Hence, they do not represent the nations they serve.[26] Others pointed out the problem is not with the institutions themselves but with the policies they advocate. For example, the IMF's conditionality went too far at the end of the twentieth century and made it difficult for developing countries to focus on their own priorities.[27]

Other critics view the problem as stemming from the intersection of what IOs do and what states can accomplish with respect to their own economies. James Mittelman argues that as globalization progressed, states lost power. To aggregate their power, states established a highly institutionalized system. More IOs appeared. Although different states had varying capacities to confront the global economy, all wanted to lower barriers. In this environment, IOs proliferated to face new problems, such as with transnational organized crime and the United Nations Interregional Crime and Justice Research Institute. Or they sought common rules, such as the OECD's efforts at negotiating "national treatment" for global corporations through the Multilateral Agreement on Investment, which would have constrained developing countries from restricting the foreign ownership of land and property. Informally, world leaders, central bankers, presidents, prime ministers, and some scholars met at the annual gathering of the World Economic Forum in Davos, Switzerland.[28] These processes became a source of deep social tension as governments became less accountable, citizens became less responsible, and certain groups were marginalized.

Thus, multilateral interventions were both necessary and futile. Disparate as it was, the first wave of the antiglobalization movement put the issue of the Bretton Woods institutions and global cooperation firmly on the agenda. It began to draw important connections among the promotion of human rights—particularly with respect to workers and workplace conditions—the environment, and democratic institutions in such a way that revealed both the positive and negative aspects of globalization and its attendant multilateralism. The movement drew clear distinctions between winners and losers. It was no longer assumed that either the post–World War II or post–Cold War liberal agendas were unmitigated goods for international society.

Stress on the UN and NATO after 9/11

The antiglobalization movement took a dramatic turn after September 11, 2001. The events were perpetrated by an international network against the core of the world's financial and political system. The victims were from all over the world. The events were significant to the unfolding history of multilateralism, as we saw in chapter 5, because American wars followed in Afghanistan and Iraq. Moreover, the energy of the antiglobalization movement was overtaken by the subsequent wars, insofar as many opponents of economic globalization organized against the conflicts.

Just as the nature of capitalism had changed with the distinct nature of globalization at the time, so the type of adversary also changed. In the post-9/11 world, Americans faced antagonists based in as many as sixty countries and not bound by any national allegiance. Yet the new forms of digital communication allowed the enemy to keep in close contact with its members. Polls conducted in the years that followed the attack revealed that many Americans were not aware of the degree of anti-Americanism in the world. While some figures, such as Michael Jordan, might be widely popular, the culture and products he represented were disliked or caused serious misunderstandings.[29] Thus, globalization no longer seemed to offer a universal good. In trying to thwart terrorists, governments limited immigration, which had the effect of preventing the movement of cheap labor from one country to another. They also imposed new regulations on the movement of goods and money.

Multilateral institutions attempted to address the challenge. The United Nations Security Council adopted Resolution 1373, thus establishing the Counter-Terrorism Committee. Five years later, the General Assembly agreed on a common framework to fight terrorism resting on four pillars: addressing the conditions conducive to its spread; preventing and combatting it; building member states' capacities to fight it; and ensuring respect for human rights and the rule of law. The UN Counter-Terrorism Center supports these goals.[30]

Yet the United States, the UN's most powerful member and erstwhile champion, was ambivalent about the organization in the wake of the attacks. Briefly reviewing the events of chapter 5, as members of the George W. Bush administration debated military action in Iraq, they also debated whether to seek Security Council authorization for the use of force. President Bush was scheduled to speak to the General Assembly on September 12, 2002. When he delivered the speech, he pledged that the United States would work with the Security Council to reimpose and enforce a weapons inspections regime on Iraq. Thus, he did not completely disregard the organization. However, if the UN did not take the action desired by the United States, the United States would enforce its resolutions with whatever allies would join. On September 8, Security Council Resolution 1441 found Iraq to be in material breach of prior UN resolutions and threatened serious consequences if Iraq did not cooperate with the inspectors. Some members wanted a second resolution, however, if and when the United States could demonstrate that Iraq actually possessed the weapons of mass destruction the United States claimed it did. When Secretary of State Colin Powell returned to the Security Council in February 2003, he was unable to convince the body that sufficient evidence was there. In March, the United States nonetheless launched an attack on Iraq in defiance of the United Nations.[31]

After the initial US invasion was complete, a guerrilla war ensued in Iraq, and the United States returned to the United Nations. Relations between the United States and the international body were strained by the circumstances leading to the war and the Security Council's skepticism that the United States' desire to seek a multilateral approach was sincere. Donors wanted a say in Iraq policy. Thus, despite the initial American avoidance of the UN, the Iraq invasion demonstrated that the UN still held the ability to confer international legitimacy on an operation. By spring 2004, the United States concluded that in order to create a plan for a transitional Iraqi government, it would have to give way to a UN-led process. The UN would create enough credibility to guide the new country through the days before elections held in January 2005. The UN representative, Lakhdar Brahimi, would negotiate among the Iraqi factions to form an interim government, and a new Security Council resolution would be sought to legitimize the new government. Despite ongoing problems with the US occupation and hard feelings at the UN over the situation, the United States eventually succeeded in getting a unanimous Security Council resolution (SC Res. 1546) that conferred international legitimacy on the new government, spelled out its powers, and set terms for ending the authority to govern. The occupation ended formally on June 28, 2004, despite a considerable continuing US presence.[32]

On the Iraqi side, the UN was not popular due to its association with the Oil-for-Food program. The Security Council created the program in 1995 to lessen the effects of international economic sanctions on ordinary citizens that remained from the 1990 intervention under the George H. W. Bush administration. Implemented in 1996, the program allowed Iraq to sell oil, with payments going into an escrow system rather than to the Iraqi government. The money could then be used for specific operations approved by the UN. Despite its intentions, the Oil-for-Food program was besieged by accusations of corruption and hurt the UN's reputation with broad segments of the Iraqi population. On August 21, 2003, a bomb targeting the UN Assistance Mission in Iraq killed twenty-two people, including UN Special Representative Sérgio Vieira de Mello. A car bomb later killed a security guard near the UN headquarters in Baghdad. Although Kofi Annan stated that the bombing would not stop the UN's efforts to rebuild the country, the UN relocated its efforts to Jordan and worked remotely.[33] Yet the image of the buildings serve as a potent reminder of the limits of the UN's work (fig. 9.1).

Therefore, the role of the UN in relation to the new global terrorist threat has been ambiguous at best. Other multilateral organizations have likewise met equivocal futures. As we also saw in chapter 5, NATO appeared to be strengthened by the 9/11 attacks. In the immediate response, allies invoked the treaty's Article 5 defense guarantee that an attack on one would be considered an attack on all for the first time in its history. Yet for military and political reasons, the United States did not ask for a NATO operation in its military campaign in Afghanistan. The United States had sufficient military

Fig. 9.1. Damage to the United Nations Headquarters building in Baghdad, Iraq, following a truck bombing during Operation Iraqi Freedom, August 21, 2003. Camera Operator MSGT James M. Bowman, USAF. Combined Military Service Digital Photographic Files. Courtesy of the National Archives and Records Administration (6647425).

capacity to project force, and it did not want interference from the eighteen allies. The campaign revealed the gaps in capabilities between the United States and its allies. When the United States increased its defense budget to combat terrorism, the amount exceeded any single European country's entire defense budget. Without a Soviet threat, NATO's existence was again called into question.[34] After 2008, the Bretton Woods order was overwhelmed by the size of the crises occurring in the global financial system. Although the existing network of political and economic institutions were asked to intervene, they could only deal with them in a superficial way.

The Global Refugee Crisis and Pressure on the EU

The wars in Afghanistan and Iraq contributed to the next fundamental challenge to multilateralism at the grassroots level. After 2011, the number of the world's displaced people rose dramatically as a result of these two conflicts and the Syrian civil war that broke out that year. The initial spark for that war came from the government of Syria's suppression of protestors. Troops killed some, and others took up the call. Early diplomatic efforts did not end the fighting, and calls for the country's leader, Bashar al-Assad, to step down were unsuccessful. Of the estimated total of thirteen million displaced by May 2016, seven million remained inside Syria, six million outside, including around one million in Lebanon and around one million in Europe. At first, those Syrian refugees that left the country went to Turkey, Lebanon, and Jordan. Therefore, most of the refugees remained in the region with the crisis. The refugees took up one quarter of Jordan's public spending.[35] This distribution follows the global pattern: most displaced people depart from, and remain in, developing countries.

Yet after 2011, the situation changed due to the geography of the conflicts, technology, and domestic politics in Europe. Whereas previous refugees to Europe received generous treatment by global standards, those who attempted to migrate to European democracies after 2011 encountered citizenries divided and strained by the effects of the financial crisis and recession that followed. By May 2016, the global displaced population stood at a postwar record of sixty million people, twenty million of whom were stranded outside of their own countries. The problem has only grown worse since then, fed by continuing conflicts in Syria, Somalia, and South Sudan.[36] Therefore, the global refugee crisis has amplified existing opposition not only toward the Bretton Woods institutions but toward the European Union and United Nations agencies as well.

Multilateral Efforts on Behalf of Refugees

As with the other growing threats, refugees and problems associated with their relocation are nothing new. And states have made attempts at cooperative arrangements to address them. After World War II, in 1950, states created the office of the United Nations High Commissioner for Refugees (UNHCR) in order to aid the millions of Europeans who had fled or lost their homes. Thus, when the UN's 1951 Refugee Convention was devised, it covered Europeans who had been displaced before 1951. The UN had not assisted the millions displaced by the partition of India or the 1948 Arab-

Israeli War. Nonetheless, the UNHCR was a useful instrument in the West for refugees fleeing communist or Soviet states. The High Commissioner assisted many Hungarians who fled the Soviet Union even though they were not covered. Many resettled in the United States. Thus, the existing framework was created by Americans and Europeans, mostly for Europeans, following World War II and during the Cold War.

The original UNHCR had three years to complete its work and received the Nobel Peace Prize for its efforts in 1954. Later crises followed the 1956 revolution in Hungary. Revised in 1967, the convention became a strong instrument of international law. It obligated signatories to refrain from sending people back to countries where they are in danger. The UNHCR operated during the decolonization of Africa in the 1960s and Asian and Latin American conflicts in the 1960s and 1970s, leading to a second Nobel Peace Prize in 1981. Therefore, rather than being disbanded, the UNHCR celebrated its sixty-fifth anniversary in 2015 in a world that is dramatically different than it was when the commission was founded.[37]

The Contemporary Refugee Crisis

In the Iraq, Afghan, and Syrian wars of the twenty-first century, refugees face a difficult choice that the existing multilateral arrangements could not have envisioned in the twentieth century when they were devised: stay closer to home in developing countries that most likely have not signed the 1951 convention or survive a more brutal trip to Europe with a much better payoff in terms of legal status and public services at the end. Many who remain in geographically proximate countries must live in camps with barely subsistence level standards. The underfunded and unaccountable humanitarian organizations and the UNHCR must care for them, in a role they were not intended to play. However, these refugees might have a better chance at integration into local societies in these countries and might be more likely to return home if and when peace comes. In addition, if they are assisted, developing countries can act as hosts at a fraction of the cost in developed countries.[38]

For refugees who went to Europe after 2011, the legal payoff conditions changed because citizenries held different attitudes toward the displaced people themselves and the agencies helping them than they had held in the 1950s and 1970s. In the minds of some citizens in the West, the origin of these refugees in Syria, Afghanistan, Iraq, and Turkey became conflated with terrorist attacks and the religion of Islam, even if such connections are nonexistent. The result is that the refugee regime has been challenged by the cultural differences between the displaced people and their host societies and the asymmetries in standards of living between the two groups. Two IOs were hit particularly hard by the burst of displaced people that headed for Europe: the UNHCR and the European Union. Neither organization had been created to address the combination of circumstances they faced.

Not surprisingly, their response has been clumsy at best. While the 1951 Refugee Convention calls on signatories to act in a "spirit of international cooperation," it does not specify obligations on countries in the world community that do not have an immediate influx of refugees. The European Union created its own forms of protection that did not exactly add up to full protection, but did help victims of war and other forms of violence outside the Refugee Convention's strict definitions. Notable among them, the Dublin agreement requires applicants in Europe to apply for asylum in the first country they reach and have their case adjudicated there. Thus, the southern EU countries faced a more immediate problem than northern member states because most of the refugees landed first in those jurisdictions. In August 2015, German chancellor Angela Merkel extended a welcome to Syrian refugees. Yet her generosity backfired politically when it became clear that other EU countries were sending refugees to Germany and Sweden (which had also opened its doors).[39] After five years in the EU, refugees can usually become permanent residents, giving them the freedom to move anywhere in Europe. Governments usually find it difficult to send them back.

But in the interim, many European governments have made it harder for asylum seekers to reach them. In March 2016, the EU signed a deal with Turkey that obliges asylum seekers who reach Greece to return to Turkey, where some may not be adequately protected and others may be returned home to dangerous circumstances. In exchange for the deal, Turkey received money, a promise of visa-free access for Turks, and other perks. Other efforts seek to stop the inflow of people from Libya who are seeking economic opportunity, a fine line from those seeking political asylum. Although pushing back boats carrying refugees is forbidden under international law and upheld by European courts, naval vessels from individual states began to try to intercept them closer to the Libyan coast and pull, rather than push, them back.[40]

In the breach, European voters feared a loss of control over the influx of refugees, exacerbating anti-immigrant sentiments that already existed.[41] Although the EU had constructed asylum and border rules, the refugees flouted them. Polling data showed that Europeans overwhelmingly disapproved of how the EU dealt with the crisis—with the highest levels of disapproval coming from Greece (94 percent), Sweden (88 percent), and Italy (77 percent). The country showing the strongest support for the EU's management was the Netherlands, with just 31 percent approval.[42]

American politics have not been immune from the crisis. The issue played a role in the US presidential campaign in September 2016, when the Obama administration announced that it would accept up to ten thousand Syrian refugees. Democratic candidates Hillary Clinton and Martin O'Malley, as well as Republican Lindsey Graham, stated that the United States should accept many more. Others on the Republican side essentially agreed, including Marco Rubio, Rand Paul, and Carly Fiorina. Republicans John Kasich and Donald Trump argued that the situation was a European matter.[43] After the November 2015 terrorist attacks at the Bataclan concert hall and other locations in Paris, candidate Trump went further, calling for surveillance of mosques and barring Syrian refugees. In December, he proposed an outright ban on Muslim immigration to the United States.[44]

Populism and International Organizations

As we saw at the beginning of the chapter, the amorphous antiglobalization movement at the turn of the twenty-first century had its own internal contradictions, many of which came from the disparate localities where the grassroots opposition had arisen. Yet after the Berlin Wall fell in November 1989, the West lacked a common enemy to rally against. Terrorism after 9/11 was not easily confined to one state or group of states. The sequence of the 2008 financial crisis, followed by the European sovereign debt crisis, followed by an onslaught of refugees was particularly toxic in Western democracies, where globalization had sown the seeds of cultural and economic insecurity. Most areas already contained some kind of job loss in concentrated sectors that amplified the anti-immigrant element. Not surprisingly, particularly virulent nationalist elements pushed back against multilateral efforts and sought to return control to local municipalities and states. In addition to the strains on the European Union and UNHCR associated with the refugee regime, more grassroots pressure in opposition to multilateralism came from a resurgent populist movement in the United States against the transatlantic alliance and in the United Kingdom against membership in the European Union.

Populism everywhere involves some notion of "the people" against an established elite, or "us" against "them." For almost all forms of populism, "us" excludes foreigners and immigrants. "Them" includes any intrusion into local or national control. Therefore, multilateralism in all its forms is at best a source of suspicion for populists and at worst an outright target. The combination of job loss, terrorism, and refugees hit three populist themes in the United States and Europe that threaten the post–World War II alliance structure that has kept the peace for so many years.

American Populism and the Transatlantic Alliance

Populism in the United States is not confined to the right, left, or center of American politics. There are right-wing, left-wing, and centrist populist parties, united by a language that conceives of ordinary people as a noble group mobilized against self-serving, undemocratic elites. In his study of the phenomenon, John Judis depicts left-wing populists as viewing the world divided in two main groups: "the people" arrayed against an elite or establishment. Right-wing populists add a third dimension. "The people" work against an elite that coddles this additional group—which could be, for example, immigrants, Islamists, or African Americans.[45] For Martin Wolf, right-wing populists believe that certain ethnicities are "the people" and that foreigners are the enemy. Left-wing populists identify workers as "the people" and the rich as the enemy.[46] Thus, there is no agreement on who constitutes "the people." They could be blue-collar workers, small business owners, students with high levels of debt, or the poor or middle class. The elites could be financial powers, intellectuals, or the 1 percent of highest income earners.

In the United States, populists have taken issue with the growth of international trade deals and immigration. We saw in chapter 4 that downward pressure on American wages has origins in the 1960s and 1970s trade laws, which advanced a neoliberal agenda without destroying the New Deal social programs. In addition, changes in immigration law meant that in the 1960s, immigrants came to the United States from Latin America and Asia. Many of these newcomers worked in the agriculture, food processing, meatpacking, construction, hotel, restaurant, and other industrial sectors. Businesses used both documented and undocumented workers and fought attempts to penalize their hiring of these people. Shortly thereafter, in the 1970s, American labor unions became concerned about competition from imports and the activities of American multinational corporations that invested overseas, where labor was cheaper. Nonetheless, both political parties came to accept major components of the neoliberal agenda, and job loss persisted.

Populist challenges in the electoral system followed in 1992, from Texas businessman Ross Perot and political commentator Pat Buchanan, and again in 1996 from Pat Buchanan. Fewer jobs materialized from the free trade deals than the number they threatened, and they did not stop the flood of immigrants entering the country. Perot questioned the George H. W. Bush administration's decision to intervene in Kuwait. Buchanan criticized the administration for raising taxes and not addressing the country's economic challenge from Western Europe and Japan. Neither candidate fit the conventional Democrat-Republican rubric, and both men pointed to the mainstream parties' lack of attention to concerns about American manufacturing, immigration, and lobbying in Washington.[47] Both questioned the neoliberal agenda.

After the financial crisis of 2008, Barack Obama was elected president. He did not directly attack the financial services industry and delayed introducing reform measures. When he did push legislation, he pushed for a stimulus bill and a plan to provide health insurance to all Americans. The plan that resulted was a combination of mandating individuals to buy insurance from exchanges, subsidizing uninsured lower-income individuals, and expanding Medicaid eligibility. Like other New Deal social policies, the Affordable Care Act addressed the needs of lower-income groups. But it did not appear to offer as much to the middle class or senior citizens, who were told that the act would be financed by reductions in the growth of Medicare spending. The anti-health-insurance reaction fed the growth of the Tea Party movement, which was never a unified organization but did share the idea that the country is divided between those who make things and those who live off of their enterprise.[48] On the right, the Tea Party attacked the Republican Party. On the left, Obama came under attack from a group of protestors who called for an occupation of Zuccotti Park near Wall Street. These organizers failed to pursue unified goals but shared the slogan that the 99 percent of lower-income people would no longer tolerate the greed and corruption of the top 1 percent. The symbolic impact was large, and the movement spread to Europe, Greece, and Spain in particular.[49]

Signs of cracks in the American commitment to leading the world economy were apparent late in the Obama administration. In 2014, China pursued plans to create a "World Bank" for Asia that would focus, at least initially, on building a new "silk road" to revive ancient trade routes connecting Asia and Europe. China would provide most of the funding for the new Asian Infrastructure Investment Bank, and lending would be directed at infrastructure projects across the region.[50] At first, the United States convinced some large countries not to join the effort, citing its ambiguous nature.[51] However, American allies quickly broke ranks, ironically pushing the bank in a direction that is more favorable to US interests.[52] Once the bank began operations, prominent American former officials including Robert Zoellick (who had served as head of the World Bank and as US trade representative) criticized the administration's actions as a strategic mistake.[53]

In the security arena, the end of the Cold War had left the United States without a major enemy. Yet both political parties sought to maintain the Cold War alliance system and American military intervention in support of the world system. This rough agreement on goals fell apart when Donald

Trump began his presidential bid. He argued that American allies were getting protection from the United States that they were not paying for, to the disadvantage of American farmers, the sick, and the homeless. In the 2016 campaign, he repeatedly attacked NATO as an alliance that was obsolete and expensive.[54] Trump picked up the themes of Buchanan and Perot in opposing NAFTA, the WTO, and the Trans-Pacific Partnership agreement. He also wanted to restore American manufacturing and stood against illegal immigration.[55] His candidacy threatened the traditional Republican coalition, and its foreign policy establishment in particular.

Once elected president, Trump took a dramatic turn against multilateralism in a series of maneuvers. In June 2017, he pulled the United States out of the Paris Agreement. At a NATO meeting, he questioned the US commitment to the alliance's collective security arrangement. Whereas the WTO had been in a state of decline after the Doha Round negotiations failed, and China did not adhere to the WTO's market principles, President Trump's actions pushed the world community definitively away from the framework of WTO rules with his announcement of steel and aluminum tariffs.[56] Later that month, he effectively bypassed the WTO by announcing a plan to impose tariffs on as much as sixty billion dollars' worth of Chinese imports. China threatened to retaliate with tariffs of its own. Given that the United States would impose these tariffs without first adjudicating its grievance in the WTO, it would flout WTO rules. Likewise, China's retaliation would also do so.[57] In May 2018, Trump ended the exemption for US allies on the tariffs on steel and aluminum. He withdrew from a deal that had been negotiated among seven countries to prevent Iran from acquiring a nuclear weapon.[58] He withdrew his signature from the G7 communiqué the next month.

The Trump administration's policy shift was so dramatic that it has not been clear how strongly it marks a permanent departure from the prevailing principles. At the same time that the administration defied the WTO's rules, the US trade representative announced his plan to file a case at the WTO to halt China's policy of forcing foreign investors to transfer technology.[59] The United States announced its departure from the Paris Agreement, but the terms of the agreement do not allow for departures before November 4, 2019. The administration also announced that an American delegation will attend all the Paris-related meetings between then and 2020.[60] The day after Trump pulled his endorsement of the joint G7 communiqué, Senator John McCain (R-AZ) tweeted a message: "To our allies: bipartisan majorities of Americans remain pro-free trade, pro-globalization & supportive of alliances based on 70 years of shared values . . . Americans stand with you, even if our president doesn't."[61] Since Senator McCain was a member of the president's party, the direction of the party was likewise called into question. And in a further sign of the cross-directions of policy, Trump next stated that the United States might end all trade with its allies if they didn't submit to his demands over reduced trade barriers.[62]

European Populism and the European Union

European populist movements have grown during the same years. They have been fostered by a different sequence of causes than those in the United States but are nonetheless related in the sense that globalization has threatened people's sense of security, prosperity, and national community. Immediately after World War II, Western European governments reached a consensus on alignment with the United States in the Cold War, the need for integration, and the benefits of a strong welfare state. In the 1980s, populist thinking began to make a mark, prompted by mass immigration and growing unemployment. In France, in particular, the country's National Front promised to return the country to its past glory.[63] While populism in Europe is not necessarily antidemocratic, it is illiberal, particularly in its disdain for minority rights, pluralism, and the rule of law.[64]

When the EU was founded, it embraced the concept of the free movement of people and businesses for member states. This concept became enshrined in the Schengen Agreement of 1985, which led to the creation of the Schengen Area, wherein internal borders are largely nonexistent. The free movement of peoples helped both businesses that needed lower-wage labor and the European project, which tried to forge a common identity among the peoples of Europe who had fought two hegemonic wars. The notion of free movement of labor in the EU was conceived at a time when living standards were roughly even and European economies were being rebuilt after the war. There was little backlash against these people because they did not compete with natives for jobs, and they were viewed as temporary residents who would return home. In the 1970s, when labor surpluses arose, Western Europe ended the recruitment of foreigners. While some returned home, others remained. Many from Africa and the Middle East brought their families to live with them. In the 1980s and 1990s, refugees from Africa and Asia further raised the proportion of non-European immigrants, a trend that persisted into the twenty-first century.[65]

Circumstances changed even more when the Cold War ended. Eleven countries from central and Eastern Europe were admitted to the EU between 2004 and 2011. No one could have predicted what would happen when controls were lifted on east European countries; yet it is not surprising that many people sought opportunities where wages and living standards were so much higher. The EU and its institutions appeared to foster the new waves of immigration, and its perceived lack of democratic accountability made it even more of a target for populist rage. Anti-immigrant sentiment began to appear in European polling in the early 1990s. Immigrants were said to make crime worse, receive social benefits that they had not paid for in taxes, and take jobs from natives. The system established among bureaucrats in Brussels shielded the EU's administration from those that disagreed. European leaders and the European Commission generally ignored these sentiments, leaving no political outlet for anti-immigrant sentiment, a void that was eventually filled by populist parties on the right.[66]

Among the EU's institutions, only the European Parliament has direct elections, and its powers are limited.[67] Yet signs of widespread dissatisfaction were even evident in the electoral outcomes for the EU's legislature, as shown by the allocation of seats in 2009 and 2014 in the European Parliament (fig. 9.2). Only four groups gained seats allocated in 2014: one that is critical of the EU and European integration (the European Conservatives and Reformists group), one that is populist and Eurosceptic (Europe of Freedom and Direct Democracy group), the nonattached members group, and the European United Left–Nordic Green Left group. The other mainstream groups all lost seats. In the 2019 elections, these trends continued, albeit not as anticipated. With the highest voter turnout in twenty years, the center-right European People's party and center-left Socialists and

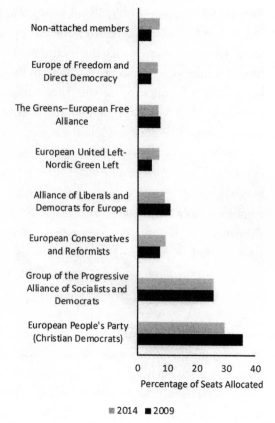

Fig. 9.2. Group party allocation of seats in the European Parliament following the 2009 and 2014 elections. Source: Results by Group in European Parliamentary Elections, 2009 and 2014, European Parliament, http://www.europarl.europa.eu/elections2014-results/en/election-results-2014.html.

Democrats lost their combined majority for the first time in a generation to the benefit of the Greens and Liberals. The Eurosceptic and far-right parties made gains, but not as large as expected.[68]

Thus, European populism initially emerged on the right. These parties tend to last longer than their American counterparts because many European countries have multiparty systems at the national level, many with proportional representation. These systems send representatives to a parliament according to the proportion of the vote they receive, and not according to the highest number received in each district (where parties with low proportions do not win seats). Hence, smaller European parties send representatives to a legislature even with low polling numbers. These parties accused elites of indulging communists, welfare recipients, or immigrants. Later, they emerged on the left as well, directing their anger against the establishment in their own country or the EU in Brussels.[69] Some arose from antitax groups, whereas others have uncertain ties to former fascists and Nazis. During the European sovereign debt crisis, leftist populist groups were more predominant in the less prosperous southern member states, while right-wing groups were concentrated more heavily in more prosperous northern and central Europe.[70]

The result is that much of Europe appears ungovernable. Voters do not see an ability to influence policy and have lashed out against the traditional center.[71] Although the phenomenon has spread across Europe, populism has some distinctive features in each country. Moreover, it has been strengthened by public sentiment following nine terrorist attacks in Europe between December 2010 and March 2016. Many of the worst were in France and Brussels.

In France, the immigration debate has become enmeshed in cultural issues connected to Islamic integration. Yet the connection between French populism and the welfare state has evolved over time. Along with some other European populist parties, Jean-Marie Le Pen's National Front began to defend the welfare state as he built a coalition among working-class voters. His daughter Marine Le Pen took over the party and reoriented it away from its anti-Semitic origins. Nonetheless, she remained vehemently opposed to immigration and Islam, arguing that the newer immigrants set up their own communities within France and governed themselves by their own codes and traditions.[72] Her economic program sought to defend French sovereignty against intrusions by the EU.

In other parts of Europe, anti-immigrant sentiments likewise originated in earlier eras. In the Netherlands in 1997, Hans Janmaat, the leader of the Center Democrats, was indicted and convicted for inciting racial hatred. Another candidate associated with anti-Islamic views was assassinated. In 2006, Geert Wilder's Party for Freedom emerged.[73] One of the strongest anti-immigrant parties has been the Danish People's Party. Denmark has one of the EU's most generous welfare systems. Since jobs were available in Denmark, those sympathetic to the Danish People's Party were concerned that immigrants would not work and would thus become free riders on the system. As more Muslim immigrants arrived, these concerns grew to include crime and religious practices. Those holding these anti-immigrant sentiments felt that residents living in Denmark before the inflow shared the same values of work and family and would not take advantage of the state.[74]

Italy has been hit particularly hard by immigration pressures and the euro crisis, given its geographic location and economic difficulties. The new-style politicians do not accept the legitimacy of EU-wide rules. The March 2018 Italian elections crushed hope that a moderate center would reemerge in European politics. More than half of Italians voted for antiestablishment parties. As with the other European elections, the principal center-left party lost a large number of voters. The two parties that won a majority at the polls constructed a government that is a coalition of the populist left and populist right, friendly to Russia, and confrontational with Brussels.[75]

The British Exit (Brexit) from the European Union

Antimultilateral populist efforts have arguably been the most successful in the United Kingdom, where a combination of anti-immigrant and anti-EU sentiment fueled the country's withdrawal. Some argued that in joining the EU, Britain had abandoned its sovereignty. Anti-EU sentiment spread to the working-class areas in northern and eastern England that had supported the Labour Party in the past. They began to back the United Kingdom Independence Party, despite the falling unemployment rate. These voters felt left behind in the country's economic advance.[76] While some parts of the country welcomed immigrants, other parts were concerned that they put pressure on public services and lowered wages. Other opposition was cultural. By the 2014 EU parliamentary election, the Independence Party claimed that it was supporting those left behind against elites in London. It comprised a major bloc of the Europe of Freedom and Direct Democracy group (see fig. 9.2). The party proposed taking the funds that the United Kingdom contributed to the EU and using them for the National Health Service.[77]

The anti-EU sentiment culminated with the British referendum to leave the European Union in 2016. Though few accurately predicted the outcome, in retrospect, signs of dissatisfaction were clearly evident. Britain had always struggled with its European identity. It was an outlier to the original six members of the EEC.[78] By 2001, the rest of the EU's members had grown far more diverse. Britain did not appear to stand as far apart as it had at the beginning. Nonetheless, British public opinion polls at the time rejected the notion that the country was fully committed.[79]

The referendum was the result of Prime Minister David Cameron's desire to renegotiate the terms of the United Kingdom's membership in the European Union. Although initially Cameron had been reluctant to hold the referendum, the Independence Party gained influence. Many Conservative members of Parliament encouraged him, thinking that the UK would also seek a package of changes in its membership that were intended to take effect after the UK would vote to "remain." Cameron acceded in order to measure public support and, it was hoped, demonstrate the support of the British people for the EU. When the Conservative Party won the 2015 general election, it introduced legislation to enable the referendum, albeit with Cameron favoring remaining in a reformed EU. When the results were announced on June 24, 2016, with a majority voting to leave, Cameron resigned, and the United Kingdom formally submitted a letter notifying withdrawal for 2019.

Once the negotiations began for the British exit, or Brexit, the same policies that had prompted the campaign to leave reappeared. Immigration figured prominently in the debates over Britain's continued participation in the European Single Market. The efforts of the country to find a way out have bolstered the Scottish independence movement.[80] After the vote to leave the EU, Tony Blair argued that the UK Independence Party's rise was a part of a broader rejection of the neoliberal worldview.[81] Although by 2017 Britain was the only EU member that sought to stop the free movement of people, the principle has been eroded elsewhere in Europe in some respects, chiefly with limits on welfare benefit entitlements. Germany, the Netherlands, and others have won cases in the European Court of Justice allowing them to adjust the entitlement for people from poorer east European countries if they exceed median wages at home.[82]

Conclusion

In the twenty-first century, what is old is new again. Nationalist pressures on efforts at multilateralism have existed since the nineteenth century when efforts at cooperation emerged along with the industrialization of nation-states in Europe. What is new is the way these nationalist protests are conducted—through new forms of social media, marches, and occupation of public space. We have seen that technology is not intrinsically good or evil. It can be used as a force for either. The same technology that ties the globalization project together also binds its dissent. In recent years, that dissent has achieved remarkable success in halting the advance of multilateralism as a mechanism to promote coordination in the world. Local democratic institutions seek more local control. Yet these same activist networks have also sought to eradicate some of the world's worst human rights abuses and practices. Just as state members have changed in the twenty-first century, so too will the multilateral forms they create need to reconstitute themselves in response.

TEN

The Past and Future of Multilateralism

In the course of the past two hundred years, the world community has bonded in a common search for peace and prosperity. It has also been unglued by nationalism, populism, and divisions of wealth and power. The underlying challenges of multilateralism come from the progress of industrialization that pushes forward across time and geographic space, altering politics within individual states and international society as it goes. The benefits of science and mass production have changed the course of history by making it possible for growing numbers of people to live longer, healthier, more productive lives. Notions of the fundamental worth and dignity of every person have likewise advanced. Yet these same developments have a harmful side, too. They have transformed the nature of war, commerce, and consumption in such ways that it is possible to end all human life with nuclear weapons and damage the ecosystem to the extent that the planet could become uninhabitable to human life.

At present, multilateralism appears deadlocked. The post–Cold War expansion of the NATO alliance fosters security for some states and insecurity for others. The United Nations suffers from repeated scandals. Its peacekeepers provoked a cholera epidemic in Haiti after the 2010 earthquake that killed more than ten thousand people; its denial of any involvement for five years contributed to a lack of response to the epidemic in other countries. In 2014, the UN faced a sex abuse scandal by French peacekeepers in the Central African Republic.[1] There are no shared ideas about what produces collective economic security in a globalized economy. Democratic market-based economies, authoritarian capitalist states, and less industrialized countries all make domestic growth and jobs their top political priorities. There has not been a major multilateral trade agreement since the Uruguay Round concluded in 1994, and the United Nations failed to offer any radical policy initiatives in the wake of a series of financial crises during the beginning of the twenty-first century.[2] The Washington consensus on appropriate policies to reform the economies of developing countries in crisis is no longer a consensus, yet nothing new has taken its place. Each government builds its own domestic security and prosperity to fit its distinctive geographical, cultural, and historical circumstances.[3] These trends push states, not toward common solutions, but toward nationalist ones.

Nevertheless, we have seen that the domestic debates associated with multilateralism are far from static. Over time, IOs can construct new constituencies for their policies in advanced, industrial democracies. For example, the initial opposition to the Bretton Woods Agreement Act in Congress objected to putting US money into a fund with an international board where the United States had a minority vote. Nor did opponents want to vote for any plan that would require the government to restrict or regulate foreign-exchange transactions. Yet within two decades after the IMF was established, the same American bankers that had opposed its creation numbered among its top supporters on Capitol Hill.[4] International organizations and the liberal world order can also gain new defenders in countries where political authority is increasingly centralized and regulations control the flow of ideas, culture, and capital. For example, China proposed the creation of the Asian Infrastructure Investment Bank under the leadership of Xi Jinping. President Xi and the current Chinese leadership have shed the formerly low-profile foreign policy of Deng Xiaoping for initiatives that will reshape the global order at the same time that many of Deng's political, social, and economic reforms have been gradually reversed.[5] Thus, contemporary China poses the paradox of becoming an increasingly illiberal state fighting Western liberal values while at the same time positioning itself as a champion of the institutions of a liberal world order.[6]

As a result, the multilateral project presses forward into unknown terrain with a new mix of nationalist, internationalist, liberal, and illiberal combinations. The account offered here provides important insights into successive efforts at achieving cooperation among a number of states in the world community, based on shared principles among them. Yet any multilateral effort is only as good as its members and the values they do have in common. Just as the form multilateralism takes constantly changes, so too do the state members. They change in terms of their own democratic features, who votes, what welfare benefits they provide, how they make decisions internally, and what activities they are willing to cooperate with other states on.

This concluding chapter looks back on the forms that we have seen multilateralism take over the past two centuries and the interplay among state and nonstate actors. Next, it considers the evolving participation of less industrialized countries in multilateral forums and the same actors. Then, it looks forward at the trends that will influence the future of multilateralism. The chapter closes by considering how multilateralism can achieve legitimacy going forward in light of these changes in states and forms.

Successive Efforts at Multilateral Cooperation

Since the end of the Napoleonic era, every major European war has been followed by efforts among the leading states to reconstruct the international system in such a way that would avoid future cataclysmic conflict. Despite the numerous setbacks in these episodes, multilateral efforts are significant because countries keep trying. Moreover, states have expanded the range of areas where they seek cooperative ventures, ranging from the rights of individuals to climate change to medicine to digital technology, as science and industry have progressed. Analysts break down these efforts into successive stages.[7] For our purposes, they have progressed through five: eighteenth-century conference diplomacy, interwar efforts at comprehensive solutions, Cold War alignments in formal IOs, post–Cold War American intervention through IOs, and the contemporary splintering and deepening of both institutions and participants as principles and alignments are shuffled.

Stages of Multilateralism

In the first era, foreign policy was the province of families of monarchs, and elite networks conducted diplomacy. The Congress of Vienna ushered in a transformation of European diplomacy because it initiated the conference system, with the leading powers holding conferences—as opposed to two states at a time negotiating between themselves. Even though the formal efforts associated with the Concert of Europe ended rather quickly, conference diplomacy remained. In the notable meetings held on many topics later in the nineteenth century, the Great Powers began to treat Europe as a political community.[8] Even as the Concert broke down toward the end of the nineteenth century, states sought multilateral solutions by attempting to introduce legal rules that would require them to submit their disputes to arbitration.[9]

Those who constructed the Concert of Europe were not constrained by the domestic political pressures that hemmed in those who followed. For the most part, they did not have to worry about public opinion; most citizens could not vote. Governments were also free from pressure by organized economic interests because most early industrialists adopted a laissez-faire ideology and wanted governments to steer clear of their activities. In addition, armies were limited in the nineteenth century, and comprised professional soldiers as opposed to individuals drafted into service. Technology limited their discrete destructive capability. Finally, the Great Powers shared values and responsibilities among themselves.[10] Nonetheless, the system was not immune to war.

The second era came after World War I and was infused with the vision of Woodrow Wilson and the League of Nations at its center.[11] In the interwar period, the number of states increased and suffrage was extended in many industrial democracies, and thus the number of citizens paying attention to foreign policy multiplied. Citizens criticized the secret diplomacy they perceived to have contributed to the start of World War I and wanted information about their governments' activities on the world stage. So-called little nations had a voice at the League of Nations, establishing a new challenge to elites who did not respect all countries equally.[12] In response, foreign ministries had to work to influence public opinion to build political coalitions among domestic pressure groups and shape what they perceived to be an emergent world public opinion.[13]

Now a formal international organization, the League of Nations and its associated agencies were created and directed by states with the supposition that their existence and operation would be useful to them.[14] Even when they disagree about how to order some of the ideas associated with their thought, the liberal internationalists who promoted IOs both then and now assume that peoples and governments share a common interest in establishing a cooperative world order, grounded in principles of restraint, reciprocity, and sovereign equality. They argue that trade and exchange have a modernizing and civilizing effect on states and strengthen the fabric of the international community. Liberals also share the belief that democracies are particularly willing and able to operate within an open, rule-based international system and cooperate for mutual gain.[15]

In the third era after World War II ended, the United States relaunched the international project but reasserted a more formal role for the most powerful states in it. The order that gradually came to fruition in this era was far more complex than originally planned insofar as it was more Western-centered, multilayered, and institutionalized. Moreover, it put the United States into the direct political and economic management of a system that was far more bureaucratic than previous efforts had been. The institutionalized international environment was so important to American interests that the United States may well have pursued it even without the Soviet threat. That is, the United States needed to build a world environment in which the behavior of states would be structured so that it became a part of world culture and the American system could survive and flourish.[16]

The American conceptualization of international problems and their solutions in legal terms strongly influenced the postwar order. In short: Americans wanted to regulate the world in a similar fashion to the way they regulated their domestic economy in the New Deal.[17] According to this understanding, the Franklin D. Roosevelt administration created administrative agencies that would combine separate legal and executive functions to create new forms of government to regulate American life. The US policy makers involved in planning for the postwar order envisioned a wide scope for IOs to come, yet each IO was associated with a specialized regulatory agency that could be established with other United Nations members.[18] For scholars of international law, the world community moved from a more restrictive international law of coexistence to a more expansive international law of cooperation. People, as well as states, became the subjects of that law. Whereas previous forms of international law had a negative function—to restrain states so that they could pursue their national interests with minimum interference from others—the postwar international law of cooperation is an instrument of collaborative ends—one that creates a system of positive inducements to facilitate and structure cooperative action.[19]

Postwar multilateralism sought to include the many and to advance principles opposed to bilateral or discriminatory arrangements that were thought to disadvantage the weak and make conflict more likely. The open admission to multilateral institutions implied that membership would level the field among participants. After decolonization progressed, the notion that sovereign states are equal became associated with the concept.[20] At least in terms of their institutional designs, the new IOs offered a role for less powerful states in decision making that they would not have held otherwise. However, the reality of most IOs in the immediate postwar period was one in which a much smaller number of states collaborated within a larger multilateral institution, and bilateral or regional spinoffs were commonplace. When big multilateralism began to falter in the 1980s, it did so because more powerful countries were no longer willing to accept free riding by weaker countries on the minilateral bargains that had been struck.[21] The United States would continue to seek cooperation, but in pursuit of principles it dictated.

Thus, America's preeminent geopolitical position both facilitated and impeded a truly open, rule-based liberal order. The United States was the organizer and manager of the Western liberal order. The US political system became fused to the wider world order. While the United States supported the rules and institutions of that order, it also received special privileges from it.[22] And the uneven response of the members of the League of Nations' successor, the United Nations, to obligations under Article 43 (that is, making armed forces, assistance, and facilities available to the Security Council for the purpose of maintaining peace and security) show that few states are willing to commit to *any* situation where the Security Council might decide to intervene. Only a few countries have earmarked and trained specific units for the UN. Most members reserve their right to decide in each case whether to intervene. The largest UN peace enforcement operations—the Korean War and the Gulf War—were undertaken by coalitions dependent on US leadership and military power. Throughout the Cold War, the United States played a similar role, either through the UN or through regional alliances. Even the NATO commitment was credible only with the United States in the alliance. Although the United States did not *only* act where its own vital interests were at stake, it did not act through any one particular organization. Rather, the United States used multilateral vehicles according to the circumstances at hand and the strategic or tactical options the IO offered American planners.[23]

Thus, from 1945 to 1990, relative differences in military capabilities defined the global balance of power. Raw military power put the Soviet Bloc into a preeminent position in the international system. Notions of collective security still tend to be associated with NATO and the role it played in delivering peace and prosperity to Western Europe. Neither the nuclear powers nor other actors have been able to reach universal agreement on a regime for nuclear nonproliferation to halt the spread of the world's most dangerous weapons and technologies. Global defense policy has been mostly a zero-sum game, as one country or bloc maximizes its defense capabilities in ways that challenge the military preeminence of its rivals.[24]

The end of the Cold War changed the playing field and ushered in the fourth era of subsequent attempts at multilateralism, as the former adversaries put many of their differences aside and confronted new threats from rising nationalism in some parts of the world and from terrorism in others. The Warsaw Pact disbanded, and Russia joined the G7 industrial grouping of states for a period, in an effort to build a world community based on shared norms of democratic governance and capitalist principles. President Bill Clinton pursued a policy of assertive multilateralism. The United States would try to build a legitimate international order based on close cooperation with other countries' respect for international law and strong IOs. As the

Cold War receded in time, however, American policy grew more unilateral, and IOs appeared to play a supporting role in US intervention across a range of conflicts. As digital technology became cheaper and more widely available, it also became easier for journalists and nonjournalists alike to report on events around the globe. Notions of human rights evolved. The international community now takes a much more active interest in what goes on inside other countries and can monitor atrocities in real time. The idea of a responsibility to protect has advanced, contributing to an erosion of norms of sovereignty in the community of states. Domestic constituencies in the Western democracies began to question commitments to foreign wars and the distribution of benefits in the new world order and integrated economy that appeared to accrue disproportionately to a cosmopolitan world elite.

Currently, in the fifth era, multilateralism both expands and shrinks as its underlying principles are questioned. The Western alliance is under attack, evidenced by the kind of world summits that previously emphasized unity and set a common agenda in the third (Cold War) era and into the fourth (assertive multilateral) era. For example, the G7 shared a common set of values that understood democracy and market-driven capitalism to be the best paths toward lasting peace and prosperity. However, the incentive for the United States and its allies to cooperate has been weakened by the absence of a common Soviet threat. We saw that the G7 became the G8 when the group invited Russia to join, in order to prevent the country from returning to communism or militarist nationalism. It became the G7 again after the Russians violated these principles with their invasion of Ukraine. In June 2018, after leaving the meeting in Canada, President Trump retracted his endorsement of the G7 communiqué.

Similar strains can be seen in the G20. The G20 overtook the G8 after the global financial crisis of 2008 when the greatest new threat appeared to be economic. The new world economy has elevated non-Western economies such as China and India.[25] China currently supports liberal international institutions, yet some indications are that it will attempt to revise them in accordance with its domestic model of control and coercion.[26] Thus, G20 countries benefit from the liberal global order but do not necessarily advocate for the same norms that underpinned the original Western market-based alliance. As the financial crisis recedes into history, they have become more conflicted among themselves and less accepting of the burdens of leadership.

In the fifth era, weapons of mass destruction are no longer held only by states. Hence, nonstate actors have shifted the way that violence presents itself. A threat to peace still comes from Great Powers engaged in security competition with each other. But it also comes from terrorist groups and rogue nations determined to undermine the global order, at times with no clear alternative to reshape it in mind. Moreover, activist networks have resumed their protests of summit meetings. When the G20 met in Hamburg in July 2017, leaders were met with signs saying, "Welcome to Hell." The alliance of anticapitalist groups who organized the protests ironically shared Trump's distrust of globalization.[27]

The outcome of these trends is that new groupings among states are not emerging in the current era, leaving the world with what Ian Bremmer and Nouriel Roubini call a "G-Zero World," or one in which no single country or bloc of countries has the political and economic capability, or will, to drive an international agenda as the United States had in the immediate aftermath of the Cold War.[28] In this world, voters in advanced industrial democracies elect politicians who appeal to nationalist sentiments and advocate a retreat from multilateralism.

The retreat from multilateralism has been particularly profound in the United States. When elected president, Donald Trump told the NATO alliance's leaders that members must contribute their fair share. Although European members of NATO agreed to devote 2 percent of their countries' gross domestic product to defense by 2024, only five of the twenty-nine members currently do so. Trump repeatedly uses the term "obsolete" to describe NATO after the collapse of the Soviet Union. On the economic front, the Trump administration renegotiated NAFTA. Although the treaty needed to be modernized, were the United States to withdraw completely, it could result in significant disruption of North American production chains and cause job losses in all three countries.[29] If the United States does not ratify the successor agreement—the US–Mexico–Canada Agreement—the trading status among NAFTA signatories may fall into limbo. Trump's announcement that he would impose steep tariffs on steel and aluminum left him isolated among G7 allies a year before his actions at the 2018 Canada meeting.[30]

Outside the United States, in the European Union, some citizens perceive cooperation to be more harmful to their well-being than their leaders do. We saw that in the 2016 UK referendum on EU membership, David Cameron, who then led the Conservative government, wanted to stay in. Most members of Parliament supported remaining in the EU. And large businesses, including Britain's influential financial sector, campaigned to remain. Yet those wanting to leave the EU carried the day, arguing that the EU imposes too many rules on business and brings little in return for the membership fees the United Kingdom pays. Immigration figured prominently in the debates, with those wanting to leave also wanting the United Kingdom to resume full control of its borders and restrict the influx of new immigrants. Many wanted Parliament to make all of the United Kingdom's own laws, as opposed to sharing decision making with other EU states.[31] The 2018 Italian national elections likewise raised questions about future EU collaborations when voters supported politicians who openly questioned the wisdom of using the euro.

Yet on some issue areas, such as the environment, citizens have forged ahead, seeking cooperation where states have been unable to act. After the US president vowed to withdraw from the United Nations climate talks in November 2017, a group of Americans attended nonetheless. Michael R. Bloomberg, the former mayor of New York, donated more than a million dollars in private funds toward an American pavilion, where participants vowed to commit the United States to reducing planet-warming CO_2 emissions, setting up an odd competition with the official US delegation, which took a less public profile. One group associated with Bloomberg issued a report that if the institutions working with him were a separate country, it would be the third largest in the world, after the United States and China.[32]

Nonstate Actors across Time

Across each historical stage of multilateralism, a range of both public and private actors have participated in efforts at global cooperation. At the most basic level, states participate through official representatives who vote on specific policy programs. Actors outside the state have participated through a variety of official and unofficial activities. Prominent individuals can serve on international delegations in a private or official capacity even if the state is not itself a member. Individuals in democracies can belong to voluntary organizations that seek certain goals within international forums, and they can donate financial resources to these organizations. Nongovernmental organizations can hold official status, such as they do in UN forums, and they can protest other official gatherings where they do not, such as at meetings of the World Economic Forum. NGOs also work in concert with IOs to provide services. Prominent philanthropies can provide monies directly to the organizations in question, or to NGOs, so that they can represent alternative views at meetings. For-profit entities such as banks and other firms can attend meetings in an official capacity, and they can act in concert with other organizations by providing private development finance, such as they do when they purchase the bonds of the World Bank or provide additional funds in IMF standby arrangements. Moreover, they can also work behind the scenes through political institutions, for example, legislatures, in powerful countries to influence results in IOs. Even governments engage in a range of participatory activities, depending on the diplomatic rank of individuals selected to represent the state at a meeting or conference.

In addition, individuals, groups, and institutions increasingly participate in IOs and influence outcomes even when a given state is not a formal member of the organization and has no voting rights attached. We saw that as far back as the 1920s, private American citizens and philanthropies donated resources to the League of Nations, despite the lack of formal US membership. Indigenous peoples of trust territories sought to influence the workings of the early UN, despite the lack of sovereign statehood. Other examples of participation without membership abound, such as postcolonial states' de facto status in the GATT before the Uruguay Round.[33]

New problems will only continue to emerge and new efforts will accompany them, with an ever-widening range of individuals, groups, and institutions participating. For example, the effects of climate change have accelerated the melting of sea ice in the Arctic, opening a region that had previously been protected by its harsh environment. In 1996, states with territories in the Arctic agreed to organize these issues into a forum, and that year, the Arctic Council was officially established, albeit without its own legal personality.[34] They included six organizations representing Arctic indigenous peoples as Permanent Participants, including the Aleut International Association, Arctic Athabaskan Council, Gwich'in Council International, Inuit Circumpolar Council, Russian Association of Indigenous Peoples of the North, and Saami Council.[35] In 2013, at its ministerial meeting in Kiruna, Sweden, the Arctic Council agreed to grant non-Arctic states permanent observer status, whereas previously they had been ad hoc observers.

Democratic or undemocratic, states offer activists a limited range of institutions they can approach to influence policy. The international system broadens that range exponentially. When one venue is unfavorable, they can try somewhere else.[36] One of the key insights of international relations has been that states take their interests to IOs where they hold a strategic advantage in voting outcomes.[37] Keck and Sikkink demonstrate that nonstate activist networks can take an issue out of a domestic venue where it has been blocked and try to move it into an international or foreign venue where pressure can then be brought to bear from outside.[38] Along the same lines, yet connected to a completely different set of states and interest groups, both for-profit and not-for-profit global actors from within advanced industrial states similarly shift venues to suit their strategic advantage. These newer actors have begun to participate in policy debates by voicing their concerns. Nonetheless, older actors continue to operate behind the scenes by providing money for financial activities that suit their interests.[39]

Yet just because interest groups operate in the public sphere, they are far from equal, depending on the audience they seek to influence and their position in the social hierarchy. Studies of domestic interest groups in the United States note that powerful groups seek private resolution of their demands and weaker groups seek public resolution. By going public, weaker groups raise the visibility of a given conflict, widen its scope, and make certain that the power ratio among private interests will not prevail. Nonetheless, if literally *everyone* were *equally* involved the pressure system, there would be a stalemate where they all converged.[40]

In IOs, a range of interest groups operates both inside and outside the public sphere to resolve political issues, and the activities of some actors either consciously or unconsciously can reinforce barriers to the public airing of some conflicts. Many authors take a relatively sanguine view of participation as beneficial to the world community when the participants are NGOs because they understand them to be motivated by a common good.[41] Observers of IOs from outside the academy take a less sanguine view. They question the representative nature of NGOs participating in economic development, due to their intrinsic lack of accountability to the populations affected by global policies.[42] Any consideration of domestic political institutions immediately reveals that some countries have associations or groups that are independent of the government, and others do not.[43] Marxist criticisms characterize NGOs as a new petite bourgeoisie who seek to lead and "speak 'for' the poor" yet fail to acknowledge their own role in the class struggle.[44] At the extreme end of these criticisms, authors emphasize the role of transnational corporations as well as NGOs in international agenda setting and argue that their activities are responsible for the imposition of broader patterns of economic and cultural globalization.[45]

Given this distribution of independent associations that could qualify as NGOs, nongovernmental organizations tend to have a northern global orientation, and their success in generating norms and change in societal relations at the social level cannot be separated from their origins and funding in the North when viewed from the South.[46] However, the weaker NGOs do not necessarily represent the entire world community simply because they are weaker. Most of the world community may, in fact, be completely excluded from the international pressure system. Having access to the system requires financial resources, as well as access to offices in Washington, DC, or New York, depending on the issue. These requirements are not practical for most NGOs from the global South, which are dependent on northern-based NGOs for funding and a presence in Washington or New York.[47] Sangeeta Kamat points out that national and international agencies can serve to legitimate certain NGOs at the expense of others. However, these legitimated NGOs are really only one specific kind, even though the term NGO is used as if it were universal.[48] Therefore, entire groups may not be represented at all.

Less Industrialized Countries

State members of IOs from developing countries have had a different relationship with IOs and NGOs throughout all of their respective histories. For at least the first one hundred years we have examined, much of the world's population lived under some type of colonial arrangement. The European member states that originally constituted the multilateral form did not transmit the same notions of territory, sovereignty, and nationality to colonial states.[49] African colonial territories in particular were considered sovereign voids where the most lasting legacy of the period is territory.[50] The colonial state had no distinctive interests of its own, except as part of the larger empire.[51]

Decolonization brought sovereignty to these territories, but it also created states that were limited in their capacity or desire to provide the civil and socioeconomic goods and welfare benefits that their former colonial authorities could offer. Thus, international society supported them, and they became members of the UN. But true political and economic independence was less easily obtained.[52] In the view of some analysts, IOs took on the colonial powers' tasks, with the exception of directly administering them; development became the task of a set of agencies to provide material support that the colonial power formerly had offered.[53] Representatives of these states organized into blocs and pressed for their concerns as a group, yet the diversity of this group prevented it from articulating specific common goals.

In the years after the decolonization movement ended, different areas of the developing world industrialized at varying rates and with different degrees of success. The former third world is no longer a collective monolith attempting to pursue the same goals.[54] Some states have profited from regional efforts at multilateralism, whereas others have failed to develop state capacity and have had to cope with declining aid flows since 1993.[55] Efforts to organize collective action along the lines that initially appeared with the Bandung Conference and the UNCTAD conferences of the 1960s have fallen apart as new groupings have emerged in their place based on shared economic or geographic circumstances. Some former developing countries, such as China, act as global lenders in the contemporary world economy and have private sources of finance available, calling into question why they would even approach an entity like the World Bank for loans. Other countries, such as the Heavily Indebted Poor Countries, are left with almost no other options than to borrow from bilateral or multilateral sources. Reform efforts seek to resolve these conundrums but meet with entrenched political opposition in developed and developing countries alike.

Yet the enduring geographical division of states preserves some aspects of the G77 in the UN development system and impedes reform. States continue to try to maximize their bilateral influence at the expense of the benefits that accrue to multilateral cooperation.[56] Despite calls for necessary reform, donor and recipient states fail to endorse any ambitious proposals to the system. Both sides are reluctant to delegate authority to an IO because they fear that a more autonomous UN development system will disadvantage their position in the United Nations against their global counterparts.

The Future of Multilateralism

What conclusions can we draw from an examination of the history of multilateralism? The concept includes a range of governmental, quasi-governmental, and private, citizen-based activities wherein states act deliberately with others to realize objectives in particular issue areas. These arrangements have defined and stabilized the international property rights of states, managed coordination problems among them, and helped to resolve the problems with collaboration. However, the mostly task-specific IOs created after World War II are in retreat. In the absence of distinct jurisdictions, IOs can appear to do more and do less simultaneously. Some IOs can become so bureaucratized that they can appear to suffer from their own unique pathologies. In the years following their creation, they do not necessarily do what their creators intended. Rather, they hold a type of power that is independent of their creators, and they construct entirely new categories of actors and interests.[57]

Our first conclusion, therefore, is that multilateralism is constantly being reorganized and renegotiated. The social dislocation of war and the advances of the Industrial Revolution create problems that states attempt to solve with domestic politics, yet they cannot solve many of these problems alone. Over time, peoples and states have attempted to address obstacles with networks of individuals, international social movements, philanthropic associations, and international organizations. When it seems as if the concept of multilateralism has met an insurmountable impediment, such as World War I or World War II, new forms of the old solutions have arisen in its wake and have tried to realize objectives in particular issue areas.

As multilateralism has become embedded in formal IOs after World War II, these IOs take on some tasks and discard others in response to the needs and interests of the major world powers, their own funding capacities, and the broader global context. Trade, for example, has been handled through treaties and then through competing IOs, UNCTAD and the GATT, as each sought to serve as the platform for negotiations and dispute settlement. Eventually, the GATT emerged as the main forum, with UNCTAD adjusting to take on a complementary role. After World War II, the OECD, IMF, and BIS each handled an aspect of the governance of global finance. By the late twentieth century, the OECD found a niche as a research organization with a special competence as a statistical agency. The BIS hosts several groupings of states on banking-related themes and retains a role in international banking activities. Informal groupings such as the Financial Stability Forum bring together officials from finance ministries and central banks. The IMF has likewise altered its responsibilities, shifting from stabilization fund to crisis fighter to facilitating the activities of crisis management. A significant amount of overlap in responsibilities has been seen among the UN, UNDP, World Bank, and IMF in the field of development. Perhaps the roles of the IOs addressing national security have changed the most, with different opportunities, possibilities, and failures among NATO and the UN Security Council in the postwar era. Finally, most IOs have taken a role in the governance of some aspect of the environment, while new IOs altogether have been created to address these same problems.

A second, related conclusion is that as a result of these shifts among IOs, future issues will not be handled in discrete IOs, and principles associated with them will become further intermingled. For example, animal, human, and environmental health are connected to one another in such a way that new concepts, such as "one health," are used as a way of understanding why disease outbreaks occur, when and where they do, and how to stop them from spreading. Interconnected initiatives do not just require states to cooperate. Academic disciplines, professional associations, and bureaucratic agencies that may not have seen themselves as pursuing the same endeavors in the past are reconsidering their connections to one another and the global ecosystem.[58] The environmental devastation of war has generally been considered a byproduct of conflict; however, it is also a strategy in war. Whereas scholars of humanitarian law and human rights have tended to focus on efforts to prevent and punish a set of egregious crimes against humanity, international humanitarian law can also be used to formulate a distinction between legitimate and illegitimate destruction of nature, wherein nature can be seen not only as property but as a combatant and even a victim. Such reconceptualizations bring together insights from scholars of environmental justice with those studying the laws of war and international criminal justice.[59]

A third conclusion is that the range of governmental, quasi-governmental, and private, citizen-based activities associated with multilateralism will continue to widen, foster, and fund its activities. International organizations have never solved the dilemma of consistent access to revenue streams independent of power politics. Private philanthropies have filled the gaps since the early twentieth century. In the contemporary era, we have seen that private philanthropies have stepped up to fund multilateral activities through a range of mechanisms, be it through collaboration with programs, individual contributions, research, or outright payments. Likewise, citizen activist groups have existed and contributed to multilateralism as long as both have existed. We saw that they grew with the explosion of activism in the United States in the 1970s connected to the end of the war in Vietnam, the civil rights movement, environmental activism, and eventually poverty relief. Yet they became more transnational at the end of the Cold War. Even as formal IOs have confronted serious obstacles, the work of NGOs has cut across state borders through individual appeals to citizens in advanced industrial economies. Moreover, they have worked in coalitions on behalf of IOs through domestic democratic mechanisms to influence policy outcomes on issues, such as debt relief for poor countries and human rights, that were previously unimaginable.

A fourth conclusion concerns the ambivalent role of the United States in multilateral efforts. Although the current American posture toward IOs may seem novel, US reticence with respect to multilateralism is long-standing. We saw that individual Americans, businesses, and philanthropies have supported such initiatives across time, yet presidential administrations have pursued unilateral policies, and Congress has exhibited outright hostility to some IOs since their founding. For example, the US rejection of membership in the League of Nations that was the brainchild of the American president speaks to this ambivalence. In order to compensate for the official position, Americans frequently devise unique solutions to participation, such as we saw with private American banks taking up the US subscription to the Bank for International Settlements in the interwar period, or with American philanthropies making major gifts to the League of Nations despite the lack of the nation's membership. This tradition continues. For example, we saw that Michael R. Bloomberg has made large personal donations toward transnational environmental activism in both public and private spheres.

As the United States retreats, other countries move on without it. Thus, US participation in multilateral efforts strengthens them, but it is not the only factor required. In November 2017, eleven countries announced that they would resurrect the Trans-Pacific Partnership after the United States withdrew; among them were Mexico and Canada—the American NAFTA partners. The United States may have lost its leadership role, but the American loss is far from a repudiation of multilateralism in trade. China's rise as a regional and economic power has propelled other nations in the region to join with it or to counter it. Even without the United States, the Trans-Pacific Partnership would be the largest trade agreement in history, increasing protections for intellectual property in some countries while opening more markets to free trade in agricultural products and digital services. The effects of its provisions on improving working conditions are debated.[60]

The future of Russia and the West remains an open question. The 1990s' expansion of NATO occurred against the wishes of the Russian leadership and despite assurances that such an expansion would not occur.[61] The question of the future of NATO heated up over the Russian invasion of Ukraine in 2014 and its meddling in elections in the United States and France, indicating renewed Russian aggression toward the West. In his own defense, Putin argues that these actions were necessary to respond to a Western plot to isolate, humiliate, and eventually destroy Russia.

Conclusion

The contemporary world order poses a new paradox for advanced industrial economies. How can international bodies and agreements build authority and capacity at the international level without threatening the accountability and responsiveness in liberal democratic states at home? We have seen that the progress that accompanies scientific advances and industrial production alters politics within individual states and international society. Thus, it creates problems across time and geography and in an ever-growing number of areas. Difficulties constantly appear, and new efforts at management or resolution are necessary to accompany them—sometimes successfully, sometimes not. If we understand multilateralism to be the coordination of relations among three or more states in accordance with certain principles, the dilemmas of the earliest multilateral efforts persist because disagreement on the principles persists.

Looking back at the League of Nations and forward at the United Nations in 1946, David Mitrany argued that "society will develop by our living it, not by policing it."[62] For Mitrany, peace-building activities develop and succeed not only by preventing conflict—as important as that is—but also by working on the real tasks of our common society: the conquest of poverty, disease, and ignorance.[63] In our day, the old national loyalties continue to tug at cosmopolitan solutions, particularly in advanced industrial democracies where voters can influence policy outcomes. Digital technology brings information to the masses, and misinformation along with it. The flow of people, goods, services, knowledge, and environmental conditions have dramatically altered the spatial dimensions of global health. Contemporary wars have produced refugee crises around the globe that compound the suffering of so many. Thus, the search for multilateral solutions remains compulsory because we live in an international society, and not just because we need to police it. Despite setbacks, catastrophes will also drive states and citizens to attempt future progress. While incremental reform will not be enough to meet the challenges of multilateralism, new forms will undoubtedly appear and present new ways of going forward.

1782   Scottish engineer James Watt patents a double-acting steam engine with a piston that pushes as well as pulls. Improvements on existing machines allow the steam engine to power a wide range of manufacturing machinery and fuel the Industrial Revolution in subsequent years.

1815   After the Napoleonic Wars, the Congress of Vienna is held and ushers in the concert system of diplomatic consultations among the European Great Powers.

1848   Gold is discovered in California.

1851   Gold is discovered in Australia.
        The first International Sanitary Conference is held in Paris in order to harmonize and reduce the conflicting maritime quarantine restrictions of European countries.

1853   The Crimean War begins in the Balkans.

1856   The Crimean War ends with the Treaty of Paris.

1859   The Second Italian War of Independence (Italian campaign) is fought, and the Battle of Solferino inspires Henry Dunant to propose an international humanitarian organization.

1861   The American Civil War begins with the Battle of Fort Sumter.

1862   Henry Dunant publishes *A Memory of Solferino*.

1863   The organizing conference for a Red Cross is held in Geneva, Switzerland.

1864   The first Geneva Convention for the Amelioration of the Condition of the Wounded in Armies in the Field is held. Participants adopt the first of four treaties of the Geneva Conventions, which are linked to the International Committee of the Red Cross.

1865   The American Civil War ends in April with Robert E. Lee surrendering to Ulysses S. Grant at Appomattox Courthouse, Virginia.

The International Telegraph Union is established by agreement at a convention in Paris in May. It establishes a set of standards, such as Morse code for international transmissions.

1871   Germany is unified following the Franco-Prussian War and adopts the gold standard.

1872   Yellowstone National Park is created in the United States, the first of its kind intended to be set aside so that it would not become spoiled with commerce as Niagara Falls had been.

1874   The General Postal Union (the original name of the Universal Postal Union) is established with headquarters in Bern, Switzerland.

1884   The International Meridian Conference is held in Washington, DC, to determine a prime meridian for international use.

1892   The first International Sanitary Convention, addressing cholera, is ratified and comes into force at the seventh International Sanitary Conference held in Venice. Later conventions at subsequent conferences relate to cholera and the prevention of the spread of plague.

Pierre de Coubertin proposes restoring the Olympic games.

1896   The first modern Olympic games are held in Athens, Greece.

1899   The First Hague Convention is signed. The Permanent Court of Arbitration is established as part of the convention in order to facilitate arbitration for differences not settled by diplomacy.

1902   The American republics establish the International Sanitary Bureau, later renamed the Pan American Sanitary Bureau.

1906   Additional treaties are added to the original Geneva Convention.

1907   The International Office of Public Hygiene is established in Paris.

The Second Hague Peace Conference revises and improves rules set forth in the first.

1910   President Theodore Roosevelt proposes a League of Peace in his Nobel Prize address.

The John D. Rockefeller Foundation establishes a Division of Medical Education.

1913	The Rockefeller Foundation creates the International Health Commission to promote public sanitation and the spread of scientific medicine.
1914	The assassination of the Archduke Franz Ferdinand of Austria in Sarajevo triggers World War I.
1915	The League to Enforce Peace is formed at a conference held in Philadelphia.
1918	President Woodrow Wilson outlines his Fourteen Points in a speech to Congress.
	An influenza pandemic infects millions all over the world.
	An armistice ends the fighting of World War I on November 11.
1919	The Treaty of Versailles is signed.
	The International Labour Organization is established.
1920	The League of Nations is founded as a result of the Paris Peace Conference.
1921	The Permanent Court of International Justice is established in The Hague, Netherlands.
1923	The League of Nations Economic and Financial Organization is formed.
1924	The League of Nations Health Organization is formed.
1929	Two additional agreements are added to the Geneva Conventions.
	In October, the US stock market crashes, ushering in the Great Depression of the 1930s.
1930	The Young Plan is accepted at a conference held in The Hague. The Bank for International Settlements subsequently begins operations in Basel, Switzerland.
	The United States imposes the Smoot-Hawley Tariff, the highest in its history.
1931	Japan invades Manchuria, commencing hostilities associated with what became the Second Sino-Japanese War.
1933	Adolf Hitler takes power and withdraws Germany from the League of Nations.
	Japan withdraws from the League of Nations.
1934	The United States joins the International Labour Organization.
	The United States enacts the Reciprocal Trade Agreement Act, giving the president the power to negotiate bilateral trade agreements without receiving prior congressional approval.

1935   Italian leader Benito Mussolini invades Abyssinia (modern-day Ethiopia) and Ethiopian emperor Haile Selassie asks the League of Nations for help.

1936   Germany occupies the Rhineland in direct violation of the Versailles Treaty.

1937   Japan embarks on a full-scale invasion of China, marking the beginning of the Second Sino-Japanese War.

1939   World War II breaks out in Europe when Hitler invades Poland in September.

The League of Nations Assembly transfers enough power to the secretary-general to allow the League to continue to exist legally and carry on reduced operations during the war.

US officials push for the creation of a permanent Inter-American Financial and Economic Advisory Committee to include financial experts from each country.

The Permanent Court of International Justice holds its last public sitting in December.

1940   The Inter-American Financial and Economic Advisory Committee establishes the Inter-American Development Commission in Washington, DC, to aid in Latin American economic diversification and promote complementary enterprises.

1941   President Franklin D. Roosevelt gives his Four Freedoms speech to Congress in January.

Germany invades the USSR in June.

Roosevelt and Prime Minister Winston Churchill release the Atlantic Charter in August, providing a broad statement of American and British war aims, including an outline of a postwar international system.

Japan invades Thailand and attacks the British possessions of Malaya, Singapore, and Hong Kong in December. Japan also attacks Pearl Harbor, Wake Island, Guam, and the Philippines, effectively commencing world war in the Pacific.

1942   Countries at war with the Axis Powers sign the "Declaration by United Nations," pledging to combine their resources to wage war.

1943   The Big Three meet in Tehran, Iran, and agree to create a general international organization designed to promote international peace and security.

1944   The United Nations Monetary and Financial Conference is held in Bretton Woods, New Hampshire, in July, laying the grounds for the future International Monetary Fund and World Bank.

The Dumbarton Oaks talks to formulate a postwar United Nations are held in Washington, DC, from August to October.

1945 Germany surrenders in May and Japan surrenders in August, ending World War II in the Atlantic and Pacific spheres.

The United Nations San Francisco Conference is held from April to June.

1946 The Greek Civil War continues. President Harry Truman argues that the United States has a duty to support free peoples associated with the war, adding to tensions among former allies after World War II that eventually became the Cold War.

The inaugural meetings of the International Monetary Fund and International Bank for Reconstruction and Development are held in Savannah, Georgia.

The Permanent Court of International Justice is dissolved and replaced with the International Court of Justice, the principal judicial organ of the UN system.

The UN Sub-Commission on the Promotion and Protection of Human Rights is created.

1947 India gains independence from Britain, marking the start of the postwar decolonization movement.

The original GATT treaty is signed, anticipating future negotiations to establish an international trade organization.

1948 The United States launches the European Recovery Program, or Marshall Plan.

The Organisation for European Economic Co-operation is established in Paris.

The United Nations Conference on Trade and Employment in Havana, Cuba, ends with the creation of a charter for an International Trade Organization.

The World Health Organization is created as a specialized agency of the UN.

The Universal Declaration of Human Rights is adopted.

1949 Truman delivers his Four Point inaugural speech introducing the concept of development in US foreign policy.

Twelve founding members sign the North Atlantic Treaty in April.

European states establish the Council of Europe as a consultative body in May.

The Geneva Conventions instruct the Red Cross to encourage compliance with international humanitarian law and set out explicit rules for civilian protection.

1950   North Korea invades South Korea in June, triggering the Korean War. The UN Security Council approves a resolution calling for armed force to repel North Korea, approving the use of military force for the first time.

The Truman no longer pursues approval of the International Trade Organization charter, leaving the GATT treaty as the primary multilateral instrument governing trade.

The Office of the UN High Commissioner for Refugees is established in December. It seeks to provide protection for refugees and find permanent solutions for them.

1951   The UN Refugee Convention is approved in July and establishes the principle that signatories will not forcibly return refugees to the country from which they fled.

The European Coal and Steel Community is formed in July.

1952   The Allied military occupation of West Germany ends.

1954   West Germany enters NATO.

1955   The Soviet Union creates the Warsaw Treaty Organization, or Warsaw Pact, in response to West German inclusion in NATO.

The African-Asian Bandung Conference is held in Indonesia.

1957   The Treaties of Rome are signed, establishing the European Economic Community and the European Atomic Energy Community.

1961   Amnesty International is founded.

1962   The Group of Ten industrial countries form to augment the IMF's resources with the General Agreements to Borrow.

1964   The first United Nations Conference on Trade and Development is held.

1966   French president Charles de Gaulle withdraws French troops from NATO but does not withdraw from the alliance.

1967   Negotiators complete the Kennedy Round of multilateral trade negotiations, the high point of tariff negotiations in GATT.

1969   An oil spill devastates the coast of California and prompts the environmental movement in US politics.

1970   The first Earth Day is held on April 22.

1971   Developing countries establish the Group of Twenty-Four to coordinate their positions on monetary and financial development issues in the IMF and World Bank.

The Foreign Trade and Investment Act (Burke-Hartke Bill) is introduced in Congress. Although it does not pass, it would have imposed comprehensive import quotas on goods that competed with American-made products.

President Richard Nixon ends the convertibility of gold for dollars in August.

1972   The United Nations Conference on the Human Environment is held in Stockholm to address environmental issues.

1973   The Tokyo Round of multilateral trade negotiations begins.

The Library Group of finance ministers forms to discuss global monetary issues, which eventually becomes the Group of Seven and Group of Eight when additional states are added and then removed.

1974   Two banking crises—Bankhaus Herstatt and Franklin National Bank— prompt the creation of the Basel Committee on Banking Supervision.

1975   The Basel Committee reaches an agreement—the Concordat—on bank supervision in a consultative capacity.

1977   Additional protocols on the protection of civilians and those no longer able to fight are added to four existing Geneva Conventions.

1979   The Tokyo Round of multilateral trade negotiations is concluded.

Congress reorganizes the Office of the Special Trade Representative. Helsinki Watch is founded.

The European Monetary System becomes operational among European Community members and creates the European Currency Unit.

1981   Peaceful protests take place against US plans to deploy short- and intermediate-range nuclear missiles in West Germany, challenging the NATO alliance from within.

The first cases of AIDS appear in advanced industrial countries.

1982   Mexico approaches default on its sovereign debt, triggering a crisis among international lenders and later crises in Latin American states during the 1980s.

1983   President Ronald Reagan proposes his "Star Wars" initiative, threatening another round of the arms race.

More than a million people in West Germany protest the US deployment of Pershing II and cruise missiles scheduled for December.

1984 In the presidential election held in November, trade becomes a major issue between Republican Ronald Reagan and Democrat Walter Mondale, thus introducing an element of partisanship into the issue where it had not been prominent before.

1985 The Schengen Agreement allowing the free movement of people in Europe is signed.

1986 The Uruguay Round of multilateral trade negotiations begins with a ministerial declaration agreed to in Punta del Este.
The Single European Act in Europe creates a Western European market.

1987 The World Bank creates an Environment Department.
The Montreal Protocol is signed in August to mandate a freeze in the production of substances that deplete the ozone layer of the atmosphere.
The United States and USSR conclude the Intermediate-Range Nuclear Forces treaty in December.
The United States and Canada agree to a bilateral free trade agreement in December.

1988 The Intergovernmental Panel on Climate Change is established.
In the Canadian federal election, the passage of the Canada-US Free Trade Agreement emerges as a contentious issue, making some call it the "free trade election."

1989 The Brady Plan converts Latin American debt into bonds.
The Berlin Wall falls in November, symbolically ending the Cold War.

1990 Iraq invades its neighbor Kuwait in August.
Germany reunifies in August.
The UN Security Council authorizes the use of force against Iraqi leader Saddam Hussein's military in November.

1991 Operation Desert Storm is launched when the United States leads a coalition against Iraq in the Gulf War in January.
Coalition forces and the Iraqi Army sign an armistice in April.
The United States and the Russian Federation sign the Strategic Arms Reduction Treaty in July.
In August, the former Soviet republics become independent states, including Ukraine—and Crimea as part of it.

NATO issues a new Strategic Concept in November, outlining the alliance's nature, purpose, and fundamental security tasks in the new landscape.

The Warsaw Pact and Comecon self-liquidate in December.

Russian president Mikhail Gorbachev survives a coup attempt and resigns in December.

The USSR dissolves in December.

1992   Europeans sign the Maastricht Treaty in February intending to create a single currency as one among many aspects of deeper integration.

The United Nations Conference on Environment and Development, or Earth Summit, is held in June in Rio de Janeiro, Brazil.

The text of the North American Free Trade Agreement (NAFTA) is approved in August.

Eastern European "economies in transition" request working parties to GATT be established.

The UN issues *An Agenda for Peace*, its plan for how to respond to conflict in the post–Cold War world.

The United States intervenes in Somalia in December.

1993   The United States turns over the Somali operation to the UN in May.

The UN Security Council establishes the International Criminal Tribunal for the Former Yugoslavia in May.

The World Conference on Human Rights is held in Vienna in June. As a result, the UN General Assembly creates the UN Office of the High Commissioner for Human Rights.

The Maastricht Treaty comes into force and the EEC is incorporated and renamed as the European Union in November.

Congress approves NAFTA in November.

1994   The Uruguay Round of multilateral trade negotiations ends when the Marrakesh Accords are signed in April. The ministerial Decision on Trade and Environment adopted in Marrakesh calls for the creation of a Committee on Trade and Environment to study the impact of environmental policies on trade.

The UN General Assembly creates an Office of Internal Oversight Services to address issues related to fraud, waste, and abuse.

The UN establishes the International Criminal Tribunal for Rwanda in November.

1995   The World Trade Organization is established under the terms of the
        Uruguay Round in January.
        The Oil-for-Food program is created by a resolution of the UN Secu-
        rity Council. It is intended as a temporary measure to allow Iraq to sell
        enough oil to pay for food and other necessities for its population then
        suffering under UN sanctions after the 1991 Gulf War. The program is
        implemented in 1996 and later becomes plagued with scandals.
        NATO intervenes against Serb actions in Bosnia and Serbia in July.
        The Dayton Peace Accords are signed in the former Yugoslavia in
        December.

1996   States form the Arctic Council to address melting sea ice and open-
        ing of the region to commerce.

1997   Russia and the West sign the NATO-Russia Founding Act in May,
        giving Russia a consultative standing in the organization.
        The Asian financial crisis emerges in July and spreads to Russia and
        Latin America.
        The Kyoto Protocol is signed in December. Signatories agree to cut
        carbon emissions.

1998   The Rome Statute of the International Criminal Court is signed in
        July. The United States is among the signatories.

1999   Eleven continental European states replace their national currencies
        with the euro in January.
        NATO intervenes against Serb forces in Kosovo in March.
        Poland, Hungary, and the Czech Republic become full members of
        NATO in March.
        The Financial Stability Forum initially convenes in April.
        Large-scale WTO protests take place in Seattle, Washington, in
        November.
        The Group of Twenty finance ministers meet to discuss issues among
        leading industrial and emerging-market countries in December.

2000   The Bill and Melinda Gates Foundation is created through the
        merger of existing foundations.
        The Jubilee 2000 campaign leads to the cancellation of the debt of
        thirty-five of the world's poorest countries.

2001   Large-scale antiglobalization protests take place at the G8 summit in
        Genoa, Italy, in July.

On September 11, a series of terrorist attacks occurs in the United States.
The United States and United Kingdom launch Operation Enduring
Freedom in Afghanistan, later joined by other forces, in October.
The Doha Round of multilateral trade negotiations begins in
November.

2002   The United States withdraws its signature from the Rome Statute of
the International Criminal Court in May.
Former US president Bill Clinton conceives of the Clinton HIV/
AIDS Initiative (now Clinton Health Access Initiative) at the International Aids Conference in July.
The International Criminal Court begins to function in July.
The Global Fund to fight HIV/AIDS, Tuberculosis, and Malaria—
the Global Fund—is founded as a partnership among governments,
civil society, the private sector, and people affected by the diseases.

2003   The United States launches an attack on Iraq in defiance of the UN.
Later, the United States gives way to a UN-led process to create a
transitional Iraqi government.
A bomb targets the UN Assistance Mission in Iraq in August.

2004   Seven new members—Bulgaria, Estonia, Latvia, Lithuania, Romania, Slovakia, and Slovenia—formally become members of NATO in
March.
The US occupation of Iraq formally ends in June.

2005   Iraqi elections are held.

2006   The UN Human Rights Commission is replaced by the UN Human
Rights Council.
The UN General Assembly adopts the Convention on the Rights of
Persons with Disabilities.

2007   The Chiang Mai Initiative creates a currency swap network among
members, and they agree to pool foreign exchange reserves in order
to lessen their reliance on the IMF.

2008   The global financial crisis begins in US housing markets.

2009   Albania and Croatia become members of NATO in April.
The Financial Stability Board succeeds the Financial Stability
Forum in April.
Greek election results in October trigger a sovereign debt crisis in
Europe.

The Copenhagen Climate Change Conference is held in December.

2010   The European sovereign debt crisis unfolds.

2011   The UN Human Rights Council issues a report on gay rights.

The Syrian civil war breaks out, contributing to a growing global refugee crisis.

2012   Amid the ongoing European sovereign debt crisis, ECB president Mario Draghi states that the bank will do whatever it takes to preserve the euro, effectively ending the crisis.

2014   The UN faces a serious sex abuse scandal by French peacekeepers in the Central African Republic in January.

Russia invades Crimea in March, prompting international censure.

An Ebola virus outbreak commences in West Africa in March.

European parliamentary election returns in May show rising support for Eurosceptic parties.

Malaysia Airlines Flight 17 is shot down in July. The Dutch-led investigation team concludes that the weapon used had been transported from Russia on the day of the crash, thus holding Russia accountable for the incident.

China proposes plans for an Asian Infrastructure Investment Bank in November.

The United States and NATO combat missions in Afghanistan formally end in December, yet a military presence remains.

2015   The Paris Agreement is signed with the goal of working through voluntary pledges to reduce CO_2 and other gases on climate change.

2016   The EU signs an agreement with Turkey in March obligating asylum-seekers who reach Greece to return to Turkey, challenging the principles of the asylum regime.

NATO allies vote to rotate four battalions through Poland and the Baltic states. They increase air patrols over the same areas in May.

Citizens in the United Kingdom vote in June to leave the EU, commencing Brexit.

The UN Human Rights Council agrees in June to appoint an independent expert to determine the causes of violence and discrimination against people due to their gender identity and sexual orientation.

A series of terrorist attacks at the Bataclan concert hall and other locations in Paris occur in November.

2017   Montenegro becomes a member of NATO in June.

"Welcome to Hell" protests are held at the G20 summit in Hamburg, Germany, in July.

In August, the Donald Trump administration announces its decision to exit the Paris Agreement on climate change.

The Council of Europe issues an International Convention in September against trafficking in human organs.

2018   The Italian elections held in March result in the later formation of a government increasingly confrontational with the EU.

The US declines to sign the G7 summit communiqué in May.

The US imposes tariffs on steel and aluminum in June, threatening a broader global trade war.

2019   British prime minister Theresa May is unable to gain parliamentary passage of a Withdrawal Agreement between the United Kingdom and the EU in the largest majority against a British government in history.

In the May European parliamentary election, mainstream blocs lose their majority for the first time, ceding ground to Greens and Liberals.

NOTES

Preface

1. Michael N. Barnett and Martha Finnemore, "The Politics, Power, and Pathologies of International Organization," *International Organization* 53 (1999): 707–9.
2. John Gerard Ruggie, "Multilateralism: The Anatomy of an Institution," in *Multilateralism Matters: The Theory and Praxis of an Institutional Form*, ed. John Gerard Ruggie (New York: Columbia University Press, 1993), 8.

1 Early Movements toward Multilateralism

1. John Gerard Ruggie, "Multilateralism: The Anatomy of an Institution," in *Multilateralism Matters: The Theory and Praxis of an Institutional Form*, ed. John Gerard Ruggie (New York: Columbia University Press, 1993), 8.
2. Graham Evans and Jeffrey Newnham, *The Penguin Dictionary of International Relations* (New York: Penguin Books, 1998), 340.
3. Craig N. Murphy, "The Last Two Centuries of Global Governance," *Global Governance* 21 (2015): 189.
4. Edward Vose Gulick, *Europe's Classical Balance of Power* (New York: W. W. Norton, 1955), 290.
5. Evans and Newnham, *Penguin Dictionary of International Relations*, 90–91. See also Paul W. Schroeder, *The Transformation of European Politics, 1763–1848* (Oxford: Clarendon Press, 1994); Brian E. Vick, *The Congress of Vienna: Power and Politics after Napoleon* (Cambridge, MA: Harvard University Press, 2014), 4–5.
6. Schroeder, *Transformation*, 802.
7. Murphy, "Last Two Centuries," 190.
8. Barry Eichengreen, *Globalizing Capital: A History of the International Monetary System*, 2nd ed. (Princeton, NJ: Princeton University Press, 1996), 15.

9. Ibid., 17.

10. Ibid., 29.

11. Ibid., 30.

12. Ibid., 40.

13. Craig N. Murphy, *International Organization and Industrial Change: Global Governance since 1850* (New York: Oxford University Press, 1994), 54.

14. Ibid.

15. Ibid., 47.

16. "The 1865 International Telegraph Conference," International Telecommunication Union, http://handle.itu.int/11.1004/020.2000/s.138.

17. "About History," Universal Postal Union, http://www.upu.int/en/the-upu/history/about-history.html.

18. Derek Howse, *Greenwich Time and the Discovery of the Longitude* (New York: Oxford University Press, 1980), xvi.

19. Ibid., 105.

20. Kelley Lee, *Globalization and Health: An Introduction* (London: Palgrave Macmillan, 2003), 48.

21. Ibid., 49.

22. Jeremy Youde, *Global Health Governance* (Cambridge: Polity Press, 2012), 14.

23. Ibid., 15.

24. Ibid., 16.

25. Lee, *Globalization and Health*, 55.

26. Youde, *Global Health Governance*, 13.

27. Schroeder, *Transformation*; Vick, *Congress of Vienna*.

28. Schroeder, *Transformation*, 803.

29. Arthur Pine Van Geider, *History of the Explosives Industry in America* (New York: Columbia University Press, 1927), 930.

30. Devin Poore, "Civil War Submarines," Opinionator (blog), January 27, 2015, https://opinionator.blogs.nytimes.com/2015/01/27/civil-war-submarines.

31. James Joll, *The Origins of the First World War* (New York: Longman, 1984), 125.

32. Ben Cosgrove, "Crimea: Where War Photography Was Born," *Time*, November 30, 2014, http://time.com/3881577/crimea-where-war-photography-was-born/.

33. Vaughn Wallace, "The Backstory: 150 Years Later: Picturing the Bloody Battle of Antietam," *Time*, September 17, 2012, http://time.com/3791584/150-years-later-picturing-the-battle-of-antietam/.

34. Martin Gumpert, *Dunant: The Story of the Red Cross* (New York: Oxford University Press, 1938), 101.

35. Ibid., 77.

36. Violet Kelway Libby, *Henry Dunant: Prophet of Peace* (New York: Pageant Press, 1964), 106.

37. Ibid., 107.

38. Ibid., 115.
39. Ibid., 108.
40. Charlotte Mohr, "Clara Barton," International Committee of the Red Cross, September 27, 2018, http://blogs.icrc.org/cross-files/clara-barton/.
41. Bronwyn Leebaw, "The Politics of Impartial Activism: Humanitarianism and Human Rights," *Perspectives on Politics* 5 (2007): 225.
42. Frederick W. Holls, *The Peace Conference at The Hague and Its Bearing on International Law and Policy* (New York: MacMillan, 1900), 150–51.
43. "History," Permanent Court of International Justice, http://www.icj-cij.org/en/history.
44. Betsy Baker, "Hague Peace Conferences (1899 and 1907)," in *The Max Planck Encyclopedia of Public International Law*, ed. Rüdiger Wolfrum, vol. 4 (Oxford: Oxford University Press, 2009).
45. Inis L. Claude, *Swords into Plowshares: The Problems and Progress of International Organization*, 4th ed. (New York: Random House, 1971), 29.
46. Baker, "Hague Peace Conferences."
47. John J. MacAloon, *This Great Symbol: Pierre de Coubertin and the Origins of the Modern Olympic Games* (Chicago: University of Chicago Press, 1981), 113.
48. Ibid., 137.
49. Norbert Muller, "Coubertin's Olympism," in *Pierre de Coubertin, 1863–1937: Olympism, Selected Writings*, ed. Norbert Muller (Lausanne, Switzerland: International Olympic Committee, 2000), 38.
50. MacAloon, *This Great Symbol*, 268.
51. Ibid., 262.
52. Ibid., 127.
53. Margaret E. Keck and Kathryn Sikkink, *Activists beyond Borders: Advocacy Networks in International Politics* (Ithaca, NY: Cornell University Press, 1998), 34.
54. Ibid., 76.
55. Murphy, *International Organization and Industrial Change*, 159.
56. Hamilton Holt, "The League to Enforce Peace," *Proceedings of the Academy of Political Science in the City of New York* 7 (1917): 258.
57. Ibid., 68.
58. William Howard Taft, "The Proposal for a League to Enforce Peace: Affirmative," Faculty Scholarship Series, Paper 3939 (1916). https://digitalcommonslaw.yale.edu/fss_papers3939 9.
59. Denna Frank Fleming, *The United States and the League of Nations: 1918–1920* (New York: G. P. Putnam's Sons, 1932), 43.
60. See Raymond B. Fosdick, *Letters on the League of Nations from the Files of Raymond B. Fosdick* (Princeton, NJ: Princeton University Press, 1966), vii, 118.
61. Kathryn C. Lavelle, "Exit, Voice, and Loyalty in International Organizations: US Involvement in the League of Nations," *Review of International Organizations* 2 (2007).

62. Charles Howard Howard-Ellis, *The Origin, Structure and Working of the League of Nations* (New York: Houghton Mifflin, 1929), 122.
63. "History," Permanent International Court of Justice.
64. "Origins and History," International Labour Organization, http://ilo.org/global/about-the-ilo/history/lang–en/index.htm.
65. Paul Weindling, "The League of Nations Health Organization and the Rise of Latin American Participation, 1920–40," *História, Ciências, Saúde—Manguinhos* 13 (2006).
66. Louis W. Pauly, "The League of Nations and the Foreshadowing of the International Monetary Fund," *Essays in International Finance* 201 (1996).
67. Martin Hill, *The Economic and Financial Organization of the League of Nations: A Survey of Twenty-Five Years' Experience* (Washington, DC: Carnegie Endowment for International Peace, 1946), 22.
68. Ibid., 4.
69. Fosdick, *Letters on the League*.
70. See Raymond Fosdick, "The League of Nations as an Instrument of Liberalism," *Atlantic Monthly*, October 1920. See also Raymond Fosdick, *Chronicle of a Generation: An Autobiography* (New York: Harper and Brothers, 1958), 225.
71. Fosdick, *Chronicle of a Generation*, 217.
72. Lee, *Globalization and Health*, 57.
73. Youde, *Global Health Governance*, 22.
74. Weindling, "League of Nations Health Organization," 7.
75. Lavelle, "Exit, Voice, and Loyalty," 378.
76. Ibid., 380.
77. Gianni Toniolo, with the assistance of Piet Clement, *Central Bank Cooperation at the Bank for International Settlements, 1930–1973* (New York: Cambridge University Press, 2005), 25.
78. Roger Auboin, "The Bank for International Settlements, 1930–1955," *Essays in International Finance* 22 (1955): 2.
79. Toniolo, *Central Bank Cooperation*.
80. Beth A. Simmons, "Why Innovate? Founding the Bank for International Settlements," *World Politics* 45 (1993): 394, n. 91.
81. Auboin, "Bank for International Settlements," 4.
82. Ibid., 7.
83. Eichengreen, *Globalizing Capital*, 70.
84. Ibid., 76.
85. Martin D. Dubin, "Toward the Bruce Report: The Economic and Social Programs of the League of Nations in the Avenol Era," in *The League of Nations in Retrospect: Proceedings of the Symposium, Geneva, 6–9 November 1980* (Berlin: Walter de Gruyter, 1983), 63.
86. Townsend Hoopes and Douglas Brinkley, *FDR and the Creation of the U.N.* (New Haven: Yale University Press, 1997), 13.

87. Gary B. Ostrower, "The United States and the League of Nations, 1919–1939," in *The League of Nations in Retrospect: Proceedings of the Symposium, Geneva, 6–9 November 1980* (Berlin: Walter de Gruyter, 1983), 124–25.

88. "History," Permanent International Court of Justice.

89. "ILO during the Second World War, 1940," International Labour Organization, http://www.ilo.org/legacy/english/lib/century/index2.htm.

90. Lavelle, "Exit, Voice, and Loyalty."

91. "Origin and Development of Health Cooperation," World Health Organization, http://www.who.int/global_health_histories/background/en/.

92. Toniolo, *Central Bank Cooperation*, 201.

93. Ibid., 214.

94. Ibid., 257–58.

2 The Embryonic Plan for Postwar Multilateralism

1. Four republics established the USSR following the Russian Revolution of 1917. Additional union republics were set up later. The USSR as a whole was under the control of the Supreme Soviet in Moscow. It ceased to exist in this form in 1991, and several successor states have joined IOs in their own capacities.

2. Townsend Hoopes and Douglas Brinkley, *FDR and the Creation of the U.N.* (New Haven: Yale University Press, 1997), 45.

3. Ibid., 9.

4. Anne-Marie Burley (now Slaughter), "Regulating the World: Multilateralism, International Law, and the Projection of the New Deal Regulatory State," in *Multilateralism Matters: The Theory and Praxis of an Institutional Form*, ed. John Gerard Ruggie (New York: Columbia University Press, 1993), 130.

5. David Mitrany, *A Working Peace System: An Argument for the Functional Development of International Organization*, 4th ed. (London: National Peace Council, 1946), 6.

6. John Gerard Ruggie, "Multilateralism: The Anatomy of an Institution," in *Multilateralism Matters: The Theory and Praxis of an Institutional Form*, ed. John Gerard Ruggie (New York: Columbia University Press, 1993), 23.

7. Ibid.

8. Mark Mazower, *No Enchanted Palace: The End of Empire and the Ideological Origin of the United Nations* (Princeton, NJ: Princeton University Press, 2009). See also his *Governing the World: The History of an Idea* (New York: Penguin, 2012).

9. Hoopes and Brinkley, *FDR and the Creation of the U.N.*

10. Charles Prince, "The U.S.S.R. and International Organizations," *American Journal of International Law* 36 (1942): 444–45.

11. Georg Schild, *Bretton Woods and Dumbarton Oaks: American Economic and Political Postwar Planning in the Summer of 1944* (New York: St. Martin's, 1995), 73.

12. Ibid., 57.
13. Lars Schoultz, *Beneath the United States: A History of U.S. Policy toward Latin America* (Cambridge, MA: Harvard University Press, 1998), 290.
14. Ibid., 295.
15. Eric Helleiner, "Reinterpreting Bretton Woods: International Development and the Neglected Origins of Embedded Liberalism," *Development and Change* 37 (2006): 946.
16. James Desmond, *Nelson Rockefeller: A Political Biography* (New York: MacMillan, 1964).
17. Kathryn C. Lavelle, "Exit, Voice, and Loyalty in International Organizations: U.S. Involvement in the League of Nations," *Review of International Organizations* 2 (2007).
18. Helleiner, "Reinterpreting Bretton Woods," 964.
19. Ibid., 961.
20. Schoultz, *Beneath the United States*, 308.
21. Ibid., 308-9.
22. Ibid., 312.
23. This history is covered in several historical and theoretical accounts. See Eric Helleiner, *States and the Reemergence of Global Finance: From Bretton Woods to the 1990s* (Ithaca, NY: Cornell University Press, 1994); Jacqueline Best, *The Limits of Transparency: Ambiguity and the History of International Finance* (Ithaca, NY: Cornell University Press, 2005); and Robert Skidelsky, *John Maynard Keynes: Fighting for Freedom, 1937–1946*, vol. 3 (New York: Viking, 2000).
24. Ariel Buira, "The Governance of the IMF in a Global Economy," in *Challenges to the World Bank and IMF: Developing Country Perspectives*, ed. Ariel Buira (New York: Anthem Press, 2003), 19.
25. Ibid., 15.
26. Helleiner, "Reinterpreting Bretton Woods," 961.
27. Jacques Fomerand, "Mirror, Tool, or Linchpin for Change: The UN and Development" (Waterloo, ON: Academic Council on the United Nations System, 2003).
28. Eric Helleiner, "The Development Mandate of International Institutions: Where Did It Come From?," *Studies in Comparative International Development* 44 (2009): 204.
29. For a discussion of the differences, see Schild, *Bretton Woods and Dumbarton Oaks*, 142.
30. Hoopes and Brinkley, *FDR and the Creation of the U.N.*, 145.
31. Schild, *Bretton Woods and Dumbarton Oaks*, 187.
32. Hoopes and Brinkley, *FDR and the Creation of the U.N.*, 193.
33. Cary Reich, *The Life of Nelson A. Rockefeller: Worlds to Conquer, 1908–1958* (New York: Doubleday, 1996).

34. Darlene Rivas, *Missionary Capitalist: Nelson Rockefeller in Venezuela* (Chapel Hill: University of North Carolina Press, 2002).

35. Reich, *Life of Rockefeller*, 332.

36. Ibid., 355.

37. John Toye and Richard Toye, *The UN and Global Political Economy: Trade, Finance, and Development* (Indianapolis: Indiana University Press, 2004), 36–37.

38. Reich, *Life of Rockefeller*, 332.

39. Bruce Muirhead, *Against the Odds: The Public Life and Times of Louis Rasminsky* (Toronto: University of Toronto Press, 1999), 115.

40. This episode is considered significant in the history of the family because it revealed that John D. Rockefeller Jr. still controlled the family's money. Reich, *Life of Rockefeller*, 387.

41. Brian Hocking and Dominic Kelly, "Doing the Business? The International Chamber of Commerce, the United Nations, and the Global Compact," in *Enhancing Global Governance: Towards a New Diplomacy*, ed. Andrew F. Cooper, John English, and Ramesh Thakur (New York: United Nations University Press, 2002), 214.

42. Walter R. Sharp, *The United Nations Economic and Social Council* (New York: Columbia University Press, 1969), 36.

43. Inis L. Claude, *Swords into Plowshares: The Problems and Progress of International Organization*, 4th ed. (New York: Random House, 1971), 77.

44. Hoopes and Brinkley, *FDR and the Creation of the U.N.*, 86.

45. Stephen C. Schlesinger, *Act of Creation: The Founding of the United Nations* (Boulder, CO: Westview, 2003), 53.

46. Schild, *Bretton Woods and Dumbarton Oaks*, 183. This discussion of the domestic American efforts to secure passage of Bretton Woods draws heavily on Kathryn C. Lavelle, *Legislating International Organization: The U.S. Congress, the IMF, and the World Bank* (New York: Oxford University Press, 2011).

47. Helleiner, *States and the Reemergence of Global Finance*, 47–48.

48. Ibid., 43–44.

49. Muirhead, *Against the Odds*, 110.

50. Ibid., 111.

51. Sidney Dell uses the term "grandmotherly" to describe the desired characteristic of the IMF. See Sidney Dell, "On Being Grandmotherly: The Evolution of IMF Conditionality," *Essays in International Finance* 144 (1981).

52. Ibid., 10.

53. Richard E. Rupp, *NATO after 9/11: An Alliance in Continuing Decline* (New York: Palgrave Macmillan, 2006), 40. Causes for the Cold War are debated. For an early review of different historical understandings, see Arthur Schlesinger Jr., "Origins of the Cold War," *Foreign Affairs* 46 (1967).

54. Wayne C. McWilliams and Harry Piotrowski, *The World since 1945: A History of International Relations*, 7th ed. (Boulder, CO: Lynne Rienner, 2009), 42, 45.

55. Ibid., 45.
56. Rupp, *NATO after 9/11*, 41.
57. McWilliams and Piotrowski, *World since 1945*, 43.
58. Ibid., 63–64.
59. Rupp, *NATO after 9/11*, 45.
60. Ibid.
61. Ibid., 46–47.
62. Ibid., 48.
63. "Founding Treaty," North Atlantic Treaty Organization, January 30, 2017, http://www.nato.int/cps/en/natolive/topics_67656.htm.
64. Lord Ismay quoted in Joseph S. Nye Jr., *The Paradox of American Power: Why the World's Only Superpower Can't Go It Alone* (New York: Oxford University Press, 2002), 33.
65. McWilliams and Piotrowski, *World since 1945*, 80.
66. Ibid., 83.
67. Ibid., 84.
68. Ibid., 86.
69. Desmond Dinan, "How Did We Get Here?," in *The European Union: How Does It Work?*, ed. Elizabeth Bomberg, John Peterson, and Richard Corbett (New York: Oxford University Press, 2012), 25.
70. Ibid.
71. Richard Woodward, *The Organisation for Economic Co-Operation and Development (OECD)* (New York: Routledge, 2009), 14.
72. The successor to the OEEC is the Organization for Economic Cooperation and Development (OECD).
73. Woodward, *Organisation for Economic Co-Operation and Development*, 15–16.
74. Paul Kubicek, *European Politics*, 2nd ed. (New York: Routledge, 2017), 77.
75. Graham Evans and Jeffrey Newnham, *The Penguin Dictionary of International Relations* (New York: Penguin Books, 1998), 158.
76. Dinan, "How Did We Get Here?," 27; Kubicek, *European Politics*, 77.
77. Derek W. Urwin, "The European Community: From 1945 to 1985," in *European Union Politics*, ed. Michelle Cini and Nieves Perez-Solorzano Borragan (New York: Oxford University Press, 2013), 16.
78. Dinan, "How Did We Get Here?," 30.
79. Urwin, "European Community," 18.
80. Roger Scully, *Becoming Europeans? Attitudes, Behaviour, and Socialization in the European Parliament* (New York: Oxford University Press, 2005), 22–23.
81. Dinan, "How Did We Get Here?," 32.
82. Ibid., 35; Kubicek, *European Politics*, 80.
83. Urwin, "European Community," 20.
84. Ibid., 13.

3 Decolonization and Development

1. Kathryn C. Lavelle, *The Politics of Equity Finance in Emerging Markets* (New York: Oxford University Press, 2004).

2. For some examples from different parts of the world, see Albert O. Hirschman, "The Political Economy of Import-Substituting Industrialization in Latin America," *Quarterly Journal of Economics* 83 (1968): 6; Peter Evans, *Dependent Development: The Alliance of Multinational, State, and Local Capital in Brazil* (Princeton, NJ: Princeton University Press, 1979); Ralph Austen, *African Economic History: Internal Development and External Dependency* (Portsmouth, NH: Heinemann, 1987); and John H. Coatsworth, "Economic Institutional Trajectories in Nineteenth-Century Latin America," in *Latin America and the World Economy since 1800*, ed. John H. Coatsworth and Alan M. Taylor (Cambridge, MA: Harvard University Press, 1998).

3. Robert H. Jackson, "The Weight of Ideas in Decolonization: Normative Change in International Relations," in *Ideas and Foreign Policy: Beliefs, Institutions, and Political Change*, ed. Judith Goldstein and Robert Keohane (Ithaca, NY: Cornell University Press, 1993), 136.

4. Robert H. Jackson, *Quasi-States: Sovereignty, International Relations, and the Third World* (New York: Cambridge University Press, 1990), 16.

5. Ibid., 113.

6. Eric Helleiner, "The Triffin Missions: American Financial Advisors and the Good Neighbor Policy" (paper presented at the Annual Meeting of the International Studies Association, San Diego, CA, 2006).

7. Gary B. Ostrower, *The League of Nations from 1919 to 1929* (Garden City, NY: Avery, 1996), 79.

8. "Consideration of Questions Affecting the Participation of Indigenous Inhabitants in the Work of the Trusteeship Council," page 1, box 4, DAG 5/2.2 S-504-0038, United Nations Archives, New York.

9. Sir Arthur Salter, "Foreign Investment," *Essays in International Finance* 12 (1951): 47.

10. Benyamin Neuberger, *National Self-Determination in Postcolonial Africa* (Boulder, CO: Lynne Rienner, 1986), 20.

11. Ibid., 7.

12. Ibid.; Jackson, "Weight of Ideas in Decolonization," 122.

13. Jackson, *Quasi-States*, 5.

14. See "India and United Nations," Ministry of External Affairs, Government of India, http://www.mea.gov.in/india-and-the-united-nations.htm.

15. David Williams, *International Development and Global Politics* (New York: Routledge, 2012), 12.

16. Stephen Browne, *United Nations Development Programme and System* (New York: Routledge, 2011), 9.

17. Ibid., 3.
18. John Toye and Richard Toye, *The UN and Global Political Economy: Trade, Finance, and Development* (Bloomington: Indiana University Press, 2004), 113, 25. See also Richard Jolly et al., *UN Contributions to Development Thinking and Practice* (Bloomington: Indiana University Press, 2004).
19. D. John Shaw, "Turning Point in the Evolution of Soft Financing: The United Nations and the World Bank," *Canadian Journal of Development Studies* 26 (2005): 44.
20. Ibid., 48.
21. Craig Murphy, *The United Nations Development Programme: A Better Way?* (New York: Cambridge University Press, 2006), 58.
22. B. E. Matecki, *Establishment of the International Finance Corporation and United States Policy* (New York: Frederick A. Praeger, 1957), 46; Robert E. Asher, Walter M. Kotschnig, and William Adams Brown Jr., *The United Nations and Economic and Social Co-Operation* (Washington, DC: Brookings Institution, 1957), 216; Kathryn C. Lavelle, "The International Finance Corporation and the Emerging Markets Funds Industry," *Third World Quarterly* 21 (2000).
23. Jonas Haralz, "The International Finance Corporation," in *The World Bank: Its First Half Century*, ed. Devesh Kapur, John P. Lewis, and Richard Webb (Washington, DC: Brookings Institution Press, 1997), 811.
24. Ibid., 819.
25. K. P. Saksena, *Reforming the United Nations: The Challenge of Relevance* (London: Sage, 1993).
26. Karl P. Sauvant, *G-77: Evolution, Structure, Organization* (New York: Oceana, 1981), 1.
27. Ibid., 10.
28. Robert Cutler, "East-South Relations at UNCTAD: Global Political Economy and the CMEA," *International Organization* 37 (1983): 24.
29. A. S. Friedberg, *The United Nations Conference on Trade and Development of 1964: The Theory of the Peripheral Economy at the Centre of International Political Discussions* (Rotterdam: Rotterdam University Press, 1969).
30. Ibid., 98.
31. Sauvant, *G-77: Evolution, Structure, Organization*, 37. See also Kathryn C. Lavelle, "Sovereign Debt Restructuring: Alliances Crossing the Financial Services Industry, States, and Non-Governmental Organizations," in *The Challenges of Global Business Authority: Democratic Renewal, Stalemate, or Decay?*, ed. Tony Porter and Karsten Ronit (Albany: SUNY Press, 2010).
32. Craig N. Murphy, *The Emergence of the NIEO Ideology* (Boulder, Colorado: Westview Press, 1984), 40.
33. Ibid. See also Kathryn C. Lavelle, "Ideas within a Context of Power: The Africa Group in an Evolving UNCTAD," *Journal of Modern African Studies* 39 (2001).

34. See Sauvant, *G-77: Evolution, Structure, Organization*; Robert L. Rothstein, *UNCTAD and the Quest for a New International Economic Order* (Princeton, NJ: Princeton University Press, 1979); Jeffrey Hart, *The NIEO: Conflict and Cooperation in North-South Economic Relations, 1974–1977* (New York: St. Martin's Press, 1983); Craig N. Murphy, *International Organization and Industrial Change: Global Governance since 1850* (New York: Oxford University Press, 1994); and Robert L. Rothstein, "Epitaph for a Monument to a Failed Protest?," *International Organization* 42 (1988).

35. Friedberg, *Theory of the Peripheral Economy*, 96.

36. Chakravarth Raghavan, *Recolonization, GATT, the Uruguay Round and the Third World* (Atlantic Highlands, NJ: Zed Books, 1990), 51.

37. Ibid., 63.

38. Kevin Watkins, *Fixing the Rules: North-South Issues in International Trade and the GATT Uruguay Round* (London: Catholic Institute for International Relations, 1992), 36.

39. In 1988 (and for purposes of the Uruguay Round), the least developed countries contracting parties were Bangladesh, Benin, Botswana, Burkina Faso, Burma, Burundi, Central African Republic, Chad, Gambia, Haiti, Lesotho, Malawi, Maldives, Mauritania, Niger, Rwanda, Sierra Leone, Tanzania, Togo, and Uganda. De facto contracting parties were Cape Verde, Equatorial Guinea, Guinea-Bissau, Kiribati, Mali, Mozambique, São Tomé and Principe, Tuvalu, and Yemen Democratic Republic. Seven other least developed countries had a "working relationship" with the GATT.

40. Sauvant, *G-77: Evolution, Structure, Organization*, 5.

41. The membership of the G24 is segmented into regions. When it was established, the African Group's members were Algeria, Côte d'Ivoire, the Democratic Republic of Congo, Egypt, Ethiopia, Gabon, Ghana, Nigeria, and South Africa. The Latin America and the Caribbean Group's members were Argentina, Brazil, Colombia, Guatemala, Mexico, Peru, Trinidad and Tobago, and Venezuela. The membership of the Asian Group comprised India, Iran, Lebanon, Pakistan, the Philippines, Sri Lanka, and the Syrian Arab Republic. China joined in 1981 as a "Special Invitee," and Ecuador, Haiti, Kenya, and Morocco were added in 2017.

42. See Albert Fishlow, "A New International Economic Order: What Kind?," in *Rich and Poor Nations in the World Economy*, ed. Albert Fishlow et al. (New York: McGraw-Hill, 1978); Hart, *NIEO: Conflict and Cooperation*.

43. Jochen Kraske, *Bankers with a Mission: The Presidents of the World Bank, 1946–91* (New York: Oxford University Press, 1996), 22.

44. Kai Bird, *The Chairman: John J. McCloy* (New York: Simon and Schuster, 1992), 283.

45. Kathryn C. Lavelle, "American Politics, the Presidency of the World Bank, and Development Policy" (policy research working paper, World Bank, Washington, DC, 2013).

46. Lavelle, *Legislating International Organization: The US Congress, the IMF, and the World Bank* (New York: Oxford University Press, 2011), 70.

47. Ibid., 68.

48. Edward S. Mason and Robert E. Asher, *The World Bank since Bretton Woods* (Washington, DC: Brookings Institution, 1973), 134.

49. Ibid., 570.

50. Robert W. Oliver, *George Woods and the World Bank* (Boulder, CO: Lynne Rienner, 1995).

51. Robert S. McNamara, *The McNamara Years at the World Bank: Major Policy Addresses of Robert S. McNamara, 1968–1981* (Baltimore: Johns Hopkins University Press, 1981), 49.

52. Robert S. McNamara, interview by John Lewis, Richard Webb, and Devesh Kapur, April 1, May 10, October 3, 1991, transcript, World Bank History Project, Brookings Institution, Washington, DC, p. 2.

53. Patrick Allan Sharma, *Robert McNamara's Other War: The World Bank and International Development* (Philadelphia: University of Pennsylvania Press, 2017), 5–6.

54. Browne, *United Nations Development Programme and System*, 18–19.

55. Ibid., 34.

56. Kathryn C. Lavelle, "Invisible Hand, Invisible Continent: Liberalization and African States in the United Nations Conference on Trade and Development" (Ph.D. diss., Northwestern University, 1996).

57. Browne, *United Nations Development Programme and System*, 43–45.

58. Ibid., 49–50.

59. See Rothstein, "Epitaph for a Monument to a Failed Protest?"; *UNCTAD and the Quest for a New International Economic Order*; Murphy, *Emergence of the NIEO Ideology*; and Hart, *NIEO: Conflict and Cooperation*.

60. Arturo Escobar, "Power and Visibility: Development and the Invention and Management of the Third World," *Cultural Anthropology* 3 (1988); Arturo Escobar, "Reflections on 'Development': Grassroots Approaches and Alternative Politics in the Third World," *Futures*, June 1992.

4 Restoring Free Trade in the World Economy

1. A. Claire Cutler, "Locating 'Authority' in the Global Political Economy," *International Studies Quarterly* 43 (1999): 72.

2. Robert Gilpin, *Global Political Economy: Understanding the International Economic Order* (Princeton, NJ: Princeton University Press, 2001), 218.

3. Ibid., 219–20.

4. Robert Gilpin, *The Political Economy of International Relations* (Princeton, NJ: Princeton University Press, 1987), 239.

5. Ibid., 245.

6. Terence Stewart, ed., *The GATT Uruguay Round: A Negotiating History (1986–1992)* (Boston: Kluwer Law and Taxation, 1993), 1899. See also John Jackson, *The World Trading System: Law and Policy of International Economic Regulations* (Cambridge, MA: MIT Press, 1989).

7. Stewart, *GATT Uruguay Round*, 1906.

8. Kent Jones, *Who's Afraid of the WTO?* (New York: Oxford University Press, 2004), 69.

9. Derek W. Urwin, "The European Community: From 1945 to 1985," in *European Union Politics*, ed. Michelle Cini and Nieves Perez-Solorzano Borragan (New York: Oxford University Press, 2013), 12–13.

10. Ibid., 15.

11. I. M. Destler, *American Trade Politics: System under Stress* (Washington, DC: Institute for International Economics, 1986), 16–19.

12. Ibid., 143–44.

13. Steve Dryden, *Trade Warriors: USTR and the American Crusade for Free Trade* (New York: Oxford University Press, 1995), 34.

14. Ibid., 6.

15. Destler, *American Trade Politics*, 10.

16. Gilpin, *Global Political Economy*, 220.

17. Gilpin, *Political Economy of International Relations*, 231.

18. Gilpin, *Global Political Economy*, 278–79.

19. Jens-Uwe Wunderlich and Meera Warrier, *A Dictionary of Globalization* (New York: Routledge, 2007), 218.

20. Robert Gilpin, *US Power and the Multinational Corporation: The Political Economy of Foreign Direct Investment* (New York: Basic Books, 1975).

21. Gilpin, *Political Economy of International Relations*, 232.

22. Ibid., 233.

23. Wunderlich and Warrier, *Dictionary of Globalization*, 220.

24. Gilpin, *Political Economy of International Relations*, 235.

25. Destler, *American Trade Politics*, 46–47.

26. Ibid., 144.

27. Kent H. Hughes, *Building the Next American Century: The Past and Future of American Economic Competitiveness* (Washington, DC: Woodrow Wilson Center Press, 2005), 34.

28. Ibid.

29. Dryden, *Trade Warriors*, 171.

30. Destler, *American Trade Politics*, 48.

31. UNCTAD, *Assessment of the Results of the Multilateral Trade Negotiations Report by the Secretary-General of UNCTAD*, Annex: Countries That Participated in the Multilateral Trade Negotiations, 1980, TD/B/778/Rev.1, p. 34.

32. Jones, *Who's Afraid of the WTO?*, 71.
33. Destler, *American Trade Politics*, 87.
34. Ibid., 108–9.
35. Ibid.
36. Ibid., 151.
37. Nitsan Chorev, *Remaking U.S. Trade Policy: From Protectionism to Globalization* (Ithaca, NY: Cornell University Press, 2007), 152.
38. M. Peter Sutherland, "The World Trading System after the Uruguay Round: Promises and Challenges" (address to the Programme d'études stratégiques et de sécurité internationale, Graduate Institute of International Studies, Geneva, November 29, 1994).
39. Tropical products are products produced exclusively in the tropical zone (between the Tropics of Cancer and Capricorn). If a product can be produced elsewhere, it is not considered to be tropical. These products are treated separately because they don't compete directly with the agricultural products of developed countries—that is, all tropical countries are considered to be "developing."
40. Terry Noyelle, "Revamping World Trade: What's in It for the South?," *Choices*, June 1994, 27–31.
41. Thomas G. Weiss, "UNCTAD: What Next?," *Journal of World Trade Law* 19 (1985): 252.
42. Ibid.
43. Ibid., 256.
44. Kevin Watkins, *Fixing the Rules: North-South Issues in International Trade and the GATT Uruguay Round* (London: Catholic Institute for International Relations, 1992).
45. Murray Gibbs, "Continuing the International Debate on Services," *Journal of World Trade Law* 19 (1985): 216.
46. Ibid., 200.
47. Chakravarthi Raghavan, "UNCTAD VII: Cooperation or Confrontation?," *Interpress Service*, July 7, 1987, 77.
48. Gilpin, *Political Economy of International Relations*, 204.
49. Gilpin, *Global Political Economy*, 341.
50. M. Angeles Villareal and Ian F. Fergusson, "The North American Free Trade Agreement (NAFTA)" (CRS Report R42965, Congressional Research Service, Washington, DC, 2017), 2.
51. Dryden, *Trade Warriors*, 370.
52. Ibid.
53. Villareal and Fergusson, "NAFTA," 5.
54. Dryden, *Trade Warriors*, 376.
55. Villareal and Fergusson, "NAFTA," 16.
56. Ibid., 19.

57. Sylvia Ostry, *Governments and Corporations in a Shrinking World* (New York: Council on Foreign Relations, 1990), 18.
58. Ibid., 19.
59. Edmund Pratt, "Intellectual Property and United States Trade Policy" (speech before the Intellectual Property Rights Conference, Conference Board, New York, October 3, 1989), as quoted in Ostry, *Governments and Corporations*, 23–24.
60. Ibid., 25.
61. Philip Evans and James Walsh, *The EIU Guide to the New GATT* (London: Economist Intelligence Unit, 1994).
62. Article 26:5(c) offers accession to a customs territory that was formerly part of an existing CP.
63. Chris Brummer, *Minilateralism: How Trade Alliances, Soft Law, and Financial Engineering Are Redefining Economic Statecraft* (New York: Cambridge University Press, 2014).
64. Christina L. Davis, "Overlapping Institutions in Trade Policy," *Perspectives on Politics* 7 (2008): 25.
65. Ibid., 26.
66. In November 1991, Canada, the EC, and Mexico issued a joint proposal that was used as the basis to continue negotiation. See Stewart, *GATT Uruguay Round*, 1943.
67. Ibid., 1944 and n. 295.
68. Ibid., 1949.
69. Jones, *Who's Afraid of the WTO?*, 81.
70. "Regional Trade Agreements: Facts and Figures," World Trade Organization, https://www.wto.org/english/tratop_e/region_e/regfac_e.htm.
71. Davis, "Overlapping Institutions," 26.
72. Ibid., 28.

5 The End of the Cold War and Changing Security Alignments

1. Kathleen Thelen, *How Institutions Evolve: The Political Economy of Skills in Germany, Britain, the United States, and Japan* (New York: Cambridge University Press, 2004), 34, 36.
2. Jeffrey A. Engel, *When the World Seemed New: George H. W. Bush and the End of the Cold War* (New York: Houghton Mifflin Harcourt, 2017), 17; Richard N. Haass, *A World in Disarray: American Foreign Policy and the Crisis of the Old World Order* (New York: Penguin, 2017), 52.
3. Timothy J. Colton, *Russia: What Everyone Needs to Know* (New York: Oxford University Press, 2016), 80–84.
4. Engel, *When the World Seemed New*, 50.
5. Ibid., 318–19.

6. William K. Domke, Richard C. Eichenberg, and Catherine M. Kelleher, "Consensus Lost? Domestic Poliitcs and the 'Crisis' in NATO," *World Politics* 39 (1987): 382.

7. Ibid., 400–401.

8. Engel, *When the World Seemed New*, 78–79.

9. Richard E. Rupp, *NATO after 9/11: An Alliance in Continuing Decline* (New York: Palgrave Macmillan, 2006), 53.

10. Ibid., 54.

11. Engel, *When the World Seemed New*, 397.

12. Ibid., 418.

13. Ibid., 425.

14. Ibid., 436–38.

15. Ivo H. Daalder, "The Clinton Administration and Multilateral Peace Operations" (Pew Case Studies in International Affairs, Institute for the Study of Diplomacy, Georgetown University, Washington, DC, 1994).

16. Rupp, *NATO after 9/11*, 73.

17. Daalder, "Clinton Administration."

18. Christina L. Davis, "Overlapping Institutions in Trade Policy," *Perspectives on Politics* 7 (2008).

19. Daalder, "Clinton Administration."

20. David Skidmore, "Who Is at the Helm? The Debate over U.S. Funding for the United Nations" (Pew Case Studies in International Affairs, Institute for the Study of Diplomacy, Georgetown University, Washington, DC, 2000).

21. Kathryn C. Lavelle, *Legislating International Organization: The US Congress, the IMF, and the World Bank* (New York: Oxford University Press, 2011).

22. Skidmore, "Who Is at the Helm?"

23. Ibid.; Alison Bond, "U.S. Funding of the United Nations: Arrears Payments as an Indicator of Multilateralism," *Berkeley Journal of International Law* 21 (2003): 707.

24. Rupp, *NATO after 9/11*, 67.

25. Ibid., 69. NATO's military structure is divided between two strategic commands. One, the Supreme Headquarters Allied Powers Europe, is located near Mons in Belgium. The other, the Allied Command Transformation, is located in Norfolk, Virginia. The supreme allied commander Europe oversees all NATO military operations and is always a US officer. Although the alliance has an integrated command, most remain under their individual national authorities until an operation begins.

26. Ibid., 74.

27. Ibid., 77.

28. Sten Rynning, *NATO in Afghanistan: The Liberal Disconnect* (Stanford, CA: Stanford University Press, 2012), 31.

29. Rupp, *NATO after 9/11*, 80.

30. Ibid., 94.
31. Ibid., 96–97.
32. M. J. Williams, *The Good War: NATO and the Liberal Conscience in Afghanistan* (New York: Palgrave Macmillan, 2011), 51–52.
33. Bond, "U.S. Funding," 710–11.
34. Rynning, *NATO in Afghanistan*, 44.
35. Ibid., 73.
36. Ibid., 75. See also David P. Auerswald and Stephen M. Saideman, *NATO in Afghanistan* (Princeton, NJ: Princeton University Press, 2014), 36.
37. Rupp, *NATO after 9/11*, 100–101.
38. Ibid., 103.
39. Rynning, *NATO in Afghanistan*, 46.
40. Rupp, *NATO after 9/11*, 156.
41. Williams, *Good War*, 98.
42. Curtis H. Martin, "Going to the United Nations: George W. Bush and Iraq" (Pew Case Studies in International Affairs, Institute for the Study of Diplomacy, Georgetown University, Washington, DC, 2005).
43. Rupp, *NATO after 9/11*, 123.
44. Martin, "Going to the United Nations."
45. Rupp, *NATO after 9/11*, 124.
46. Martin, "Going to the United Nations."
47. Rupp, *NATO after 9/11*, 130.
48. Ibid., 137.
49. Martin, "Going to the United Nations."
50. Ibid.
51. Isabel Coles and Courtney McBride, "Iraq Urges Pompeo to Maintain U.S. Troop Presence in Country," *Wall Street Journal*, January 9, 2019.
52. Auerswald and Saideman, *NATO in Afghanistan*, 2.
53. Rupp, *NATO after 9/11*, 56–57.
54. Ibid., 61.
55. Kimberly Marten, "Reducing Tensions between Russia and NATO" (Council on Foreign Relations Special Report, Center for Preventive Action, Council on Foreign Relations, New York, 2017), 10.
56. Ibid., 11.
57. "NATO Enlargement—A Case Study," Center for Strategic and International Studies, https://medium.com/center-for-strategic-and-international-studies/nato-enlargement-a-case-study-c380545dd38d.
58. Rupp, *NATO after 9/11*, 60.
59. Marten, "Reducing Tensions between Russia and NATO," 5.
60. R. G. Gidadhubli, "Expansion of NATO: Russia's Dilemma," *Economic and Political Weekly* 39, no. 19 (2004).

61. "Why Crimea Is So Dangerous," BBC News, March 11, 2014, http://www.bbc.com/news/world-europe-26367786.

62. Marten, "Reducing Tensions between Russia and NATO," 4.

63. Neil MacFarquhar, "A Powerful Russian Weapon: The Spread of False Stories," *New York Times*, August 28, 2016.

64. Peter Pomerantsev, "Russia and the Menace of Unreality: How Vladimir Putin Is Revolutionizing Information Warfare," *Atlantic*, September 9, 2014, https://www.theatlantic.com/international/archive/2014/09/russia-putin-revolutionizing-information-warfare/379880/.

65. Marten, "Reducing Tensions between Russia and NATO," 4.

66. Ibid., 5.

67. Jonathan Masters, "The North Atlantic Treaty Organization (NATO)," Council on Foreign Relations, April 2, 2019, https://www.cfr.org/backgrounder/north-atlantic-treaty-organization-nato.

68. Rupp, *NATO after 9/11*, 80.

69. Martin S. Indyk, Kenneth G. Lieberthal, and Michael E. O'Hanlon, "Scoring Obama's Foreign Policy," *Foreign Affairs* 91 (2012): 29.

70. Jeffrey Goldberg, "The Obama Doctrine," *Atlantic*, April 2016, 78. See also Indyk, Lieberthal, and O'Hanlon, "Scoring Obama's Foreign Policy," 30.

71. Obama quoted in Goldberg, "Obama Doctrine," 78.

72. Ibid., 81.

73. Marten, "Reducing Tensions between Russia and NATO," 7.

74. Masters, "NATO."

6 Wellness of People and the Planet

1. Sophie Harman, "The Bill and Melinda Gates Foundation and Legitimacy in Global Health Governance," *Global Governance* 22 (2016): 349.

2. "Our History," Rockefeller Foundation, https://www.rockefellerfoundation.org/about-us/our-history/.

3. "History of 1918 Flu Pandemic," Centers for Disease Control and Prevention, https://www.cdc.gov/flu/pandemic-resources/1918-commemoration/1918-pandemic-history.htm.

4. Allan Mitchell, *The Divided Path: The German Influence on Social Reform in France after 1870* (Chapel Hill: University of North Carolina Press, 1991), 46.

5. Ibid., 61–62.

6. Ibid., 160.

7. James W. McGuire, *Wealth, Health, and Democracy in East Asia and Latin America* (New York: Cambridge University Press, 2010), 113.

8. Joseph Wong, *Healthy Democracies: Welfare Politics in Taiwan and South Korea* (Ithaca, NY: Cornell University Press, 2004).

9. Jeremy Youde, *Global Health Governance* (Cambridge: Polity Press, 2012), 30.

10. "Constitution of WHO: Principles," World Health Organization, http://www.who.int/about/mission/en/.

11. Nitsan Chorev, *The World Health Organization: Between North and South* (Ithaca, NY: Cornell University Press, 2012), 4.

12. Ibid., 6–7.

13. Youde, *Global Health Governance*, 39–40.

14. Ibid., 43.

15. See Chorev, *World Health Organization*, 151, and Youde, *Global Health Governance*, 45.

16. Youde, *Global Health Governance*, 50.

17. Ibid., 64.

18. Ibid., 54.

19. Ibid., 51.

20. Sophie Harman, *Global Health Governance* (New York: Routledge, 2012), 58.

21. "Bill and Melinda Gates Foundation," 355.

22. Harmon, *Global Health Governance*, 64.

23. Youde, *Global Health Governance*, 86. See also "Clinton Foundation History," Clinton Foundation, https://www.clintonfoundation.org/about/clinton-foundation-history.

24. Kelley Lee, *Globalization and Health: An Introduction* (New York: Palgrave Macmillan, 2003), 155.

25. Youde, *Global Health Governance*, 91–97.

26. "Resilience at 10: Planetary Health and Resilient Health Systems," Rockefeller Foundation 2015 Annual Report, https://www.rockefellerfoundation.org/about-us/governance-reports/annual-reports/annual-report-2015/.

27. Lee, *Globalization and Health*, 61.

28. Frederike Ambagtsheer and Willem Weimar, "A Crimonological Perspective: Why Prohibition of Organ Trade Is Not Effective and How the Declaration of Istanbul Can Move Forward," *American Journal of Transplantation* 12 (2012).

29. Details of Treaty No. 216, "Council of Europe Convention against Trafficking in Human Organs," Council of Europe, https://www.coe.int/en/web/conventions/full-list/-/conventions/treaty/216.

30. Fikresus Amahazion, "Epistemic Communities, Human Rights, and the Global Diffusion of Legislation against the Organ Trade," *Social Sciences* 5 (2016).

31. Ken Conca, *An Unfinished Foundation: The United Nations and Global Environmental Governance* (New York: Oxford University Press, 2015), 37.

32. Thomas Hale, David Held, and Kevin Young, *Gridlock: Why Global Cooperation Is Failing When We Need It Most* (Cambridge: Polity Press, 2013), 196.

33. Garrett Hardin, "The Tragedy of the Commons," *Science* 162 (1968): 1244.

34. Ibid., 1247.
35. Kate O'Neill, *The Environment and International Relations* (New York: Cambridge University Press, 2017), 5.
36. Ibid., 34–35.
37. "The History of Earth Day," Earth Day, http://www.earthday.org/about/the-history-of-earth-day/.
38. Richard Black, "Stockholm: Birth of the Green Generation," BBC News, June 4, 2012, http://www.bbc.com/news/science-environment-18315205.
39. Adil Najam, "Developing Countries and Global Environmental Governance: From Contestation to Participation to Engagement," *International Environmental Agreements* 5 (2005): 308.
40. Ibid., 307.
41. Elizabeth R. DeSombre, *Global Environmental Institutions* (New York: Routledge, 2006), 21.
42. Ibid., 11.
43. Conca, *Unfinished Foundation*, 61.
44. Hale, Held, and Young, *Gridlock*, 224.
45. Ibid., 225.
46. Conca, *Unfinished Foundation*, 65.
47. Jane A. Leggett and Richard K. Lattanzio, "Climate Change: Frequently Asked Questions about the 2015 Paris Agreement" (CRS Report R44609, Congressional Research Service, Washington, DC, 2017), 5.
48. Najam, "Developing Countries," 314.
49. Conca, *Unfinished Foundation*, 71.
50. Leggett and Lattanzio, "Climate Change," 5.
51. Kathryn Hochstetler and Manjana Milkoreit, "Responsibilities in Transition: Emerging Powers in the Climate Change Negotiations," *Global Governance* 21 (2015): 213.
52. Leggett and Lattanzio, "Climate Change," 6.
53. Ibid.
54. "United Nations Framework Convention on Climate Change," UNFCCC, https://unfccc.int/resource/docs/convkp/conveng.pdf.
55. "List of Parties," Convention on Biological Diversity, https://www.cbd.int/information/parties.shtml. See also "Update on Ratification of the UNCCD," United Nations Convention to Combat Desertification, http://www.unccd.int/Documents/Ratification%20list%20Dec2016.pdf.
56. Conca, *Unfinished Foundation*, 76.
57. Hale, Held, and Young, *Gridlock*, 211.
58. O'Neill, *Environment*, 157.
59. Elinor Ostrom, *Governing the Commons: The Evolution of Institutions for Collective Action* (New York: Cambridge University Press, 1990).

60. Henrik Selin and Stacy D. VanDeveer, "Changing Climates and Institution Building across the Continent," in *Changing Climates in North American Politics: Institutions, Policymaking, and Multilevel Governance*, ed. Henrik Selin and Stacy D. VanDeveer (Cambridge, MA: MIT Press, 2009), 10.

61. Jessica F. Green, *Rethinking Private Authority: Agents and Entrepreneurs in Global Environmental Governance* (Princeton, NJ: Princeton University Press, 2013).

62. Selin and VanDeveer, "Changing Climates," 13.

63. Hale, Held, and Young, *Gridlock*, 259.

64. Conca, *Unfinished Foundation*, 12.

65. Ibid., 29.

7 Global Justice and Human Rights

1. Kenneth W. Abbott et al., "The Concept of Legalization," *International Organization* 54 (2000): 17.

2. Graham Evans and Jeffrey Newnham, *The Penguin Dictionary of International Relations* (New York: Penguin Books, 1998), 262.

3. Elizabeth Griffin and Başak Çali, "International Humanitarian Law," in *International Law for International Relations*, ed. Başak Çali (New York: Oxford University Press, 2010), 244.

4. Ibid., 238.

5. Juan M. Amaya-Castro, "International Courts and Tribunals," in *International Law for International Relations*, ed. Başak Çali (New York: Oxford University Press, 2010), 170.

6. See also Griffin and Çali, "International Humanitarian Law," 242.

7. Sidney B. Jacoby, "Some Aspects of the Jurisdiction of the Permanent Court of International Justice," *American Journal of International Law* 30 (1936): 234.

8. Amaya-Castro, "International Courts," 167.

9. Reinhold Niebuhr, *Moral Man and Immoral Society* (New York: Charles Scribner's Sons, 1932), 22.

10. Ibid., 49.

11. Ibid., 83.

12. Edward Hallett Carr, *The Twenty Years' Crisis, 1919–1939* (New York: Harper Torchbooks, 1964), 193.

13. Ibid., 199.

14. Ibid., 205.

15. Ibid., 236.

16. Griffin and Çali, "International Humanitarian Law," 237.

17. *Fundamental Freedoms: Eleanor Roosevelt and the Universal Declaration of Human Rights* (Brookline, MA: Facing History and Ourselves Foundation, 2010), 19.

18. Sabine C. Carey, Mark Gibney, and Steven C. Poe, *The Politics of Human Rights: The Quest for Dignity* (New York: Cambridge University Press, 2010), 17.

19. Ibid., 11.

20. Rachel Kerr and Eirin Mobekk, *Peace and Justice: Seeking Accountability after War* (Cambridge: Polity Press, 2007), 27.

21. R. J. Vincent, *Human Rights and International Relations* (New York: Cambridge University Press, 1988), 17.

22. David P. Forsythe, *The Internationalization of Human Rights* (Lexington, MA: Lexington Books, 1991), 6. See also *Fundamental Freedoms*, 226.

23. *Fundamental Freedoms*, 47.

24. Ibid., 48.

25. Ibid., 66.

26. Ibid., 103.

27. Ibid., 109.

28. Ibid., 117.

29. Ibid., 111.

30. Ibid., 148.

31. Ibid., 165.

32. Ibid., 167.

33. Ibid., 15.

34. Julie A. Mertus, *The United Nations and Human Rights: A Guide for a New Era* (New York: Routledge, 2005), 162.

35. Vincent, *Human Rights and International Relations*, 61.

36. Ibid., 62.

37. Ibid., 78.

38. Forsythe, *Internationalization*, 17.

39. Jack Donnelly, *Universal Human Rights in Theory and Practice* (Ithaca, NY: Cornell University Press, 2013), 26.

40. Mertus, *United Nations and Human Rights*, 48.

41. Ibid., 80.

42. Carey, Gibney, and Poe, *Politics of Human Rights*, 11.

43. Lawrence Ziring, Robert E. Riggs, and Jack C. Plano, *The United Nations: International Organization and World Politics*, 4th ed. (Belmont, CA: Wadsworth, 2005), 418.

44. "Who We Are: Brief History," United Nations Human Rights, Office of the High Commissioner, http://www.ohchr.org/EN/AboutUs/Pages/BriefHistory.aspx.

45. Stephen Hopgood, *Keepers of the Flame: Understanding Amnesty International* (Ithaca, NY: Cornell University Press, 2006), 2.

46. Ibid., 24.

47. Ibid., 52.

48. Ibid., 19.

49. Ibid., 18.
50. Ibid., 105.
51. Ibid., 65.
52. Ibid., 69.
53. Ibid., 79.
54. Ibid., 116.
55. "History," Human Rights Watch, https://www.hrw.org/history.
56. Hopgood, *Keepers of the Flame*, 140.
57. Ibid., 138.
58. Mertus, *United Nations and Human Rights*, 163.
59. Hopgood, *Keepers of the Flame*, 143–44.
60. Ibid., 165.
61. Patrick S. Wegner, *The International Criminal Court in Ongoing Intrastate Conflicts: Navigating the Peace-Justice Divide* (Cambridge: Cambridge University Press, 2015), 20.
62. Kerr and Mobekk, *Peace and Justice*, 26.
63. Kathryn Sikkink, *The Justice Cascade: How Human Rights Prosecutions Are Changing the World* (New York: W. W. Norton, 2011), 5.
64. Ibid., 12.
65. Ibid., 13.
66. Paola Gaeta, "International Criminal Law," in *International Law for International Relations*, ed. Başak Çali (New York: Oxford University Press, 2010), 261.
67. Ibid., 262.
68. Ziring, Riggs, and Plano, *United Nations*, 314.
69. Michael Barnett, *Eyewitness to a Genocide: The United Nations and Rwanda* (Ithaca, NY: Cornell University Press, 2002), 3.
70. Ibid., 7.
71. Ibid., 181.
72. Ziring, Riggs, and Plano, *United Nations*, 314.
73. Sikkink, *Justice Cascade*, 15.
74. Gaeta, "International Criminal Law," 264.
75. Sikkink, *Justice Cascade*, 112.
76. Ibid., 116–17.
77. Michael J. Struett, *The Politics of Constructing the International Criminal Court: NGOs, Discourse, and Agency* (New York: Palgrave MacMillan, 2008), 74.
78. Errol P. Mendes, *Peace and Justice at the International Criminal Court: A Court of Last Resort* (Northampton, MA: Edward Elgar, 2010), 16.
79. Struett, *Politics of Constructing*, 148.
80. Sikkink, *Justice Cascade*, 18; Wegner, *International Criminal Court*, 17.
81. Wegner, *International Criminal Court*, 16.
82. Ziring, Riggs, and Plano, *United Nations*, 316.

83. Ibid., 315.
84. Ibid., 406; Mendes, *Peace and Justice*, 19.
85. Wegner, *International Criminal Court*, 309.
86. Mendes, *Peace and Justice*, 166.
87. Joseph Cotterill and Edith Honan, "South Africa Withdrawal Deals Fresh Blow to ICC," *Financial Times*, October 21, 2016.
88. Wegner, *International Criminal Court*, 312–15.
89. Ibid., 303.
90. Ibid., 21; Sikkink, *Justice Cascade*, 26.
91. David Miller, "Justice," in *The Blackwell Encyclopedia of Political Thought*, ed. David Miller et al. (New York: Basil Blackwell, 1987), 222.
92. Peter Jones, "Human Rights," in *The Blackwell Encyclopedia of Political Thought*, ed. David Miller et al. (New York: Basil Blackwell, 1987).

8 Money and Finance in the New Global Economy

1. Chris Brummer, *Soft Law and the Global Financial System: Rule Making in the 21st Century* (New York: Cambridge University Press, 2012), 63–65.
2. Harold James, *International Monetary Cooperation since Bretton Woods* (New York: Oxford University Press, 1996), 181.
3. Barry Eichengreen, *Globalizing Capital: A History of the International Monetary System*, 2nd ed. (Princeton, NJ: Princeton University Press, 1996), 1–3. See also James, *International Monetary Cooperation*, 57; and Andreas F. Lowenfeld, *International Economic Law* (New York: Oxford University Press, 2002), 598.
4. Ngaire Woods, *The Globalizers: The IMF, World Bank, and Their Borrowers* (Ithaca, NY: Cornell University Press, 2006), 22.
5. Robert Gilpin, *The Challenge of Global Capitalism in the World Economy in the 21st Century* (Princeton, NJ: Princeton University Press, 2000), 114–15; John Braithwaite and Peter Drahos, *Global Business Regulation* (New York: Cambridge University Press, 2000), 88.
6. David Rogers, *The Future of American Banking* (New York: McGraw-Hill, 1993), 85. See also David Rockefeller, *Memoirs* (New York: Random House, 2002), 134.
7. Harold van B. Cleveland and Thomas F. Huertas, *Citibank: 1812–1970* (Cambridge, MA: Harvard University Press, 1985), 266.
8. Ibid., 264. See also Rogers, *Future of American Banking*, 148.
9. Robert Solomon, *The International Monetary System, 1945–1976: An Insider's View* (New York: Harper and Row, 1977), 34. See also Michael D. Bordo and Owen F. Humpage, "Federal Reserve Policy and Bretton Woods," in *The Federal Reserve's Role in the Global Economy: A Historical Perspective*, ed. Michael D. Bordo and Mark A. Wynne (New York: Cambridge University Press, 2016), 94–95.

10. Andrew Baker, *The Group of Seven: Finance Ministries, Central Banks and Global Financial Governance* (New York: Routledge, 2006), 20.

11. Robert W. Russell, "Transgovernmental Interaction in the International Monetary System, 1960–1972," *International Organization* 27 (1973): 435.

12. Ibid., 439.

13. Harold K. Jacobson, *Networks of Interdependence* (New York: Alfred A. Knopf, 1984).

14. James, *International Monetary Cooperation*, 49.

15. Gianni Toniolo, *Central Bank Cooperation at the Bank for International Settlements* (New York: Cambridge University Press, 2005), 271.

16. Ibid., 268.

17. Roger Auboin, "The Bank for International Settlements, 1930–1955," *Essays in International Finance* 22 (1955): 18.

18. Ibid., 5.

19. Solomon, *International Monetary System*, 182.

20. Baker, *Group of Seven*, 24.

21. Robert Solomon, *Money on the Move: The Revolution in International Finance since 1980* (Princeton, NJ: Princeton University Press, 1999), 5; Baker, *Group of Seven*, 25.

22. Baker, *Group of Seven*, 20.

23. Joan Edelman Spero, *The Failure of the Franklin National Bank: Challenge to the International Banking System* (New York: Columbia University Press, 1980), 7.

24. Basel Committee on Banking Supervision, "Bank Failures in Mature Economies" (working paper, Bank for International Settlements, Basel, April 2004), 5.

25. Spero, *Failure of Franklin National Bank*, 78–79.

26. Ibid., 156.

27. Ibid., 159; Braithwaite and Drahos, *Global Business Regulation*, 104; Robert Gilpin, *Global Political Economy: Understanding the International Economic Order* (Princeton, NJ: Princeton University Press, 2001), 812–13.

28. Tony Porter, *States, Markets and Regimes in Global Finance* (New York: St. Martin's Press, 1993), 59. See also Kathryn C. Lavelle, "U.S. Foreign Policy and the Governance of Finance," *Business and Politics* 21 (2018): 10–12.

29. Charles Goodhart, *The Basel Committee on Banking Supervision: A History of the Early Years* (Cambridge: Cambridge University Press, 2011), 542–46.

30. Charles Lipson, "The International Organization of Third World Debt," in *Toward a Political Economy of Development*, ed. Robert Bates (Berkeley: University of California Press, 1988).

31. James Boughton, *Silent Revolution: The International Monetary Fund, 1979–1989* (Washington, DC: International Monetary Fund, 2001), 291.

32. Ibid., 297.

33. Ibid.

34. Solomon, *Money on the Move*, 40.

35. James, *International Monetary Cooperation*, 369.

36. Randall Dodd, "Sovereign Debt Restructuring," *Financier* 9 (2002).

37. Richard B. Miller, *Citicorp: The Story of a Bank in Crisis* (New York: McGraw-Hill, 1993), 112.

38. For a review of the development of transnational civil society in this area, see Jan Aart Scholte and Albrecht Schnabel, eds., *Civil Society and Global Finance* (New York: Routledge, 2002). For a review of the activist network's work on debt relief, see Joshua William Busby, "Bono Made Jesse Helms Cry: Jubilee 2000, Debt Relief, and Moral Action in International Politics," *International Studies Quarterly* 51 (2007).

39. "Jubilee 2000," Advocacy International, http://www.advocacyinternational.co.uk/featured-project/jubilee-2000.

40. "Debt Relief under the Heavily Indebted Poor Countries (HIPC) Initiative," International Monetary Fund, March 19, 2019, http://www.imf.org/en/About/Factsheets/Sheets/2016/08/01/16/11/Debt-Relief-Under-the-Heavily-Indebted-Poor-Countries-Initiative.

41. Solomon, *Money on the Move*, 53.

42. Peter Coffey, *The Euro: An Essential Guide* (New York: Continuum, 2001), 14.

43. Solomon, *Money on the Move*, 62.

44. Ibid., 55.

45. Ibid., 63.

46. "Stages of Economic and Monetary Union," European Central Bank, https://www.ecb.europa.eu/ecb/history/emu/html/index.en.html.

47. Solomon, *Money on the Move*, 59–60.

48. Coffey, *Euro*, 23–25.

49. Eichengreen, *Globalizing Capital*, 220.

50. David M. Wood and Birol A. Yesilada, *The Emerging European Union* (New York: Longman, 2002), 125.

51. Eichengreen, *Globalizing Capital*, 193.

52. Ibid., 194.

53. Joseph E. Stiglitz, *Globalization and Its Discontents* (New York: W. W. Norton, 2002), 95–97.

54. Ibid., 89.

55. Ibid., 95–96.

56. Brummer, *Soft Law*, 71.

57. Ibid., 73.

58. Bhumika Muchhala, "Introduction," in *Ten Years After: Revisiting the Asian Financial Crisis*, ed. Bhumika Muchhala (Washington, DC: Woodrow Wilson International Center for Scholars, 2007), 10.

59. David Burton, "Asia and the International Monetary Fund: Ten Years after the Asian Financial Crisis," in *Ten Years After: Revisiting the Asian Financial Crisis*, ed.

Bhumika Muchhala (Washington, DC: Woodrow Wilson International Center for Scholars, 2007), 71.

60. Robert Winnett, "Financial Crisis: Gordon Brown Calls for 'New Bretton Woods,' " *Daily Telegraph*, October 13, 2008, http://www.telegraph.co.uk/finance/ financialcrisis/3189517/Financial-Crisis-Gordon-Brown-calls-for-new-Bretton-Woods.html.

61. Kathryn C. Lavelle, *Money and Banks in the American Political System* (New York: Cambridge University Press, 2013), 197–99.

62. Lavelle, "Bailing Out Capitalism," *Current History: A Journal of Contemporary World Affairs* 112 (2013): 304.

63. Lavelle, *Money and Banks*, 193.

64. Martin A. Weiss, *The Global Financial Crisis: The Role of the International Monetary Fund (IMF)* (Washington, DC: Congressional Research Service, 2009), 1.

65. Kathryn C. Lavelle, *Legislating International Organization: The US Congress, the IMF, and the World Bank* (New York: Oxford University Press, 2011), 160.

66. Ibid., 166.

67. Brummer, *Soft Law*, 73.

68. The High-Level Group on Financial Supervision in the EU, Jacques de Larosière, chair, "Report" (Brussels, February 25, 2009).

69. Nikki Tait, "Banker Attacks Piecemeal Oversight," *Financial Times*, March 18, 2009.

70. Pierre Briancon, "Axel Weber and Mario Draghi in Pole Positions as Fight for ECB Succession Starts," *Telegraph Investor*, February 3, 2010.

71. James Shotter, "Weber Agrees Departure Date in April," *Financial Times*, February 11, 2011; Brian Blackstone, Geoffrey Smith, and Marcus Walker, "German Shuns Top Euro Bank Job," *Wall Street Journal*, February 10, 2011.

72. Peter Müller, Christoph Pauly, and Christian Reiermann, "Jürgen Stark's Resignation Is Setback for Merkel," *Spiegel Online*, September 12, 2011, https:// www.spiegel.de/international/europe/ecb-chief-economist-quits-juergen-stark-s-resignation-is-setback-for-merkel-a-785668.html.

73. Nicolas Véron, *Europe's Radical Banking Union* (Brussels: Bruegel, 2015), 14.

74. Ibid., 18.

75. Kathleen R. McNamara, "The Forgotten Problem of Embeddedness: History Lessons for the Euro," in *The Future of the Euro*, ed. Mark Blyth and Matthias Matthijs (New York: Oxford University Press, 2015), 21–22.

9 Dissent on Globalization

1. See, e.g., Thomas L. Friedman, *The Lexus and the Olive Tree: Understanding Globalization* (New York: Farrar, Straus and Giroux, 1999). See also Robert W.

Merry, "Trump vs. Hillary Is Nationalism vs. Globalism, 2016," *National Interest*, May 4, 2016, http://nationalinterest.org/feature/trump-vs-hillary-nationalism-vs-globalism-2016-16041.

2. Ariel Buira, ed., *Challenges to the World Bank and IMF: Developing Country Perspectives* (London: Anthem Press, 2003).

3. Joseph E. Stiglitz, *Globalization and Its Discontents* (New York: W. W. Norton, 2002), 3.

4. Margaret E. Keck and Kathryn Sikkink, *Activists beyond Borders: Advocacy Networks in International Politics* (Ithaca, NY: Cornell University Press, 1998), 11.

5. Kathryn C. Lavelle, *Legislating International Organization: The US Congress, the IMF, and the World Bank* (New York: Oxford University Press, 2011), 34. See also Allan J. Cigler and Burdett A. Loomis, "Always Involved, Rarely Central: Organized Interests in American Politics," in *Interest Group Politics*, ed. Allan J. Cigler and Burdett A. Loomis (Washington, DC: CQ Press, 2002), 381.

6. Lavelle, *Legislating International Organization*, 99.

7. Leon Gordenker and Thomas G. Weiss, "Pluralizing Global Governance: Analytical Approaches and Dimensions," in *NGOs, the UN, and Global Governance*, ed. Leon Gordenker and Thomas G. Weiss (Boulder, CO: Lynne Rienner, 1996), 24.

8. Thomas M. Callaghy, "Networks and Governance in Africa: Innovation in the Debt Regime," in *Intervention and Transnationalism in Africa: Global-Local Networks of Power*, ed. Ronald Kassimir, Thomas M. Callaghy, and Robert Latham (New York: Cambridge University Press, 2001).

9. Keck and Sikkink, *Activists beyond Borders*, 36–37.

10. Jeffrey M. Berry, *The New Liberalism: The Changing Power of Citizen Groups* (Washington, DC: Brookings Institution Press, 1999).

11. Lavelle, *Legislating International Organization*, 99.

12. Walter LaFeber, *Michael Jordan and the New Global Capitalism* (New York: W. W. Norton, 2002), 56.

13. Ibid., 68–69.

14. Ibid., 72–74.

15. Ibid., 150.

16. Jagdish Bhagwati, *In Defense of Globalization* (New York: Oxford University Press, 2004), 21–24.

17. Ibid., 27.

18. Kent Jones, *Who's Afraid of the WTO?* (New York: Oxford University Press, 2004), 21.

19. Ibid., 27.

20. See Simon Jeffery, "Protester Shot Dead in Genoa Riot," *Guardian*, July 20, 2001, https://www.theguardian.com/world/2001/jul/20/globalisation.usa.

21. Transcript of Kofi Annan's recollections recorded at "Secretary-General's interview by Barbara Crossette at the Sixteenth Annual Meeting of the Academic Council on the UN System," June 12, 2003, New York, https://www.un.org/sg/en/content/sg/press-encounter/2003-06-12/secretary-generals-interview-barbara-crossette-sixteenth.

22. Martha Finnemore, *National Interests in International Society* (Ithaca, NY: Cornell University Press, 1996); Audie Klotz, *Norms in International Relations: The Struggle against Apartheid* (Ithaca, NY: Cornell University Press, 1995); Keck and Sikkink, *Activists beyond Borders*; Thomas G. Weiss and Leon Gordenker, eds., *NGOs, the UN, and Global Governance* (Boulder, CO: Lynne Rienner, 1996).

23. Stiglitz, *Globalization and Its Discontents*, 5.

24. Ibid., 10.

25. Richard Peet, *Unholy Trinity: The IMF, World Bank and WTO* (London: Zed Books, 2003), 246.

26. Stiglitz, *Globalization and Its Discontents*, 19. See also Jones, *Who's Afraid of the WTO?*, 28.

27. Stiglitz, *Globalization and Its Discontents*, 242.

28. James H. Mittelman, *The Globalization Syndrome: Transformation and Resistance* (Princeton, NJ: Princeton University Press, 2000), 233.

29. LaFeber, *Michael Jordan*, 173.

30. "United Nations Office of Counter-Terrorism," United Nations, http://www.un.org/en/counterterrorism/.

31. Curtis H. Martin, *Going to the United Nations: George W. Bush and Iraq* (Washington, DC: Institute for the Study of Diplomacy, 2005).

32. Ibid.

33. "UN to Stick by Iraq Mission," BBC News, August 20, 2003, http://news.bbc.co.uk/2/hi/middle_east/3167233.stm.

34. Philip H. Gordon, "NATO and the War on Terrorism: A Changing Alliance," Brookings Institution, June 1, 2002, https://www.brookings.edu/articles/nato-and-the-war-on-terrorism-a-changing-alliance/.

35. "Looking for a Home," *Economist*, May 28, 2016.

36. The Data Team, "The World's Refugee Crisis: Past and Present," *Economist*, May 27, 2016,.

37. "History of UNHCR," United Nations High Commissioner for Refugees, http://www.unhcr.org/en-us/history-of-unhcr.html.

38. "Looking for a Home," *Economist*, May 28, 2016.

39. "Creaking at 60: Compassion Fatigue," *Economist*, March 25, 2017.

40. Ibid.

41. "Looking for a Home." See also "Creaking at 60."

42. Phillip Connor and Jens Manuel Krogstad, "Key Facts about the World's Refugees," FactTank, Pew Research Center, October 5, 2016, http://www.pewresearch.org/fact-tank/2016/10/05/key-facts-about-the-worlds-refugees/.

43. Janell Ross, "The Politics of the Syrian Refugee Crisis, Explained," *Washington Post*, September 11, 2015.

44. Jenna Johnson and David Weigel, "Donald Trump Calls for 'Total' Ban on Muslims Entering the United States," *Washington Post*, December 8, 2015.

45. John B. Judis, *The Populist Explosion: How the Great Recession Transformed American and European Politics* (New York: Columbia Global Reports, 2016), 15.

46. Martin Wolf, "The Economic Origins of the Populist Surge," *Financial Times*, June 27, 2017.

47. Judis, *Populist Explosion*, 46.

48. Ibid., 55–56.

49. Ibid., 60–61.

50. Jamil Anderlini, "China Expands Plans for World Bank Rival," *Financial Times*, June 24, 2014.

51. Tom Mitchell, "Concerns Remain over Chinese Rival to Asian Development Bank," *Financial Times*, October 24, 2014.

52. Shawn Donnan and Geoff Dyer, "US Warns of Loss of Influence over China Bank," *Financial Times*, March 17, 2015.

53. Robert Zoellick, "Shunning Beijing's Infrastructure Bank Was a Mistake for the US," *Financial Times*, June 7, 2015.

54. Judis, *Populist Explosion*, 66.

55. Ibid., 70.

56. See Edward Alden, "Trump, China, and Steel Tariffs: The Day the WTO Died," Council on Foreign Relations, March 9, 2018, https://www.cfr.org/blog/trump-china-and-steel-tariffs-day-wto-died.

57. Peter S. Goodman, "Chief of WTO Worries about Its Role as Peacekeeper as a Trade War Brews," *New York Times*, March 24, 2018.

58. Mark Landler, "Trump Abandons Iran Pact He Long Scorned," *New York Times*, May 9, 2018.

59. Goodman, "Chief of WTO Worries."

60. Robinson Meyer, "Trump and the Paris Agreement: What Just Happened?," *Atlantic*, https://www.theatlantic.com/science/archive/2017/08/trump-and-the-paris-agreement-what-just-happened/536040/.

61. McCain quoted in Morgan Gstalter, "McCain Rips Trump over Trade," *The Hill*, June 9, 2018, http://thehill.com/homenews/senate/391524-mccain-takes-jab-at-trump-over-trade-tells-allies-americans-stand-with-you.

62. Chas Danner, "Trump Threatens to End all Trade with Allies," *New York Magazine*, June 9, 2018, http://nymag.com/daily/intelligencer/2018/06/trump-threatens-to-end-all-trade-with-allies.html.

63. Cas Mudde, "Europe's Populist Surge: A Long Time in the Making," *Foreign Affairs* 95 (2016): 26.

64. Ibid., 28.

65. Judis, *Populist Explosion*, 96.

66. Ibid., 98.

67. Ibid., 107.

68. Aleksandra Wisniewska and Billy Ehrenberg-Shannon, "The European Elections 2019 in Five Charts," *Financial Times*, May 27, 2019.

69. Judis, *Populist Explosion*, 89.

70. Ibid., 132.

71. Helen Thompson, "Want to Understand What Is Wrong with Europe? Look at Italy," *New York Times*, March 8, 2018.

72. Judis, *Populist Explosion*, 144.

73. Ibid., 102.

74. Ibid., 100.

75. Steven Erlanger, "Challenges from Abroad and Within Keep European Union on Edge," *New York Times*, June 1, 2018.

76. Judis, *Populist Explosion*, 135.

77. Ibid., 136.

78. Timothy Garton Ash, "Is Britain European?," *International Affairs* 77 (2001): 3.

79. Ibid., 10–11.

80. Elisabeth O'Leary, "Scottish Independence Case Helped by 'Brexit Chaos': Sturgeon," Reuters, October 8, 2017, https://www.reuters.com/article/us-britain-eu-scotland/scottish-independence-case-helped-by-brexit-chaos-sturgeon-idUSKBN1CD0B2.

81. Judis, *Populist Explosion*, 138.

82. "Creaking at 60."

10 The Past and Future of Multilateralism

1. See Editorial Board, "Dodging Accountability at the U.N.," *New York Times*, August 22, 2016.

2. Chris Brummer, *Minilateralism: How Trade Alliances, Soft Law, and Financial Engineering Are Redefining Economic Statecraft* (New York: Cambridge University Press, 2014).

3. Ian Bremmer and Nouriel Roubini, "A G-Zero World," *Foreign Affairs* 90 (2011).

4. Kathryn C. Lavelle, *Legislating International Organization: The US Congress, the IMF, and the World Bank* (New York: Oxford University Press, 2011), 76.

5. Elizabeth C. Economy, *The Third Revolution: Xi Jinping and the New Chinese State* (New York: Oxford University Press, 2018), 5.

6. Liselotte Odgaard, "The Rise of an Illiberal China in a Liberal World Order," *Asia Policy* 13 (2018): 150. See also Economy, *Third Revolution*, 17.

7. See, e.g., Inis L. Claude, *Swords into Plowshares: The Problems and Progress of International Organization*, 4th ed. (New York: Random House, 1971); F. H. Hinsley, *Sovereignty*, 2nd ed. (New York: Cambridge University Press, 1986), 227; G. John Ikenberry, "Liberal Internationalism 3.0: America and the Dilemmas of Liberal World Order," *Perspectives on Politics* 7 (2009); and Paul Gordon Lauren, Gordon A. Craig, and Alexander L. George, *Force and Statecraft: Diplomatic Challenges of Our Time*, 5th ed. (New York: Oxford University Press, 2014).

8. Claude, *Swords into Plowshares*, 25–26.

9. Hinsley, *Sovereignty*, 227.

10. Lauren, Craig, and George, *Force and Statecraft*, 29–31.

11. Ikenberry, "Liberal Internationalism 3.0," 74.

12. Lauren, Craig, and George, *Force and Statecraft*, 54.

13. Ibid., 55–56.

14. Claude, *Swords into Plowshares*, 13.

15. Ikenberry, "Liberal Internationalism 3.0," 72.

16. Ibid., 78.

17. Anne-Marie Burley (now Slaughter), "Regulating the World: Multilateralism, International Law, and the Projection of the New Deal Regulatory State," in *Multilateralism Matters: The Theory and Praxis of an Institutional Form*, ed. John Gerard Ruggie (New York: Columbia University Press, 1993), 126.

18. Ibid., 134–35.

19. Ibid., 127.

20. Miles Kahler, "Multilateralism with Small and Large Numbers," in *Multilateralism Matters: Theory and Praxis of an Institutional Form*, ed. John Gerard Ruggie (New York: Columbia University Press, 1993), 295.

21. Ibid., 296–97.

22. Ikenberry, "Liberal Internationalism 3.0," 72.

23. Townsend Hoopes and Douglas Brinkley, *FDR and the Creation of the U.N.* (New Haven: Yale University Press, 1997), 220.

24. Bremmer and Roubini, "G-Zero World."

25. Ikenberry, "Liberal Internationalism 3.0," 79.

26. Odgaard, "Rise of Illiberal China," 153. See also Economy, *Third Revolution*.

27. See " 'Welcome to Hell' Protesters Clash with Police outside G-20 Summit," CNBC, July 6, 2017, https://www.cnbc.com/2017/07/06/welcome-to-hell-protesters-clash-with-police-g20-summit-hamburg.html.

28. Bremmer and Roubini, "G-Zero World."

29. For an op-ed on this topic, see George P. Shultz and Pedro Aspe, "NAFTA Needs an Update, Not Repeal," *New York Times*, October 16, 2017.

30. See Steven Erlanger and Julie Hirschfeld Davis, "Once Dominant, the United States Is Now Isolated at G-20," *New York Times*, July 8, 2017.

31. See Brian Wheeler and Paul Seddon, "Brexit: All You Need to Know about the UK Leaving the EU," BBC News, May 2, 2019, http://www.bbc.com/news/uk-politics-32810887.

32. See Lisa Friedman, "Dueling US Messages at Global Climate Talks," *New York Times*, November 12, 2017.

33. Recall that if the General Agreement had been applied in a colonial territory, the postindependence state could continue to apply the GATT on a de facto basis.

34. Svein Vigeland Rottem, "The Arctic Council in Arctic Governance: The Significance of the Oil Spill Agreement," in *The New Arctic Governance*, ed. Linda Jakobson and Neil Melvin (Oxford: Oxford University Press, 2016), 149.

35. See "The Arctic Council: A Backgrounder," May 20, 2015, http://www.arctic-council.org/index.php/en/about-us.

36. Margaret E. Keck and Kathryn Sikkink, "Transnational Advocacy Networks in the Movement Society," in *The Social Movement Society: Contentious Politics for a New Century*, ed. David S. Meyer and Sidney Tarrow (New York: Rowman and Littlefield, 1998), 221.

37. Stephen D. Krasner, *Structural Conflict: The Third World against Global Liberalism* (Berkeley: University of California Press, 1985).

38. See Margaret E. Keck and Kathryn Sikkink, *Activists beyond Borders: Advocacy Networks in International Politics* (Ithaca, NY: Cornell University Press, 1998). For some later work using Keck and Sikkink, see Kenneth R. Rutherford, "The Evolving Arms Control Agenda: Implications of the Role of NGOs in Banning Antipersonnel Landmines," *World Politics* 531 (2000); and Thomas Callaghy, Ronald Kassimir, and Robert Latham, eds., *Intervention and Transnationalism in Africa: Global-Local Networks of Power* (Cambridge: Cambridge University Press, 2001).

39. Business has historically remained behind the scenes, but in recent years, its political activity has become more visible and sophisticated. Nonetheless, business as a community remains fragmented, particularly in the American context. See David Vogel, *Kindred Strangers: The Uneasy Relationship between Politics and Business in America* (Princeton, NJ: Princeton University Press, 1996), 5.

40. E. E. Schattschneider, *The Semisovereign People: A Realist's View of Democracy in America* (New York: Harcourt Brace Jovanovich College, 1975), 34.

41. Thomas Risse, "Transnational Actors and World Politics," in *Handbook of International Relations*, ed. Walter Carlsnaes, Thomas Risse, and Beth A. Simmons (Thousand Oaks, CA: Sage, 2002), 256.

42. Marina Ottaway, "Corporatism Goes Global: International Organizations, Nongovernmental Organization Networks, and Transnational Business," *Global Governance* 7 (2001): 266.

43. Helmut K. Anheier and Lester M. Salamon, eds., *The Nonprofit Sector in the Developing World* (Manchester, UK: Manchester University Press, 1998).

44. James Petras, "NGOs: In the Service of Imperialism," *Journal of Contemporary Asia* 29 (1999): 439.

45. See James H. Mittelman, *The Globalization Syndrome: Transformation and Resistance* (Princeton, NJ: Princeton University Press, 2000); James H. Mittelman, "Globalization: An Ascendant Paradigm?," *International Studies Perspectives* 3 (2002); Stephen R. Gill and David Law, "Global Hegemony and the Structural Power of Capital," *International Studies Quarterly* 33 (1989); Stephen Gill, *American Hegemony and the Trilateral Commission* (New York: Cambridge University Press, 1990); and Mark Rupert, *Producing Hegemony: The Politics of Mass Production and American Global Power* (New York: Cambridge University Press, 1995).

46. Charles Abugre and Nancy Alexander, "Non-Governmental Organizations and the International Monetary and Financial System," in *International Monetary and Financial Issues for the 1990s: Research Papers for the Group of Twenty-Four* (New Yorka: United Nations, 1998).

47. Ibid.

48. Sangeeta Kamat, *Development Hegemony: NGOs and the State in India* (New Delhi: Oxford University Press, 2002), 9.

49. Crawford Young, "The African Colonial State and Its Political Legacy," in *The Precarious Balance: State and Society in Africa*, ed. Donald Rothchild and Naomi Chazan (Boulder, CO: Westview Press, 1988), 29–30.

50. Ibid., 33.

51. Ibid., 36.

52. Robert H. Jackson, *Quasi-States: Sovereignty, International Relations, and the Third World* (New York: Cambridge University Press, 1990), 9.

53. Ibid., 113–14.

54. Kathryn C. Lavelle, "Invisible Hand, Invisible Continent: Liberalization and African States in the United Nations Conference on Trade and Development" (Ph.D. diss., Northwestern University, 1996).

55. Nicolas van de Walle, *African Economies and the Politics of Permanent Crisis, 1979–1999* (New York: Cambridge University Press, 2001), 18.

56. M. O. Baumann, "Forever North-South? The Political Challenges of Reforming the UN Development System," *Third World Quarterly* 39 (2017): 627.

57. Michael N. Barnett and Martha Finnemore, "The Politics, Power, and Pathologies of International Organization," *International Organization* 53 (1999).

58. See, e.g., "The One Health Initiative Will Unite Human and Veterinary Medicine," One Health Initiative, http://www.onehealthinitiative.com.

59. Bronwyn Leebaw, "Scorched Earth: Environmental War Crimes and International Justice," *Perspectives on Politics* 12 (2014).

60. Alexandra Stevenson and Motoko Rich, "Trans-Pacific Trade Allies Move On, without the U.S.," *New York Times,* November 12, 2017.

61. Michael Mandelbaum, "Pay Up, Europe: What Trump Gets Right about NATO," *Foreign Affairs* 96 (2017): 108–12.

62. David Mitrany, *A Working Peace System: An Argument for the Functional Development of International Organization,* 4th ed. (London: National Peace Council, 1946), 62.

63. Ibid.

ACKNOWLEDGMENTS

My work as a teacher and researcher brings me joy. This reality would not be possible for so many years without students at Case Western Reserve University whose questions, hard work, and idealism inspire me to do better every day. My hope is that each of them finds a purpose in their own lives that gives them similar satisfaction. Grace Protasiewicz provided invaluable insight into how to clarify key concepts in the book and painstakingly proofread drafts. Both American and international students have challenged me to remember that all peoples do not have the same perspectives on politics.

Several individuals provided extremely helpful assistance with specific chapters of the book. I received outstanding commentary from blind reviewers at two stages. I thank them, as well as Jeremy Youde for his suggestions on the literature on global health governance, and Jessica F. Green for her ideas about global environmental governance. Discussions with Sean Harris and Christine Young Harris on many aspects of US foreign policy in the post–Cold War world have helped me sharpen my understanding of NATO and the US-Russia relationship. My friendship and collaboration with Liselotte Odgaard compelled me to think about the future of multilateralism in the Arctic. James B. Young's unflagging enthusiasm pushed me forward constantly, from encouraging the production of "enduring material," to reading drafts as I wrote them, and to providing his own unique insight on every page with wit and wisdom.

Many centers at Case Western supported this book by providing opportunities for interdisciplinary collaboration, encouragement, and financial assistance for which I remain grateful. When our department was renovated in the summer of 2018, Shannon French, Laura Mekhail, and the Inamori International Center for Ethics and Excellence at Case Western Reserve University provided an office for me to continue to work on the book uninterrupted. Peter Knox and the Baker Nord Center for the Humanities provided funds for research on aspects of the book relating to financial governance when I had a sabbatical semester in the winter of 2016.

Special thanks go to Jaya Chatterjee at Yale University Press for coming up with the concept of the book and pointing out why I should want to write it. Her constant willingness to provide feedback has shaped the final project far beyond the editorial call of duty. I am also appreciative of the efforts of Laura Jones Dooley and Margaret Otzel, who took as much care with the manuscript in production as if it were their own.

Trump, Donald, 133, 233, 237–38, 252–53
Trusteeship Council (UN), 43–44,
60–62
tuberculosis, 7, 136–37, 144, 146
Turkey: and Iraq War (2003), 124; and
NATO, 128; refugees in, 230, 232
Turner, Ted, 121

Ukraine: Crimean Peninsula crisis (2014),
130, 252, 263; and UN, 42
UNCTAD. *See* United Nations Confer-
ence on Trade and Development
UNDP. *See* United Nations Development
Programme
UNEP (United Nations Environment Pro-
gramme), 153
UNFCCC (United Nations Framework
Convention on Climate Change), 155–
59
UNHCR (United Nations High Commis-
sioner for Refugees), 230–32, 234
Union of Soviet Socialist Republics. *See*
Soviet Union
United Kingdom: antiglobalization move-
ments in, 234, 242–43; and Bretton
Woods, 38; and Brexit, 242–43, 254; and
Cold War, 47, 54–55; and European
sovereign debt crisis, 215; as foreign
finance source in industrial era, 4–5;
and global health governance, 138, 140;
and gold standard, 4–5, 198; and IMF,
46, 194; immigration policy in, 242–43,
254; Industrial Revolution in, 2; and
International Criminal Court, 182; and
Latin American debt crises, 202; and
League of Nations, 22, 27; and NATO,
49, 130–32; as permanent member of
Security Council, 43; and post–World
War II multilateralism, 30, 32, 34, 38,
46–47, 54–55
United Nations: and Balkans conflict and
intervention, 117–20; and economic development finance, 76–78; human rights
mechanisms in, 173–77; planning for,
35–37; post–Cold War interventions by,
112–14; and postwar diplomacy, 39–45.

See also General Assembly; Security
Council; *specific organizations*
United Nations Children's Fund
(UNICEF), 116
United Nations Conference on Environ-
ment and Development, 155
United Nations Conference on Trade and
Development (UNCTAD): early years,
67–73; decline of bloc system, 75–76,
78; and changes from Uruguay Round,
82, 94–97, 152, 258, 260
United Nations Declaration of Human
Rights, 189
United Nations Development Programme
(UNDP), 76–77, 94, 260
United Nations Environment Programme
(UNEP), 153–54, 159
United Nations Framework Convention on
Climate Change (UNFCCC), 155–59.
See also Kyoto Protocol and Paris Agree-
ment
United Nations High Commissioner for
Refugees (UNHCR), 230–32, 234
United States: antiglobalization movement
in, 234–38; and Geneva Conventions,
12; and global health governance, 140–
41; and gold standard, 197–99; Great
Depression in, 25–27; and ILO, 20; and
IMF, 45–46; and International Criminal
Court, 182; and NAFTA, 98–101, 237,
253; participation in international organizations, 45–46; partisanship politics
during post–Cold War period, 114–16; as
permanent member of Security Council, 43; populism in, 234–38; trade politics in, 83–85; and Trans-Pacific
Partnership, 262
Universal Declaration of Human Rights,
170–73, 185, 189
Universal Postal Union, 6
Uruguay Round, 91–102; final agreement,
101–2; GATT evolution in, 97–102, 255;
and multinational corporations, 95–97;
and regional trading blocs, 98–100; and
transnational corporations, 100–101
USSR. *See* Soviet Union